D1357221

18 0256586 6

POSITIVE DIPLOMACY

Positive Diplomacy

Peter Marshall

Foreword by J. E. Spence

First published in Great Britain 1997 by
MACMILLAN PRESS LTD
Houndmills, Basingstoke, Hampshire RG21 6XS and London
Companies and representatives throughout the world

A catalogue record for this book is available from the British Library.

ISBN 0–333–69251–9

First published in the United States of America 1997 by
ST. MARTIN'S PRESS, INC.,
Scholarly and Reference Division,
175 Fifth Avenue, New York, N.Y. 10010

ISBN 0–312–17667–8

Library of Congress Cataloging-in-Publication Data
Marshall, Peter, 1924–
Positive diplomacy / Peter Marshall.
p.   cm.
Includes bibliographical references and index.
ISBN 0–312–17667–8 (cloth)
1. Diplomacy.   2. Diplomatic and consular service, British.
3. International relations.
JZ1405.M37 1997
327.2—dc21
97–14651
CIP

This book is printed on paper suitable for recycling and made from fully managed and
sustained forest sources.

10   9   8   7   6   5   4   3   2   1
06   05   04   03   02   01   00   99   98   97

Printed in Great Britain by
The Ipswich Book Company Ltd
Ipswich, Suffolk

In Memoriam
PRM
1927–1981

"*Just tell the press the Ambassador feels it would be inappropriate to comment until he's had time to study the complete text.*"

Drawing by Lorenz; © 1979 *The New Yorker* Magazine, Inc.

Contents

Foreword

The renaissance in diplomatic studies in British universities during the last decade calls for some explanation. During the Cold War, ideological difference and the stultifying impact of a balance of terror, freezing the status quo, produced a climate hostile to the negotiation of a grand, creative settlement of the political disputes that divided the superpowers and their allies. True, crises abounded – Cuba, Berlin, the Middle East – and skilful diplomacy played its part in defusing their worst effects. Paradoxically, the one area where diplomacy was effective was in negotiating arms control agreements where the existence of a coincidence of interest in avoiding war either by accident or design led to significant outcomes. What diplomacy could not do – through no fault of its practitioners – was engineer a major achievement of disarmament. The level of tension and distrust was simply too high to permit this benefit.

But with the end of the Cold War and the well-nigh universal acknowledgement that democratic pluralism and the free market were the building blocks of a new and stable world order, the diplomat, freed from the constraints of defending and asserting national interest in a cold-war context, now has to function in an interdependent world which calls increasingly into question the concept of sovereignty and the realism of national boundaries. Diplomacy, to quote Sir Victor Wellesley, is no longer in fetters; its practitioners – as Sir Peter Marshall rightly emphasises – have to cope not only with the political and social implications of a globalised economy but with issues, *inter alia*, of human rights, the environment and international crime. And the task is complicated by the ubiquitous spread of information technology and the emergence of a host of new international actors ranging from multinational companies to humanitarian relief organisations.

The modern diplomat, therefore, has to be something of a polymath. Apart from the traditional skills of negotiation and the traditional virtues of civility and self-restraint, the youthful entrant to a country's diplomatic corps has to acquire a sound understanding of technical areas of expertise about which his predecessors 'had not to delve or think deeply' (Wellesley). It is in this context that Sir Peter Marshall's book has much to contribute. He is that *rara avis*, a diplomat turned scholar, concerned to reflect on his experience as a distinguished practitioner in the hope that a new generation will be better equipped to cope not only with a world of 'telegrams and anger', but one which is simultaneously undergoing a social and economic transformation.

In his day, as Sir Peter readily admits, there was not much available by way of 'structured guidance' for the embryo diplomat. His generation – like its academic counterpart – was brought up on the classic texts of Harold Nicolson and, for the more discerning, the writings of the seventeenth-century theorist, François de Callières, resurrected in the 1970s by my former colleague at the University of Leicester, Maurice Keens-Soper and his Canadian collaborator, Karl Schweizer.

Today, the plethora of masters' programmes in diplomatic studies and the corresponding rise in scholarly publication bears ample testimony to the popularity of the topic and equally the recognition of the need for formal training in the art of diplomacy. Both these developments are in part a response to the changing nature of the diplomatic enterprise and a recognition that a sophisticated diplomacy combining traditional skills with technical understanding is essential if the world is to become a more tolerant and civilised international community.

The great merit of Sir Peter's work is that it combines a detailed exposition of the work of the diplomat with an explanation of how the world has changed and what is required if diplomatic theory and practice are to accommodate successfully to those changes. In this respect, *Positive Diplomacy* is far more than a manual of instruction; wit and elegance happily inform a superb analysis. Aspiring diplomats, current practitioners (and their political masters!), together with those who seek some understanding of international relations in general, will read this book with profit and pleasure.

J. E. SPENCE
Associate Fellow and former Director of Studies
Royal Institute of International Affairs

Preface

This course of lectures has evolved over a period of seven years at the Diplomatic Academy of London at the University of Westminster. It is designed to encourage, among those who have embarked, or aspire to embark, on a career in diplomacy, a professional approach to the handling of international relations. Its fundamental purpose is to nurture the capability to make policy. It is intended to complement the extended and rigorous study of international affairs which must form part of the training of a diplomat, and which is also a growing feature of higher education generally.

In the United Kingdom formal initial training is apt fairly quickly to run up against the national grain, and hence against national willingness to allocate the necessary resources to it. There are many experienced diplomats, not confined to the pragmatic Anglo-Saxon tradition, who believe that the only training of real value which a diplomat can receive is on the job. There is of course enormous advantage in watching master craftsmen at work. Even where this advantage is not available three-dimensionally, two-dimensional substitutes have their own value. Biography and autobiography, mixing, as they do, reminiscence and anecdote with analysis (albeit in proportions tending to favour the first two of these ingredients at the expense of the third) are an invaluable source for the young diplomat.

Yet even if formal training at the outset of a career is subject to rapidly diminishing returns, that is not the end of the matter. The fact that there is no substitute for experience in the development of a great painter does not mean that there is no place for art school. Even where individual flair, talent and taste are pre-eminent, technique is still a fruitful area for collective articulation and study. Those who have engaged in rigorous and systematic study of the various elements of a craft must, other things being equal, enjoy an advantage over those who have not. The problem is how to establish the useful limits of such an approach as this to the work of a diplomat. Those limits will, as already suggested, vary according to the pressures of prevailing circumstances and to available resources, as well as to more deep-seated national characteristics.

At a more detailed level, there are two sources of hesitation about the possibility of successfully translating the concept of developing the capacity to make policy into a viable course of study. First, how far does international society today have common, or indeed universal, characteristics of sufficient strength and durability to permit the realistic offer of a *table d'hôte* menu for 'policy capability', rather than *à la carte* guidance and advice, devised by individual countries to suit their own requirements? Secondly, do countries differ so widely that general prescription for the development of 'policy capability' cannot but run the risk of irrelevance? As regards the first of these questions, world interdependence and the extent to which business is transacted multilaterally rather than bilaterally – and by methods which United Nations practice has done much to standardise – mean that there is a vast range both of subject matter and of procedure of concern to virtually every diplomat, whatever country he or she may represent. The common background is great and growing. Its study at the outset of a diplomatic career is not merely desirable, it is essential. Just as in the 'Old Diplomacy' among the European powers before the outbreak of the Great War in 1914 there emerged both a great body of collective subject matter and a collective professional approach to it, so in the multifarious conditions of 'New Diplomacy' of the present century there is a web of world-wide common concern and practice.

As regards the second question, whatever its size, whatever the extent of its international involvement and whatever the scale of its professional diplomatic activity, every country is at the end of the day faced with the same facts of international substance and process. One of the pioneers of British economics, Alfred Marshall (with whom I can unhappily make no truthful claims of kinship) invented the device of the 'representative firm' as the means of studying the state of affairs in any given industry or market.[1] This device served in particular to illuminate the considerations which individual managers and entrepreneurs would have in mind in deciding their level of output. In diplomacy, the country chosen as 'representative firm' would vary according to the subject under investigation. Yet international study of diplomacy in London offers many instances where the UK can reasonably be regarded as a 'representative firm'. To the extent, moreover, that it cannot be so regarded, UK experience and practice can still be of value to the student in London in drawing conclusions of relevance to his or her own country.

Two other factors militate in favour of the international study of diplomacy in London. First, Commonwealth connections, including shared methods and traditions, add to the relevance of British experience to diplomats from other Commonwealth countries. There are some 50 Commonwealth countries. Secondly, few countries have seen such a drastic change in their relative, as well as in their absolute, international situation during the twentieth century as has Britain. The forces at work in this drastic change repay study, as much for the general background which they afford to policy-making in modern conditions as for the insight they give into the British involvement in world affairs.

Diplomacy, as these lectures insist, is a collective matter. So is diplomatic training. The reaction of the students is vital to the continuous adaptation of both regular courses and specialised programmes. What the students learn from one another may be as valuable as anything they learn from formal sessions in the lecture room. What they offer by way of comment on course content and arrangement is an indispensable guide in shaping the curriculum.

Whatever the difficulties and imperfections of diplomatic training, one general consideration militates in favour of persistence, namely the complexity of modern interdependence and the corresponding complexity of foreign policy-making. The world needs wise, prudent and responsible foreign policy from every government. It is more likely to get it if diplomats are properly trained. There is much talk today of the necessity for 'good governance',[2] a comprehensive term extending to more or less the whole range of public affairs, and emphasising administrative and democratic accountability. In an interdependent world the argument applies as directly to the conduct of foreign as to that of domestic policy.

A more personal consideration has also encouraged me to persist with these lectures. When I joined the British Foreign Service in 1949, in contrast to the situation which prevails today, I received absolutely no formal training whatever. No mechanism for providing it existed, except in the important area of 'hard' languages. One entered the pool at the deep end. When, some years later, I was first appointed to the pivotal post of Head of Chancery in a mission abroad – in my case Baghdad – there was likewise no structured guidance available as to what was expected of me. By this time however, an invaluable book, *The Foreign Office*, had been written by Lord Strang, a recently retired Permanent Under-Secretary of State.[3] From its pages I was able to gather an accurate, if daunting, idea of what was involved. I fastened in particular on Lord Strang's verdict that the Head of Chancery 'is thus always a busy man and sometimes a harassed one'. As I became immersed in my duties in Baghdad the truth of this proposition forced itself upon me. On my return home at the end of the day's work my wife had only to hear a reference to 'Strang, page 105' to understand that there was a need for the usual restoratives.

In no field of professional endeavour can learning from others be of more importance than in diplomacy. Example and encouragement are at the core of diplomatic effectiveness. The essence of what these lectures seek to convey is in some sense the common property of all diplomatic practitioners. I stand greatly in the debt of my colleagues in the British Diplomatic Service; of my colleagues in the Commonwealth Secretariat, who serve one of the world's most imaginative associations; and of those at the United Nations, whether as members of the different Secretariats or as national representatives, who see loyalty to the issues and opportunities of interdependence as the key to serving the community of nations and the governments they elect.

More specifically, I am particularly grateful to the University of Westminster, and to the Diplomatic Academy of London, whose Director, Dr Nabil Ayad, has evolved over the years a distinctive pattern of diplomatic training. I am deeply indebted to Professor Jack Spence, the Director of Studies of the Royal Institute of International Affairs at Chatham House, both for reading the text and for contributing the Foreword. I take this opportunity to record my gratitude to the Royal Institute of International Affairs for two score years of stimulus, help and encouragement. The frequency with which Chatham House figures in the Bibliography in particular is an indicator of the value of its work to the profession.

I am likewise most grateful to Mrs Sally Morphet, of the Research and Analysis Department of the Foreign and Commonwealth Office, for reading the draft and making a number of valuable comments. I also thank most warmly Mr Ian Soutar, the Head of the Library and Records Department of the Foreign and Commonwealth Office, for helping to see the draft through its official hoops, and also for the illuminating insights into the application of information technology to diplomatic practice he has provided at the annual Symposia at the University of Westminster organised by the Diplomatic Academy and the London Diplomatic Association.

The cartoon by Lorenz in the Frontispiece is reprinted by kind permission of *The New Yorker* Magazine, Inc. I am further indebted to Eagle Star for permission to reproduce their advertisement in Annex 6 and to Wide World Photos for permission to use the jacket illustration.

Because of their anonymity I am unable to express my thanks personally to the authors of Annex 7. I hope they will feel that I have done something to preserve their excellent work.

Ms Alexandra McLeod of the United Nations Office and Information Centre in London has been of great assistance in providing UN documentation. I express unstinting admiration for the composure with which Mrs Carol Savage has produced the several typed versions of the text, and in the process coped with handwriting which some people inexplicably find difficult to decipher. At a subsequent stage Miss Jo North was of the greatest help in copy-editing and in the compilation of the index.

I naturally exempt all those who have helped me from any responsibility for the shortcomings of these lectures. My hope is that, whatever their inadequacies, they will be of some interest and use to those who serve the profession in any of its many capacities.

PETER MARSHALL
London, July 1996

Introduction: Action as the End Object of Diplomacy

International affairs are, quite rightly, the subject of intense public interest and media coverage. They are, again quite rightly, studied widely and deeply at universities. But those who follow international affairs in these different ways do so by and large from the standpoint of examining what other people do. As professional diplomats, on the other hand, we are concerned with what *we* do. This, while in no way diminishing the importance of the study of international affairs, requires us to adopt a somewhat different approach to the same range of phenomena. Our watchword is Aristotle's dictum: 'we study politics not for the sake of knowledge but for the sake of action'.

If the priority is to get things done, the balance between what one most wants to do and what one is most likely to be able to achieve is of key importance. The more complex the medium in which one operates, the more important striking that balance will be. International affairs are inherently more complex than internal affairs because the medium is unfamiliar as well as complex. It is no accident that the words 'foreign' and 'strange' are synonymous. Nowhere does the writ of the Law of Unintended Consequences run more freely than in the conduct of international relations.

It is sometimes said that foreign policy is about what to do and diplomacy is about how to do it. This is an over-simplification. In reality, how to do it may determine to a very great extent what to do. The way in which nations interact is governed not solely by the substance of international affairs in the sense of the objective, distilled essence of respective national situations and interests – if, indeed, it were possible to extract such an essence from the real world. It is also governed by the nature of international society, by the manner in which nations behave and by the way in which they organise (or fail to organise) their dealings with one another. Substance and process are indeed inextricably linked. Process affects substance just as language affects thought. Anyone engaged professionally in the conduct of international relations cannot but place great emphasis on the mastery of process alongside the mastery of substance.

It is likewise said that the difference between an administrator and a manager is that an administrator keeps things going while a manager makes things go. Although this too can be criticised as an over-simplification, it is a distinction with practical value. Much discussion of diplomacy proceeds on the basis that it is more in the realm of the administrative than of the managerial. Phrases such as 'international relations', 'diplomatic practice', 'protocol' and 'international law' have a static, even a passive, ring about them. This may be salutary, if it induces in those engaged in diplomacy a certain humility about making things go the way they want, indeed about the scope for effective intervention generally. Mr Dean Rusk, a former US Secretary of State, remarked that recognition of the complexity of foreign affairs was the beginning of wisdom in diplomacy. Talleyrand, the great French statesman, went further. His oft-quoted, and frequently misquoted, injunction was: '*Surtout, Messieurs, point de zèle*' – 'Above all, gentlemen, no zeal at all.'[1] Blundering activity, in other words, was worse than no activity. There is much scope in human affairs generally for masterly inactivity. But that inactivity should be the product of prudence, not of ignorance nor of apathy. Moreover, that is only part of the truth. Politics is about power. The conduct of foreign policy represents the exercise of power in one particular area of national life, namely its international component. It is positive and proactive as well as prudent and reactive. Talleyrand himself was nothing if not positive. The work of a diplomat revolves in practice round the question, perennially asked by the minister of foreign affairs or by the ambassador, 'What is the situation and what are we going to do about it?'

POLICY CAPABILITY

A prime objective of diplomatic training must be to help make the diplomat capable of coming up with an effective answer to that perennial question: that is, to help make him or her 'policy capable'. Diplomats must have the capacity as practitioners:

(i) to analyse clearly and comprehensively the international situation, or particular aspects of it, with which they are concerned;
(ii) to examine, on the basis of a firm grasp of the relevant factors, the policy options available;

(iii) to set those options out in a manner which will facilitate the shaping of policy;

(iv) to combine with such an analysis of policy options a set of practical recommendations as to the course to be adopted, based on the one hand on national interests and pressures, and on the other hand on an understanding of the prevailing international conditions in which those recommendations would have to be applied, and hence of the prospects of their successful application; and

(v) to assist effectively both at home and abroad in the carrying out of policy when adopted, this executive function being recognised as inextricably linked with the advisory functions described in (i) to (iv) above.

To help the foreign minister to shape his or her policy, and then to help him or her carry it out, involves a whole range of skills and the capacity to use them in the right combination.[2] In particular, good ideas have to be presented in such a way that other people, probably more august, can understand them, adopt them and apply them successfully. The key supplementary question a diplomat needs to be ready to answer is 'Even if this is a good idea, will it work, and, if so, how?' There is no point in looking ahead if your feet are not on the ground.

'Policy capability' is as much an executive as an advisory affair. The executive and advisory functions are, like substance and process, inextricably mixed. Taking effective action is not a matter of discrete initiatives alone, any more than good gardening consists only of planting, without careful preparation of the ground beforehand. 'Policy capability' must reflect the continuity of international affairs and the wide variety of ongoing diplomatic activities, which in their turn reflect that continuity: the cultivation of good political relations, including personal relations with foreign leaders; the projection abroad of the national viewpoint and of national values; the strengthening of economic ties with other countries; the development of cultural links with them; and the promotion of the interests of the country's nationals abroad. All these are essential to the successful adoption of specific policies in the field of international affairs.

This interdependence of a wide range of diplomatic activities underlines a related aspect of the concept of 'policy capability'. 'Policy' is often thought of as concerned only with great all-embracing issues – affairs of state and 'high' policy. The reality of the management of international relations, as with the management of other businesses, is different. In the first place the objectives of foreign policy are pursued in a variety of different ways, many of them humdrum. Purposeful, detailed work, undertaken over a wide range of subjects, yet directed and co-ordinated on the basis of a clear overall assessment of national interest, is the essence of policy. Secondly, the nature of politics is such that a seemingly obscure or unimportant issue can suddenly become headline news and the cause of an international crisis. This possibility should never be absent from the minds of those who deal with seemingly routine matters.[3]

A FRAMEWORK FOR BUILDING POLICY CAPABILITY

The concept of 'policy capability' thus includes the whole integrated range of activities involved in the conduct of international relations. It embraces the substance of international affairs from the most general issue to the most particular, irrespective of whether the issues are political, economic, commercial, cultural, consular or concerned with 'information', that is to say, the support of policy by means of public persuasion and discussion. It embraces likewise the vital 'vocational' aspects of professional diplomacy such as proficiency in foreign languages, the acquisition of the personal skills which the individual diplomat needs, and the mastery of the technology of diplomatic organisation and management needed to enhance collective performance. It recognises the overriding importance of harnessing all this effort and expertise, individual and collective, to practical and coherent ends.

'Policy capability' must realistically be founded on the professional competence of diplomats individually in both the advisory and executive spheres. It is apparent that in large measure it can be acquired only by dint of apprenticeship and experience. But that is not the same thing as to say that formal training at the threshold, or in the early stages, of a diplomatic career has no useful part to play. Such training is a particular need in countries where administrative resources are scarce. The challenge is to make it as coherent and practical as possible. A combination of solid factual background and a valid technique of analysis can serve to develop the framework of thought which a young diplomat would find of most value while on the job.

Of what does such a framework consist? In the first place, diplomats must have a broad and clear understanding of their professional environment: that is, of what it is that they face in the interdependent world of today. In the second place, they must be familiar with the institutional topography, and the diplomatic arena in which they are called upon to act. In the third place, they must acquire the professional skills both as individuals, and as members of the Diplomatic Service and servants of the state, which will enable them to work effectively. The framework, in other words, includes analytical elements, institutional features and operational factors.

This categorisation is of course arbitrary. With an even greater incursion into the arbitrary, these analytical elements, institutional features and operational factors can be subdivided on the following lines:

(a) Analytical issues:
     (i) the evolution of diplomacy in response to rapid change and growing interdependence;
    (ii) the nature of international society today;
   (iii) national sovereignty and its limits.
(b) Institutional features:
    (iv) the United Nations system;
    (v) the world economy;
   (vi) European architecture.
(c) Operational factors:
   (vii) foreign policy-making;
  (viii) Diplomatic Service organisation;
    (ix) the acquisition of diplomatic skills: drafting.

STRUCTURE OF THE BOOK

The lectures which follow explore each of these subdivisions in turn. The final lecture – 'A Diplomat's Decade' – is of a more anecdotal character, and seeks to illustrate in practical form general points of guidance which emerge from the earlier lectures.

If there seems to be an element of the artificial about the framework, it is worth observing that the lectures are designed to be delivered separately, either in whole or in part. Their individual content may be of more practical relevance to the work of a diplomat than attempts, however beguiling intellectually, to refine their mutual relationship and perfect their collective coverage. Total conceptual clarity is in any case unattainable.

The objective can be more modestly formulated. The need to think systematically about public affairs, as a condition of acting effectively on them, is manifest. If they are in the habit of thinking systematically, young diplomats will be of much greater service to those for whom they work. The lectures are designed to develop the capacity to think simultaneously in analytical, institutional and operational terms. Each lecture includes a number of sub-headings. These are reproduced in the list of Contents, which can thus serve not only as a summary of the text, but also as a checklist, or a series of checklists, as to what goes into the making of policy. Cross-referencing in the text itself, combined with the Notes and the Bibliography, as well as the Index, is designed to help in the process.

CONCLUDING COMMENT

The elaboration of a 'policy capability framework' along the lines explored above is not an end in itself. It is, to repeat, a way of approaching the task of training those who have embarked, or who aspire to embark, on a diplomatic career. It is no substitute for rigorous academic study of the substance of international affairs. Rather, it is an accompaniment to it. The two overlap. They are indeed two sides of the same educational coin. Political and economic affairs are a splendid subject area in which to learn to think. The aim, it cannot be over-emphasised, is to lead to more effective action, which depends on a grasp of process as well as of substance. The proposition was summed up definitively in the verdict of Macaulay, the noted British historian and politician, on Machiavelli:

> The qualities of the active and the contemplative statesman appear to have been blended in a rare and exquisite harmony. His skill in the details of business had not been acquired at the expense of his general powers. It had not rendered his mind less comprehensive; but it had served to correct his speculations and to impart to them that vivid and practical character which so widely distinguishes them from the vague theories of most political philosophers.[4]

1 Diplomacy: A Child of Changing Times

Diplomatic theorists insist that precision is a key element in the conduct of international affairs. It is ironic therefore that the word 'diplomacy' is monstrously imprecise. It has at least six meanings, or groups of meanings, interrelated but distinct. At its most comprehensive, it can mean the content of foreign affairs as a whole, arising from the etymology of the word 'diploma', a folded paper or letter of recommendation, or a document, and hence the content of the document. Secondly, diplomacy can mean the conduct of foreign policy, again a comprehensive matter, involving all aspects of the impact which one country may make on another, including resort to force. Thirdly, it can mean the management of international relations by negotiation. This definition, it is important to note, narrows the meaning of diplomacy to negotiation, as distinct from the use of force, at the same time as it widens it by introducing the concept of management, and hence of the business of dealing with the dimension of international interdependence, as well as with the ramifications of the international aspect of national affairs as a whole. Fourthly, diplomacy can mean the apparatus for managing international relations, especially professional Diplomatic Services: a more limited, and also a more technical, concept. Fifthly, it can mean the manner in which international relations are managed. The definition adopted by one noted British authority, Sir Ernest Satow, is 'the application of intelligence and tact to the conduct of official relations between the governments of independent states'.[1] This definition has its normative use as a standard to which those engaged in the conduct of foreign policy should aspire. But it can scarcely be regarded as an accurate description of the sum total of the impact which one country makes on others, all of which is relevant to the management of its international relations. Finally, diplomacy can mean the art or the skill of the diplomat, with popular overtones not only of great ingenuity but also of evasiveness, dissimulation or deceit. 'A diplomat is someone who can be disarming when his or her country is not.' Stalin took this approach to its logical conclusion: 'a diplomat's words have no relation to actions – otherwise what kind of diplomacy is it? Sincere diplomacy is no more possible than dry water or wooden iron.'

If a word can simultaneously signify content, conduct, character, method, manner and art, it can fairly be said to be conducive to misunderstanding. We can of course adopt the policy of Humpty-Dumpty and aver that when we use it, a word means just what we choose it to mean – neither more nor less.[2] But such egocentricity has its disadvantages. A more co-operative approach is required in the pursuit of clarity. All six meanings, or groups of meanings, of the word 'diplomacy' are relevant. Moreover, they are relevant simultaneously. Collectively they underline the inextricable mix of substance and process in international, as in national, affairs. Collectively, too, they indicate that we are concerned with a vast range of phenomena which can be thought of as the social science of international relations, a social science to keep the company of politics or civics or economics, and which constantly overlaps with them. But if we do not use the word 'diplomacy' for all of this, is there any alternative? There exists the word 'diplomatics', which would fit the bill admirably, were it not already used principally to mean the study of diplomas or the deciphering of ancient documents.

If we are denied, at least for the moment, any comprehensive word to describe our concerns, we are all the more obliged to be clear in our minds which particular meaning we may attach at any given moment to the word 'diplomacy' and to recognise the interdependence of that particular meaning with other meanings of the word. We must avoid confusing ourselves and others.

DIPLOMACY, A CHILD OF ITS TIME: 'OLD' AND 'NEW' DIPLOMACY

The inextricable mix of substance and process is one of the foremost characteristics of diplomacy in any of the six meanings described above. Another chief characteristic of diplomacy is that it is a child of its time. Human nature may not change much. The way human beings interact may conform to certain broad patterns. But one of the benefits of civilisation is the capacity to interpret human experience in such a way as to accumulate wisdom, and in so doing favour constructive, rather than destructive, behaviour. That does not mean that progress is uninterrupted. Anarchy is never eradicated. Rather, the manner in which nations deal with one another is an uncertain amalgam of responses to current pressures and opportunities; of conditioning by a body of precedent; and of rule-making, rule-minding and rule-bending, in unpredictable combination.

If there are no absolutes in diplomacy, there are at least comparisons to be made. We can with profit look at diplomacy as practised at various times, to note the differences and to establish the reasons for those differences. It is particularly instructive for us, at the end of the twentieth century, to look at the situation at the beginning of it. The difference is vast.

For 300 years or so, from the end of the Thirty Years War in 1648 to the outbreak of the Great War in 1914, there evolved a recognisable pattern of diplomacy in Europe now generally regarded as the 'Old Diplomacy', to distinguish it from the 'New Diplomacy' ushered in at the end of the Great War, and associated in particular with the name of President Woodrow Wilson of the United States.[3] Sir Harold Nicolson, the best-known British authority on diplomacy, listed the five chief characteristics of the 'Old Diplomacy' as follows: the prime importance of Europe; the leading influence of the Great Powers, which had wider interests, 'more money and more guns'; the common responsibility of the Great Powers for the conduct of the Small Powers, including the preservation of peace between them; the existence in every European country of a professional diplomatic service on a more or less identical model; and the rule that sound negotiation must be continuous and confidential.[4] One has only to list these characteristics to see how different are the diplomatic conditions of today. There has been a great expansion in the responsibilities of government in the field of economic management and social conditions; there has been a vast increase in the volume of transactions and in the speed of communications; there has been a similar growth in the public content of international affairs and of the extent to which public opinion has to be wooed and shaped. Euro-centricity has radically declined as other power-centres have arisen. Nations previously under European sway have acquired independence. Above all, and underneath it all, there has been the rise of interdependence, which calls increasingly in question the realism of the concept of national sovereignty and the relevance of national boundaries.

The 'Old Diplomacy' was 'political', esoteric, elitist, and far from the madding crowd. It was ideologically neutral. It was oriented to patterns of trade and influence. It was ready to resort to war as a method of achieving its objectives. In the kingdoms and empires of Europe it was a matter of royal prerogative. In his essay on Civil

Government, the seventeenth-century British philosopher John Locke insisted that the good of society requires that several things should be 'left to the discretion of him that has the executive power'.[5] Fledgling independent American opinion went in the same direction. Those at the Philadelphia Convention in 1787 with experience of the realities of foreign affairs were at pains to convince their colleagues that firm executive control was essential. While they were ready to see the management of internal affairs left to a considerable extent to a popular assembly, they would take no such risk with foreign affairs. After discussing the 'absolute necessity of system' and the inadequate realisation in the public mind of its importance in national affairs, John Jay wrote in the *Federalist Papers*: 'it was wise therefore in the convention to provide not only that all power of making treaties should be committed to able and honest men, but also that they should continue in place a sufficient time to become acquainted with our national concerns and to form and introduce a system for the management of them'.[6]

The 'New Diplomacy' has none of the prevailing characteristics of the 'Old Diplomacy' described above. It has burst the bonds of European hegemony. Its concerns go far beyond traditional political questions. It is dominated by economic concerns and their social implications. It is absorbed in democracy and human rights, both individual and collective. It is populist rather than elitist. It is a matter of intense public interest and debate. The auditorium is as important as the stage.

A SERIES OF 'INVASIONS' OF THE POLITICAL FOREGROUND

How, from the point of view of the management of international relations, can one best analyse the changes which have come about during the twentieth century and the impact which these have had on the way in which nations interact with one another? Perhaps the most helpful way is to think in terms of a series of 'invasions' of the political foreground, whereby traditional activities, as epitomised by the 'Old Diplomacy', were overtaken by the developments of the modern world to which the 'New Diplomacy' is a response. These 'invasions', though logically distinct, are interdependent and overlapping. They do not present themselves in neat chronological sequence. The elements which compose them have been present and detectable all along. But in the twentieth century they have come to be perceived as of great importance, individually and cumulatively. In analytical, as much as in any strict chronological order they could be listed on some such lines as the following:

(a) the 'economic' invasion, whereby the growing interdependence and interpenetration of economies and the increasing degree of government responsibility for economic management came to dominate the content of international affairs in a manner unknown in the nineteenth century;

(b) the 'public concern and involvement' invasion, as a result of which public opinion became both a key concern and a key asset in the conduct of foreign policy;

(c) the 'self-determination and decolonisation' invasion, by which the concepts of democracy and autonomy familiar in the developed world found their logical extension to the sphere of the subject peoples of the former empires, with all that this implied for international arrangements across the board;

(d) the 'human rights' invasion, in which the treatment of individuals and of minorities became an issue of international concern, with crucial political as well as humanitarian implications;

(e) the 'social' invasion, giving prominence not only to economic development as the means of facilitating a better standard of living, but also to social development and to the pressing problems of society: poverty, unemployment, poor health, inadequate education, disadvantages suffered by women, the particular problems of children, young people, the handicapped and the aged;

(f) the 'new issues' invasion, especially the question of how to handle threats to the environment but also other collective threats which transcend national boundaries: drug abuse, terrorism, HIV/Aids;

(g) the 'information technology' invasion, which in its ubiquitous immediacy has transformed the world. The vocabulary has constantly to be changed and expanded in order to accommodate the new concepts to which the technology gives rise; and

(h) the 'multiplicity of actors' invasion, as a result of which those who are part of the process of conducting international relations have increased enormously in number, and are no longer essentially confined, as in the days of the 'Old Diplomacy', to sovereigns, ministers and professional diplomats.

I summarise these 'invasions' in turn.

(a)   The 'Economic' Invasion

The nineteenth century saw the apogee of *laissez-faire*, the economic
expression of which was minimal government involvement in the
management of the economy, with a corresponding lack of emphasis
on economic matters in the conduct of international relations. Looked
at a century later, nineteenth-century diplomacy does indeed seem to
have been something of a graceful political exercise, slow to respond to
the rapid and intensive changes in economic activity, not only within
countries but also between them. Perhaps the most profound British
analysis of the implications of these changes was contained in
Diplomacy in Fetters, published in 1944, by Sir Victor Wellesley,
Deputy Under-Secretary of State at the Foreign Office between 1925
and 1936.[7] His thesis in essence was that the Industrial Revolution had
developed national economies into a world economy of interdependence and interpenetration, fundamentally altering the background to
the conduct of foreign affairs. The machinery for the latter, however,
had remained static and hence had ceased to function effectively. In the
nineteenth century Wellesley said, 'no great economic and social
problems had come to the fore to sully the purity of the diplomats'
thought. They had not to delve and think deeply.'[8]

The twentieth century, Wellesley argued, has been different. So long
as diplomatic practitioners thought in traditional political terms, rather
than taking into account the full range of relevant factors, diplomacy
was 'in fetters'. This is a criticism which can scarcely be levelled at
diplomats today. Economic factors force their attention on governments at every turn. The world economy, discussed in Lecture 5, is at
the centre of their concerns. The task is not so much to recognise the
relevance of a wide range of factors as to reflect that recognition in wise
policy-making. Wellesley's book dealt in detail with the way in which
all these considerations needed to be reflected, not only in the
experience, training and organisation of diplomats, but also in the
machinery of government as a whole and in the conduct of
parliamentary business. Foreign policy, he maintained, could no longer
be dealt with in a vacuum and on a hand-to-mouth basis. Wellesley's
prescription cannot but seem over-elaborate. This, together with his
somewhat discursive style, may explain why his pioneering work was
not better known even among the professionals in his day, let alone
subsequently. But much of his message, at least as far as diplomatic
organisation is concerned, was contained in the proposals for British
diplomatic reform adopted at the end of the Second World War.[9]

(b)   The 'Public Concern and Involvement' Invasion

The proposition can be put succinctly: 'Where war is everybody's tragedy and everybody's nightmare, diplomacy is everybody's business.' A feature of the nineteenth century was the relative lack of public interest in foreign affairs. They were effectively the preserve of the educated minority. Since their scope was very largely political, they held little interest for the man or woman in the street and no great significance for their daily lives. Two world wars, with only an uneasy peace between them, changed all that. The everyday lives of millions of people were shattered by the upheavals of the first half of the twentieth century. Concern to avoid the horror of war combined with the increasing internationalisation of our existence to underline the public content of international affairs.

The public content of international affairs has greatly increased in two separate ways. First, there is much enhanced public interest, which democratically responsible governments must be ready to meet with an appropriate flow of information and explanation: to Parliament; to the media; to non-governmental bodies of all kinds; and to individuals. The flow must be both national and international. Disraeli remarked that 'without publicity there can be no public spirit, and without public spirit every nation must decay'. This emphasis on publicity drew its strength in great part from the feeling that secrecy was a particular defect of the 'Old Diplomacy'. President Wilson spoke of 'open covenants of peace openly arrived at'.[10] The intention was that people should not be faced with *faits accomplis* in the field of foreign policy, with possibly disastrous consequences. Rather they would know at least in general terms what was afoot and governments would have to carry their electorates with them.

This introduces the second element of the public content of foreign affairs, namely the scope for influencing opinion both at home and abroad. Freedom of the press has long been perceived as bestowing great power on journalists, at times an inconvenience to the most benevolent of governments. It was Macaulay who remarked that 'the gallery in which reporters [sit has] become a fourth estate of the realm'.[11] Today the instantaneous coverage of events by world-wide television and radio is regarded in many quarters as conferring excessive powers on the media. Some would have it that Cable News Network (CNN) is already *de facto* the sixteenth (and permanent) member of the UN Security Council. There is particular disquiet in smaller developing countries which have little by way of independent information resources. Yet it is governments which have most scope for influencing public opinion. Propaganda is very much a feature of the twentieth century, thanks to the spread of literacy and the development of mass communication. The Allies directed it with considerable effect in the First World War against discontented elements within the Austro-Hungarian Empire. The Nazis brought propaganda to a high state of effectiveness. Political theorists spoke of power over opinion as a separate element, distinct from military or economic power. Both the British Council and the External Services of the British Broadcasting Corporation (BBC) came into being to some extent as a response to hostile propaganda. Their significance for British diplomacy has been great, thanks to the enviable reputation they have established for quality and objectivity.[12]

(c)   The 'Self-Determination and Decolonisation' Invasion

A great feature of the 'Old Diplomacy' was the imperial outreach of the principal European powers, both within Europe and in other continents. The most dramatic expansion of European power outside Europe took place in the late nineteenth century in the so-called 'scramble for Africa'. The colonial occupation which this entailed was, in historical terms, of short duration. The empires within Europe were of much longer standing. The Versailles Treaty and related arrangements after the end of the Great War bestowed independence, on the basis of the principle of self-determination assiduously promoted by President Wilson, upon a number of European countries. The map of Europe was redrawn on national and ethnic lines. The results were deeply disappointing. The collective security arrangements required to validate the post-war settlement did not materialise, thanks to the shortcomings of the League of Nations. But the principle of self-determination maintained its strong appeal. Outside Europe, the end of the Great War saw no flowering of self-determination on the same scale. A number of the colonies of the defeated powers were recycled as 'mandated territories' of the League. The old Turkish Empire was carved up into spheres of influence, and indeed of occupation.

It was only after the Second World War that decolonisation gained real momentum. Membership of the UN has more than trebled since 1945. The nation-state system has blossomed to an extent never before witnessed. At the same time, however, interdependence has called that system increasingly into question. There is thus at the centre of international relations today a paradox which admits of no easy resolution. Prevailing opinion is strongly in favour of decolonisation as the logical extension of the concepts of democracy and autonomy to the people of former empires. On the other hand, the concept that accession to statehood was conditional upon the capacity to ensure, not merely self-defence, but also economic survival, without help, has come to be disregarded, especially in the cases of a number of the smallest and poorest countries. The world community contains a number of members who will be dependent on the protection and the charity of others for the foreseeable future. The question of whether or how to intervene in the affairs of such countries is never far away. It is fashionable to describe states where there is breakdown, as 'failed states'. Somalia is a case in point. The international instability that this engenders does not need to be emphasised. But it is not yet such as to weaken the present general firm allegiance to the nation-state system.[13]

(d) The 'Human Rights' Invasion

The concept of self-determination does not of course apply only to countries or to peoples. Its enduring strength is derived from belief in the rights of the individual, even if in many cases these can be safeguarded only collectively. But there is no guarantee that autonomy and self-determination at the national level will ensure the liberty and the well-being of the individual. A particular problem arises where there are significant minorities within nations – ethnic, religious, cultural, linguistic or regional – and particularly where those minorities are linked to similar minorities, or even majorities, in neighbouring states. This is the problem which has plagued Europe for centuries. It is likely to dominate the decades ahead.

As regards the practical management of international relations, concern over the rights of the individual anywhere and everywhere finds its most acute expression in the unresolved conflict between the sovereignty of states, and resistance to international intervention in matters which are essentially within the domestic jurisdiction of states, on the one hand, and international awareness that how a state treats its citizens, especially its minorities, may be of vital international significance, on the other.[14]

(e) The 'Social' Invasion

The United Nations Charter makes it crystal clear that the maintenance of world peace consists not only of avoidance of armed conflict, but also of measures to improve the lot of the individual and so remove tensions and pressures. International concern in this regard is a reflection of the acceptance by national governments of responsibilities over a very wide range of social affairs, and of their recognition that effective action depends greatly on international co-operation as well as on domestic measures. The volume of international business transacted today in the social area would dumbfound the diplomats of a century ago.[15]

(f) The 'New Issues' Invasion, especially Environmental Protection

The 'economic' invasion referred to above has, of course, a high technological content. It is also characterised by a rapid and growing rate of change. Futurologists have always existed in one form or another. But they are now perhaps more prominent and strident and better at articulating their concerns. There is at all events a growing emphasis on 'new issues', which require both the priority attention of the international community and new structures and attitudes to handle them effectively.

By far the most important of these 'new' issues is the protection of the environment. It is a massive subject, with wide diplomatic ramifications. The essential point is that popular concern over pollution and the depletion of natural resources has caused Western governments over the past 25 years or so to accord greatly increased attention to the question of protecting the environment. It is apparent that remedial measures require international co-operation on a major scale. Governments must take into account the numerous aspects of international relations with which environmental questions are interdependent. In the developing world the problem of the environment is primarily linked to population growth, poverty and related pressure on land and other natural resources. If, moreover, the remedial measures sought by the West were to include, for example, reduced emissions of 'greenhouse' gases, this would inhibit the industrial development of the poorer countries. In the view of the latter it should thus be the subject of compensation from those richer countries whose earlier industrialisation had contributed so signally to the problem. The protection of the environment, in other words, has become a further source of North–South tension.

A milestone was reached with the publication in 1987 of the report of the World Commission on Environment and Development, set up in 1983 at the request of the UN General Assembly under the chairmanship of the Norwegian Prime Minister, Mrs Gro Harlem Brundtland.

The report, entitled *Our Common Future*,[16] gave prominence to the concept of sustainable development: development which 'meets the needs of the present without compromising the ability of future generations to meet their own needs'. The concept is politically adroit, not least because it is deliberately vague. It points to international co-operation and shared costs. The Commission emphasised that sustainable global development required that 'those who are more affluent adopt life styles within the planet's ecological means – in their use of energy, for example'. Sustainable development could, moreover, 'only be pursued if population size and growth are in harmony with the changing productive potential of the ecosystem'.

The Commission was influential in mobilising the international community to tackle the manifold environmental issues on a more coherent basis. A monster UN conference on environmental questions was held at Rio de Janiero in 1992 – 'the Earth Summit' – a Framework Convention on Climate Change and a Convention on Biological Diversity having been concluded shortly beforehand. The interrelationship of environmental issues and other aspects of the world economy are considered further in Lecture 5.[17]

There are other 'new' issues, less cosmic in scale, but nevertheless of great world-wide concern and requiring co-operative international treatment and not merely national action. Of these, three spectacular examples may be quoted: drug abuse; terrorism, especially where it originates in ideological or religious differences, or springs from perceived denial of human rights; and the spread of HIV/Aids. The illicit drugs trade world-wide has been estimated to be worth some $500 billion, equivalent to 50 per cent of UK gross domestic product.[18]

(g) The 'Information Technology' Invasion

As this series of 'invasions' has suggested, interdependence takes many forms. But nothing has globalised our life as much as the revolutionary developments of the past 25 years or so, not only in communications themselves, but also in the fusion of the erstwhile separate operations of transmitting information and processing it. Progress has been so rapid and the prospects of even greater change so eye-catching that it may be hard to separate fact from fiction and sober forecasting from fantasy. Information technology is the touchstone of modern living.

Stuart Eldon, a member of the British Diplomatic Service, has recently written a book entitled *From Quill Pen to Satellite*,[19] which encapsulates the changes these developments have brought about in the work of foreign ministries. Process and substance are inextricably mixed in this, as in other, fields. The management of international relations will inevitably become more subject to the pressure of time. Its public content will rise. It will need to exploit, just as it cannot avoid being influenced by, developments in information technology. As already noted, these developments are already coming thick and fast. They will come even thicker and faster in the future.

(h)   The 'Multiplicity of Actors' Invasion

It is the inevitable consequence of the enormous expansion in international contact that those involved in the management of that contact should greatly increase in number. But the increase is a matter of cause as well as of effect. On the (highly) theoretical supposition that the vast increase in both the number of sovereign states and in the range of business handled intergovernmentally had brought about no change from the 'Old' diplomacy to the 'New', there would have been a corresponding increase in the number of diplomats and of officials in international organisations. Diplomacy would have been a growth industry on those grounds alone. But the transition to the 'New' diplomacy has been accompanied by a very great growth of public interest in, and involvement with, international relations. The actors are not only far greater in number, but also of a far greater variety, including politicians, lobbies, the media and non-governmental organisations of all kinds. Once, moreover, the concept of international relations ceases to be confined to intergovernmental activity, but is widened to include the sum total of the impact of one country on another, or indeed of one civilisation upon another,[20] the growth in the number of actors is even greater. The multiplicity must include exporters, visible and invisible, and even tourists, the activities of all of whom may have a bearing on the management of international relations. In theatrical terms, the play is no longer a classical drama on a small stage; it is an epic film with a cast of thousands.

THE IMPLICATIONS OF THE TRANSITION FROM 'OLD' TO 'NEW' DIPLOMACY

The intention of this survey of 'invasions' of the political foreground is to explain the transition from the 'Old Diplomacy' to the 'New' in response to the momentous changes in human affairs which the twentieth century has witnessed. Significant as each of the 'invasions' is individually, it is their combined impact which has transformed international relations. They are a most powerful mix of substance and process. Together they have profoundly affected diplomacy in each of the six meanings of the word referred to at the beginning of this lecture. They have enormously widened the content of international affairs. They have greatly complicated the conduct of foreign policy. They have likewise complicated the management of international relations at the same time as they have made the grisly alternative of war infinitely more destructive. As for the apparatus for the management of international relations, diplomacy has come to resemble a business enterprise, whereas, in earlier times under the 'Old Diplomacy', it may have seemed to be more of an art.[21] By the same token the manner in which relations are conducted has undergone profound transformation. Finally, the 'invasions', collectively and cumulatively, have profoundly altered the skills and knowledge required to do a diplomat's job, while not altering to the same extent the personal qualities he or she needs to do it successfully.

The lectures which follow seek to illustrate the combined impact of all these changes on the business of diplomacy, marking the transition from the 'Old Diplomacy' to the 'New'. The lectures observe the sequence set out in the Introduction, which discussed the elaboration of a framework for developing the capability to help to make policy, the key requirement for a diplomat. Lectures 2 and 3 analyse the practical effects of the transition from 'Old' to 'New', both as regards the nature of today's world and the problems which national governments encounter in organising their efforts to deal with it. They cover respectively 'The Nature of International Society Today' and 'National Sovereignty and its Limits'. Moving on to institutional features, Lecture 4 discusses the United Nations, the principal institutional expression of the 'New Diplomacy' and a vital element in the interdependent world of today. No one imagines that all our affairs can be handled exclusively by or through the United Nations and the bodies linked to it in the UN system. The UN is a necessary, but not a sufficient, condition of adequate management of today's world. What then would constitute a sufficient condition? There is, of course, no single answer. A practical way of tackling the issue is to look at the reality of the world economy and the arrangements which governments need to manage it, in full recognition of the non-economic factors – social, developmental, environmental and security – which are relevant. This is the task of Lecture 5.

Lecture 6 deals with 'European Architecture', the extraordinarily complex web of arrangements affecting not only the continent of Europe, geographically defined, but also the Atlantic and the whole of Russia, as well as Japan. This reflects not only the importance of the European dimension to the 'Old Diplomacy' and the transition to the 'New Diplomacy', but also the vital European element in securing future world peace and prosperity. An Appendix to Lecture 6 surveys the peace agreement on Bosnia and Herzegovina from the point of view of the institutional features involved.

Lectures 7, 8, 9 and 10 approach the 'New Diplomacy' from the operational aspect. They revisit the phenomena covered by the first six lectures respectively from the point of view of foreign policy formulation, the organisation of professional Diplomatic Services, and, finally, the skills of the individual diplomat. The balance of emphasis between substance and process in these final four lectures may differ to some extent from the balance in their six predecessors. The mix of substance and process remains inextricable.

The Annexes include four texts dating from the closing months of 1995. While it is clear that texts chosen for illustrative purposes should be as up-to-date as possible, any selected simply on the basis of its recent appearance is quickly vulnerable to the passage of time. For reasons which are elaborated in the lectures, 1995 is a particularly fruitful year for the study of the evolution of the 'New Diplomacy', particularly as regards the United Nations in its Golden Jubilee year and the situation in Europe in the aftermath of the Cold War and the collapse of the former Yugoslavia.

2 The Nature of International Society Today

The previous lecture traced the evolution of diplomacy from the 'Old' to the 'New', during the course of the twentieth century, in response to a series of interdependent 'invasions' of the political foreground by 'non-political' phenomena, driven by the interaction of public interest and awareness and the revolution in communications. What diplomats face today is vastly different from what their predecessors faced a century ago. Policy-making has to take account of a far wider and more rapidly changing range of phenomena, and to operate in the full glare of publicity. It is incumbent on us to be as clear as we can about the nature of international society today.

This lecture discusses four propositions which encapsulate the transition from the 'Old Diplomacy' to the 'New' and illustrate what it is that diplomats, and those whom they serve, have to take into account to a degree unfamiliar in previous centuries:

(a) 'international' is by no means the same as 'intergovernmental';

(b) the distinction between external affairs and internal affairs has been blurred, and indeed partly submerged, by the onset of interdependence and by the impact which it makes on every aspect of life;

(c) this is the age of the common man and the common woman; and

(d) more and more is demanded of governments at a time when their capacity to deliver what is expected of them in the domestic, as well as in the foreign, sphere is being continuously reduced.

These propositions will be considered in turn. As with other aspects of interdependence, it is their collective and cumulative influence, rather than their individual impact, which serves to shape international society today, and hence to condition effective policy-making. This lecture will concentrate on the practical side of the analyses, thus helping to pave the way for the survey in the third lecture of the implications for state sovereignty and the 'legitimacy' of the state's activities in the field of foreign policy.

21

'INTERGOVERNMENTAL' AND 'INTERNATIONAL'

When it first made its appearance at the end of the eighteenth century, the word 'international' in practice meant 'intergovernmental'. There is an element of the tautological about this comfortable over-simplification. It does not suggest that there was no contact across boundaries which did not take the form of intergovernmental transaction. The situation was rather that there was a great deal of such contact, but that it was essentially private and not of national, or state, concern, and hence of intergovernmental concern. Interdependence put paid to that state of affairs in two respects. First, the range of matters affecting the citizen individually as well as the economy or society as a whole, which for one reason or another became of direct concern to governments, increased enormously. Secondly, the external component of the life of the nation grew so greatly that it became a major factor in the concerns of government, virtually irrespective of its strict intergovernmental content. The change was thus one of kind as well as of degree.

The distinction between what is international and what is intergovernmental is not therefore a point of mere theoretical debate. Sound management of international relations is concerned with the safeguarding and promotion of national interest while avoiding sources of difference and dispute, and hence the danger of friction, or worse, between nations. Any source of difference or dispute, however obscure originally, may come to occupy the attention of those responsible for foreign policy and the promotion of the security and prosperity of the realm. Interdependence spreads the net very wide. In simple diplomatic models, the sources of difference may be found more or less exclusively in 'political' matters and the policies pursued in relation to them by secretive, authoritarian, sovereign governments, ruling countries with more or less self-sufficient economies. In more complex international conditions the tensions may well arise from economic problems. Economics is about scarcity. Where there is no scarcity, there need be no economics. Where there is scarcity, there will be rivalry between potential uses and users of the resources in question.

As protagonists in international relations, governments may give expression not merely to rival political or economic policies, but also to profound ideological or religious differences. Prior to the twentieth century these rivalries and differences were reflected in intergovernmental relations. During the twentieth century matters may have moved on. In a striking article in the summer of 1993 in *Foreign Affairs*, the periodical published by the Council on Foreign Relations, the noted American academic Professor Samuel Huntington posed the question whether we are now faced with a 'clash of civilisations'. His contention was that the fundamental source of conflict in the years ahead will not be primarily ideological nor primarily economic: 'the great divisions among humankind and the dominating source of conflict will be cultural . . . the clash of civilisations will dominate global politics'.[1]

As was to be expected, Professor Huntington's thesis did not go uncontested. But its central message is one which diplomats cannot prudently ignore. Nation-states and governments remain the principal actors in the management of international relations. But, as already noted, there is now a multiplicity of actors.[2] We have thus to keep an open mind about which factors should at any particular moment have prior claim on our attention. Perhaps the word 'international' should be redefined, pejoratively rather than neutrally, as 'tending, or such as may tend, to cause difficulty in an interdependent world'. 'Foreign affairs', one expert observed wearily, 'are just one damn thing after another.' The eminent British novelist E. M. Forster characterised modern politics as 'telegrams and anger'.

EXTERNAL AND INTERNAL AFFAIRS

The manifold imprecisions surrounding the word 'diplomacy', to which reference was made in the first lecture, extend to the question of defining for purposes of administration and action what is meant by 'foreign affairs', for which there is usually a very senior minister or secretary of state constitutionally responsible. What in fact we are talking about is the external component of national life, which in conditions of modern interdependence may be predominant. Hence the traditional concept that foreign affairs are a self-contained, somewhat recondite, speciality, which can be hived off from the rest of public business and handled separately from it, will no longer stand up to critical examination. It has been apparent for a century or so that the elements of this external component have to be looked at as much in relation to those aspects of domestic business to which they are akin, as to the generality of external business of which the foreign minister is both the prime mover and the residuary legatee. In other words, one has to handle foreign affairs from the standpoint of their 'affairishness' as well as from that of their 'foreignness'. Hence the necessity for effective machinery of government for the conduct of foreign policy, an issue to which we shall return in Lectures 7 and 8. But there comes a point, especially, for example, in the case of smaller countries within a closely integrated international grouping such as the European Union, where the external component is not so much the tail wagging the dog as the dog itself.

In the case of the United Kingdom, this suggests a curious similarity with the situation before the Foreign Office came into existence in 1782.[3] The office of secretary of state developed from medieval times. By the seventeenth century there were two principal secretaries of state, each responsible for aspects of both home and foreign affairs. From 1640 their functions were divided into two approximately geographical spheres, northern and southern. These roughly corresponded to the division of Europe into Catholic and Protestant states during the Thirty Years War. The Northern Department covered the Holy Roman Empire, Holland, Scandinavia, Poland and Russia, while the Southern Department covered France and other Latin countries and Turkey. For the first century and more of the 'Old Diplomacy', Britain's foreign policy was conducted in harness with domestic policy. As a result of the 1782 reforms, the Northern Department became the Foreign Office and the Southern Department emerged in effect as the Home Office, but with responsibilities for the colonies (the number of which had recently been reduced by thirteen, as a result of the American War of Independence). The rationale of this division of labour 300 years ago was the affinity between various aspects of the external and internal components of the national life, whatever the relative proportions overall of the one to the other. The more complex those aspects, the more difficult it became adequately to provide for that affinity.

THE AGE OF THE COMMON MAN AND THE COMMON WOMAN

It may seem bizarre to describe the twentieth century, which has seen previously unimaginable horrors visited on the individual, as the age of the common man and woman. Hitler, Stalin and even Mao must surely be strong contenders for the title of the 'great enemy of the human race'. The death and destruction of two world wars, culminating in the dropping of two atomic bombs on Japan, surely bear comparison in terms of human misery with anything mankind has previously endured. The combination of technology, bureaucracy and ideology has been particularly lethal, for example in the Holocaust. The twentieth century has been the bloodiest in history. Although during the last 50 years humankind has been spared any repetition of the two world wars which blighted the first half of the century, tens of millions of people have perished as a consequence of conflict. The danger of nuclear obliteration, the development of even more vicious engines of mass destruction and the refinement of chemical and bacteriological weapons are fearsome testimony to the application of technological progress to the harm, rather than to the benefit, of human beings. Terrorism, already a scourge, could become infinitely worse if it gained access to the most sophisticated weaponry. Forced migration is the most eye-catching evidence of widespread deprivation among the world's fast-growing population.

But that is not the whole story. Life will never be free of danger and want. Nor indeed is it particularly enlightening to attempt to draw up a utilitarian balance sheet between pain and pleasure in one generation as compared with another. Our concern is with the implications for the management of international relations of the characteristics of international society today. It is in this respect that the proposition that this is the age of the common man *and* the common woman is central. Perhaps the most important respect in which international society today differs from the situation addressed by the 'Old Diplomacy' is in the status of women, politically, socially and economically. The twentieth century has seen great strides not only in the political and social emancipation of one half of the human race, but also in its economic situation. A hundred years ago it was normal to talk of the 'common man' when referring to the population as a whole. Today, even with the male chauvinist assurance that 'man' should be taken as embracing 'woman', the phrase rings palpably false. There is of course a very long way to go before the status of women could be regarded as equal, on whatever definition of the term might be accepted, to that of men. But the degree of progress already achieved is symbolised by the vast gathering in Beijing in September 1995, on the occasion of the Fourth United Nations Conference on Women. The event is referred to in more detail in Lecture 5.[4]

The proposition that this is the age of the common man and the common woman can be broken down into six subordinate propositions:

(a) the lot and the welfare of the individual is the focus world-wide of policy-making, as regards both domestic affairs and international affairs, to a greater extent than in any previous age;

(b) human rights have achieved a priority not previously known;
(c) democratic institutions and the principle of the answerability of
     government to the people have likewise achieved a prominence not
     previously witnessed;
(d) the non-governmental input into the management of international
     relations is greater than ever before;
(e) the average standard of living is the highest in history; and
(f) even though it is often identified in political discussion with
     bigotry, oppression and terrorism, fundamentalism should not be
     regarded simply as a synonym for alienation or extremism. Rather
     it is a warning that individuals are the ultimate arbiters of policy.

(a)   The Focus of Policy

The first of these subordinate propositions reflects perhaps the salient
characteristic of the 'New Diplomacy', and of the twentieth century
which it serves, namely the role which the individual has come to
occupy in the priorities of policy-making, both national and international. The welfare of the individual is pinpointed in the preamble to
the Charter of the United Nations with a directness and a clarity far
removed from the 'Old Diplomacy'. The ideas of democracy and
democratic responsibility have a long and honourable history. The
American Declaration of Independence speaks of life, liberty and the
pursuit of happiness as inalienable rights. But in Europe, and in the
empires in other continents where it held sway, it was largely a matter
of sovereign and subject rather than responsible government and
citizen. In the ancient world, and indeed in the modern, slavery was the
infrastructure for the institutions of democracy. When all allowance is
made for the gap between aspiration or objective and reality, the 'New
Diplomacy' has achieved much to make the present an age in which life
is more rewarding for the groundling. 'Good governance' is an
expression of the acceptance by those who have been elected of
comprehensive responsibility for the management of affairs in the
interest of the individual rather than of the state. The corollary of the
acceptance of this responsibility is recognition that the capacity to
discharge it to the satisfaction of the electors is the ultimate source of
democratic legitimacy.
    One aspect of the focus on the individual has been of particular
significance in the management of international relations, namely that
of humanitarian concern. Quick and generous international response

to disasters, natural or man-made, has been a prominent feature of the interdependent world. For this, television – both as a means of bringing into living-rooms around the world the horror in human terms of disasters, and as a spur to the raising of funds to help with relief efforts – can take much of the credit. But this humanitarian impulse is not an isolated and ephemeral affair. It is linked to the sustained effort which is essential to assist development in the developing countries. International development co-operation is a vast and complex business. Yet the needs which it exists to help in meeting seem always to outrun it.[5]

Humanitarian concerns likewise are not something separate from economic policy and somehow superimposed upon it. Rather they are inherent in social attitudes, the existence of which was assumed by the founders of economic theory to be a necessary condition for the implementation of their recommendations. Adam Smith is described on the title page of his great economic treatise *Wealth of Nations* as 'formerly Professor of Moral Philosophy in the University of Glasgow'. His fundamental doctrine as a moral philosopher was that all our moral sentiments arise from 'sympathy', which he said, 'leads us to enter into the situations of other men and to partake with them in the passions which those situations have a tendency to excite'.[6]

(b) Human Rights

Even if society takes the individual as the focus for policy-making, that is not the same thing as guaranteeing to him or her the essential freedoms which make life more rewarding. The individual must be not simply the object, but also the subject, of society's concerns.

In this sense, for all its shortcomings, the twentieth century merits the title of the age of the common man and the common woman. The consensus reflected both in the founding texts and in the deliberations of the United Nations is that the individual should aspire to, and should be helped to achieve, social progress and better standards of life 'in larger freedom'.[7] Hence the commitment to international co-operation in 'promoting and encouraging respect for human rights and for fundamental freedoms for all without distinction as to race, sex, language or religion'. Once again, these sentiments have not burst upon the scene fully developed. They are the product of centuries of thought, of pressure and of sacrifice. Nor is their formulation in documents, however solemn, a guarantee of their implementation. Nevertheless they represent, to an extent unmatched in history, the declared aim of

the international community to respect the individual and develop his
or her potential.

(c) Democratic Institutions

A key feature of the 'New Diplomacy' is the application to the
international community of the principles of democracy and the
creation of institutions to give them expression, notably the League of
Nations and the United Nations. While it cannot be supposed that
their creation is solely aimed at boosting the age of the common man
and the common woman, the efficient functioning of international
democratic institutions is none the less highly relevant. Democracy
among sovereign states, which may include among their number those
of authoritarian character, does not, as already noted, guarantee
freedom for the individual within such authoritarian states. But the
pressure of international opinion reinforces the pressures within
individual countries for safeguarding human rights and for respect
for the individual. The common man and the common woman, in other
words, have a source of support abroad of a sort which did not
previously exist. The anti-Apartheid movement is a striking illustration
of the point. This support was also a factor of great importance to the
oppressed peoples of the former Soviet Empire. It is relevant in many
countries today.

(d) Participation in Foreign Policy-making

The point has already been made[8] that there is now a multiplicity of
actors in the management of international relations. Their respective
inputs vary considerably. The inputs may be indirect as well as direct.
As factors to be taken into account in policy-making by governments,
they are significant and likely to increase in importance. The practical
implications are referred to in Lectures 4 and 7, dealing with the United
Nations and the formulation of foreign policy. The relevant point in
the present context is not only that the scope for popular participation
in the determination of foreign policy is greater, but also that
governmental policies built on inadequate popular consultation and
support will end in failure. The Maastricht Treaty can already be seen
as a textbook case of intergovernmental consultation becoming
seriously out of touch with the opinion of ordinary people.[9]

Striking though the Maastricht Treaty may be as an example of
inadequate participation by electors, as distinct from governments, it is

eclipsed by the collapse of the Soviet Empire. Seventy years of repression, indoctrination and terror, during which there was built up the most elaborate apparatus of control, ended in humiliating failure for the governments and the collapse of the system they were concerned to defend. The Soviet Empire was not crushed by external forces nor even by the weight of its own incompetence. It was cast aside by the ordinary people.

(e) The Standard of Living and Human Development

The validity of the proposition that this is the age of the common man and the common woman needs to be tested not only in terms of collective aspiration or commitment but also in terms of results. Fine words butter no parsnips. Promises do not fill empty stomachs. The twentieth century has produced spectacular results. Living standards have risen not only in the developed world, but also in a number of emerging countries, in a way which would fill the beneficiaries with grateful awe were they not so often inclined to take it for granted.

This is not to suggest for one moment that the problems of world poverty and deprivation have been solved. Far from it. But the economic and technical, and even the political, possibilities now exist to put a minimum acceptable level of existence within the reach of the world's growing population as a whole. One of the most significant developments of recent years has been the growth of economic activity in the world's most populous countries, China and India.

China's GDP growth rate in the past decade has been of the order of 10 per cent annually. India's rate in the same period has been more than 5 per cent, a notable achievement by the traditional standards of Western economies. These two countries between them contain one-third of the world's population, hitherto assumed to face insoluble difficulties because of sheer numbers alone. It was reported that China's wealthiest province, Southern Canton, had promised to eliminate poverty by 1997, when its neighbour Hong Kong, which now enjoys one of the highest per capita incomes in the world, reverts to China.[10] If China and India can achieve spectacular progress, the more obstinate areas of poverty elsewhere, especially in Africa, present the international community with a correspondingly smaller problem.

There are frequent optimistic forecasts as to the long-term growth prospects for world GDP and per capita income. On any 'objective' analysis these forecasts, if anywhere near accurate, would yield the resources to meet the requirement of a decent standard of living for all.

The catch, however, lies in the word 'objective'. As standards rise, so do expectations. So does the threshold of acceptability as to what constitutes an acceptable standard of living. The problem is subjective as well as objective.

The standard of living is not of course a matter of income per head alone. The Charter of the United Nations, as already noted, spoke of the determination 'to promote social progress and better standards of life in larger freedom', a broader concept. In recent years the United Nations Development Programme (UNDP) has combined two other indicators – adult literacy and life expectancy – with purchasing power to produce a Human Development Index (HDI). In 1995, in the context of the UN Conference on Women in Beijing, UNDP introduced two new indices to examine gender and development; one, the Gender Development Index (GDI) adjusts the HDI to indicate the discrepancy between men and women. The other, the Gender Empowerment Measure (GEM), evaluates the advancement of women in economic and political terms. Both the indices show that gender inequality is universal.

The historian Arnold Toynbee commented shortly after the end of the Second World War that our age is the first generation since the dawn of history in which mankind dared to believe it practical to make the benefits of civilisation available to the whole human race. Whether Toynbee and his contemporaries would have been equally confident about this possibility had they known that the world population would more than double well before the end of the century is a matter for speculation. But in the event the aspirations of 50 years ago have shown themselves not to be wholly misplaced.

Toynbee spoke of the 'benefits of civilisation', a wider concept than a better standard of living, even when the inclusion of qualitative indices such as the Human Development Index supplement the purely economic criteria. The point is well taken. A rise in the standard of living may not be an unqualified good. Prosperity is excellent as a springboard to achieve self-fulfilment. It is less satisfactory when treated as a cushion, bringing with it a decline in the competence and drive which produced it in the first instance. Social security can blunt the incentive to thrift and the readiness to make sacrifices. The widespread availability of credit, while undoubtedly serving the productive process, may put gratification ahead of prudence. Voluntary indebtedness may be as harmful in its effects as involuntary indebtedness. Consumerism is self-centred. What is delightfully referred to as the 'ex-pioneer spirit' – the feeling that the efforts of one's forebears justify taking life easily one's self – is a classic example of success carrying within it the seeds of its own destruction. Overall, a rapid rise in the standard of living may be accompanied by a decline in traditional civic virtues and in a loss of common purpose and faith. That can scarcely be called progress.

At one time the word 'Westernisation' was synonymous with progress. But the second half of the twentieth century has seen that automatic acceptance under increasing challenge. Just as in conditions of modern interdependence state authority has come to be regarded as an obstacle to progress in some respects, rather than its sole source as in earlier centuries – the point is developed in Lecture 3[11] – so there is increasing resistance to the simple equation of Westernisation with progress. There has been a resurgence of what are known as 'Asian values', as expressed in the highly successful economies of the Pacific Rim. 'Democracy', to quote a former Singaporean ambassador, 'is but one virtue in the basket of virtues to be weighed.' The Asian variant of democracy was in any case unlikely to be the same as the Western model.[12] It would put more emphasis on authority and on the common good. Mr David Howell, Chairman of the Foreign Affairs Committee of the House of Commons, has written a pamphlet entitled *Easternisation*.[13] The West should be 'clear-headed' about adopting 'Confucian' values, especially those underlying the strong family ties which, Mr Howell suggests, are not only a notable feature of East Asian societies, but also a key ingredient of the success of their economies. At all events it is surely prudent to expect some adverse reaction in the West, let alone elsewhere, to what is seen as a decline in the civic virtues, a growth of flagrant disregard of obligations and unheeding over-emphasis on rights which 'progress' has appeared to tolerate, if not actually to encourage.

(f)   Fundamentalism and the Capacity to Absorb Change

Life's experience does not suggest that progress will be free of obstacles or disadvantages. While it is clear that the great developments of the twentieth century including the 'New Diplomacy' have made the lot of the individual more rewarding, there has been a price to pay. What is the principal danger of which those concerned with foreign policy-making need to take account? The simple answer, perhaps, is 'the strains and stresses imposed on people by rapid change, especially change induced from abroad over which those affected feel they have no control'. It is clear that change has a differential impact on those whom it affects. It causes strains within families, within communities, between generations, between occupations. It may be seen as a threat to established values. The threat will be the greater if it is perceived as a form of aggression from abroad, albeit cultural or economic, rather than military. Change must go with the grain, and not against it. People need roots, and need them to be nourished. Disorientation and disaffection are the symptoms of change insensitively managed.

It is in this light that 'fundamentalism' can be so misleading a term, especially as it is often used in discussion of terrorism and militancy. Yet it is not synonymous with alienation nor with violence and extremism. Rather it is a useful warning that the capacity to absorb change is uneven. Rapid change may provoke a reaction of surprising strength. For policy-makers fundamentalism is a reminder that core values need to be respected; that the common man and the common woman are the repository of these core values, however unclear may be their articulation at any given moment; and that, in this capacity as the repository of core values, the individual citizen is likely to have the last say.

THE PRESSURE ON GOVERNMENTS IN SATISFYING THEIR ELECTORATES

The practical consequence of all these features of international society today – interdependence, complexity, rapid change, instant information and the mutual impact not only of countries but of cultures, even of civilisations – is to make the task of governments very much harder in the external, as well as in the internal, sphere. The issues governments have to weigh and the measures they have to take are of great and growing difficulty. To this, however, must be added the more subjective element, in democratic countries at least, of more exigent and impatient electorates, reflecting the advent of the age of the common man and the common woman. Electorates demand more and more of their governments at the same time as the latter are less and less able to furnish what is demanded. The Charybdis of rising voter expectations accompanies the Scylla of growing governmental impotence. Those elected to govern understandably claim from time to time that the country is 'ungovernable'.

The potential for instability which such a situation offers needs no emphasis. Yet this is not to suggest that there is only one outcome, namely the increasing denial by electors of national governments' 'legitimacy'. Conspicuous governmental failures are likely to encourage not only cynicism about governments and politicians, but also greater realism about the capacity of governments to satisfy rising expectations. It is at least a plausible hypothesis that a growing gap between the services demanded of national governments on the one hand, and the services actually delivered by them on the other, will encourage the realisation that public provision is not always the answer. The essence of *laisser faire* is that, in order to govern better, it is necessary to govern less. This philosophy in the past may have concentrated attention on getting rid of restrictions on the freedom of the individual. But the principle also applies to pretensions to organise everything centrally with consequent high levels of taxation. 'Big' government as the universal provider may in fact have reached its peak in the 1960s. There may once again be a trend in favour of civil society, a concept in which citizens get on with their lives, expecting the government to do no more than ensure security and hold the ring. International civil society is an extension of the same approach.[14]

A NEW WORLD ORDER/DISORDER?

The 1991 United Nations operation 'Desert Storm' to expel Iraq from Kuwait, coming swiftly on the heels of the collapse of the Soviet bloc and the end of the Cold War, raised hopes of a New World Order. There were references to the 'End of History',[15] representing the 'final' victory of liberal democracy and the market economy over totalitarianism and socialism. This optimism, indeed triumphalism, was soon recognised as premature. The fate of the former Yugoslavia was stark evidence of the threat of a new world disorder, rather than a new world order. The Bosnian Serbs surrounded Sarajevo in April 1992, with the declared intention of 'strangling' it. There is a dreadful symmetry about that event. As a phase in history rather than an arbitrary unit of time, there is a temptation to regard the twentieth century as having begun on 28 June 1914, with the assassination in Sarajevo by a Serbian terrorist of the heir to the Habsburg throne, which provoked the outbreak of the Great War. It can be regarded as having come to an end, likewise in Sarajevo, in April 1992. The twenty-first century, in other words, would have as its inheritance an instability resulting from the end of the Cold War and the increasing misalignment between the state system and the exigencies of interdependence. The prospects, on this analysis, would be bleak. We could be faced with endless friction and discontent without the common ground and the means to tackle them collectively.

But this pessimistic outlook should not go unchallenged. The international community must learn to organise itself to deal with the situation with which it is confronted. If the peace agreement on Bosnia and Herzegovina succeeds, and the twentieth century is reckoned to have come to an end not in April 1992, with the Bosnian Serb intention of 'strangling' Sarajevo, but rather on 14 December 1995, when the peace agreement was signed in Paris,[16] then the heritage of the twenty-first century would be much more encouraging. The point is discussed in more detail in the Appendix to Lecture 6. But whatever specific legacy the twentieth century leaves the twenty-first, the ingredients of effective policy-making are discernible. Chief among them is realism and a willingness to face unpalatable facts. The last five years have taught us that the vigilance which has characterised foreign policy since 1945 is indispensable. The pace of change makes it more necessary than ever. 'Nature', it is said, 'abhors a vacuum.' It also abhors over-simplification. Rapid change is rarely simple. Meteorology offers us a relevant insight. Television viewers are familiar with isobars, lines drawn on a map joining up points of equal barometric pressure. They are probably unfamiliar with the concept of the isallobar, a line joining up points of equal change in barometric pressure during a given period, for example three hours. The significance of the isallobar is that deterioration in weather conditions is closely associated with rapid change in barometric pressure. The applicability of this proposition to the political weather is clear. In conditions of rapid change we must expect stormy political weather.

Secondly, adversity can help in as far as it spurs us to count our blessings. Economic analysis is familiar with the proposition that the value placed on any good or service may best be judged when there is a risk of losing it. This is true of politics as well as of economics. What does anarchy have to offer? The danger is not so much that, when faced with the choice, people will opt for anarchy or disorder in preference to order. Rather it is that they will not be presented with such a choice since, in conditions of breakdown of order, those who are capable of framing acceptable policies to restore the situation may have neither the incentive nor the structures to put them into effect. 'All that is necessary for evil to triumph is that good men should do nothing.'[17] The crux of international relations, as of democracy within nations, is to press experience of the past into the service of managing the present and future, especially in the nurturing of the institutions which enjoy popular support and facilitate peaceful change.

Thirdly, the experience of 50 years of peace encourages the view that 'liberal democracies do not fight one another'.[18] We are entitled to derive some satisfaction in that regard from the operation of the 'New Diplomacy'. But satisfaction is tempered by the awareness that patriotism can take violent forms when aroused. Aggression is so basic an element in human nature that it cannot safely be assumed to have been exorcised by the international application of democracy. In any case, the greater dangers today arise not so much from conflict between states as within them. Nevertheless the proposition is worth examining, since, if it is true, it is a significant pointer to the priorities which the international community should embrace in the common interest.

'LIBERAL DEMOCRACIES DO NOT FIGHT ONE ANOTHER'

It is frequently said that war between this country and that is 'unthinkable'. In the case of the countries of Western Europe, for example, the explanation may be that the savagery and destruction of the Second World War were so great that they were sufficient to blunt any natural aggressiveness for generations to come. But human nature does not change definitively in short periods of time. However, institutions, even if they do not change human nature, can influence the way in which people behave, individually and collectively.[19] Indeed the extent to which institutions recognise the consistent quality of human nature, with its weaknesses as well as its strengths, is likely to be a reliable measure of their effectiveness. These considerations underlie the approach to the United Nations, the world economy and European architecture surveyed in Lectures 4, 5 and 6 respectively. There is a certain irony in the fact that the application of the principles of democracy to international relations was less a direct attempt to find the answer to peace between countries than a by-product of the application of those principles within countries. This illustrates the point that countries think in terms of their own core values, which are largely domestic, when managing their international relations. All too often in the past those core values have had a malign effect on international relations. With democracy the effect is demonstrably benign.

Internal democratic processes, if applied to the management of international relations, will act as a shock absorber when difficulties arise. They will provide for measured consideration of the policy to be adopted. They will discourage deceit and provocation and inspire confidence and willingness to explore mutually beneficial compromise. They reflect intelligent perception of self-interest in an interdependent world. War is so destructive that the winners, if any, are likely to be the few at the expense of the many. The many, if given half a chance, will prevent recourse to it. The prizes which have led them to go to war in the past – such as access to resources, *lebensraum*, water, fertile land or sources of energy for example – can be seen to be either unobtainable by force, or more easily obtainable by peaceful means. Just as mercantilism, which assumed that it was possible to gain in trade only at the expense of others, gave way to a more co-operative international trade theory of comparative advantage,[20] so *realpolitik* is giving ground to enlightened self-interest.

Yet is this a question of chicken and egg? Has the onset of interdependence, characterised by the series of 'invasions' of the political foreground described in Lecture 1, disposed of most, if not all, of the reasons for which men fought in the past? Is it interdependence, rather than the application of democratic principles and practice to the management of international relations, which diminished the incentives to fight? Is it indeed interdependence as we know it which in the long run makes the introduction of democratic institutions inevitable for managerial reasons?

The answer to all these questions is probably 'Yes, but. . .'. Democracy may be 'the worst possible form of government except for every other that has been tried'. But it is the key to the management of interdependence on the practical plane at least, whatever reservations there may be in various quarters at a philosophical level.[21] The wisdom of the 'New Diplomacy' is to use the institutions to achieve consensus as to process, and to contain any differences there may be about substance.

3 National Sovereignty and its Limits

The first lecture dealt with the evolution of diplomacy, a child of its time, from the 'Old' to the 'New', in response to waves of change which have brought about modern interdependence. The second lecture surveyed the nature of international society today, with the ambiguities it creates by reason of the mismatch between the realities of interdependence on the one hand, and the responsibilities which none the less still fall on national governments on the other. That mismatch asserts itself at every turn. It aggravates the difficulties of statecraft, already great enough. It is likely to become still more insistent. Its consequences for the practical conduct of foreign policy are far-reaching. They can be conveniently analysed by reference to the concept of sovereignty, that is, the source of authority by which governments exercise power. This lecture will approach the issue of sovereignty in four stages:

(a) sovereignty at home;
(b) sovereignty in relation to other sovereigns;
(c) sovereignty in the international system; and
(d) sovereignty and its limits.

SOVEREIGNTY AT HOME

As already explained, the 'Old Diplomacy' was the product of the international system which came into being with the Peace of Westphalia in 1648. The core of this system was the nation-state. The essence of the nation-state in turn was sovereignty in the sense of 'absolute and independent authority'. It is, however, the inevitable consequence of interdependence that these categories have to be substantially modified if they are to reflect the realities of the twenty-first century rather than those of the nineteenth.

There is in the first place a good deal of discussion about the reality of the concept of the 'nation-state'. It is clear that there is less congruence today between the concept of the nation and the concept of the state than was the case a hundred years ago. The practical test of nationhood today is not whether the people owe allegiance, willing or unwilling, to a state and its sovereign, but rather whether the people feel a sense of identity with those in political charge. Nationhood, in other words, is bound up with a sense of belonging – with geographical, linguistic, ethnic, cultural, ideological or religious ties – a definition which applies to minorities within states as well as to nations. A nation, it has been suggested, is a community of memory, and hence a community of the loyalties which memory engenders. The state, in this perspective, is something much more utilitarian. It is a vehicle for the delivery of essential common services such as security, law and order, and social goods. Its ultimate justification is its capacity of deliver those essential common services, in addition to incorporating adequately the affinities and loyalties associated with the concept of nationhood.

The enormous increase in the membership of the United Nations brought about by self-determination and decolonisation has underlined the decline in congruence between 'nation' and 'state' on the definitions used above. It has also underlined the extent to which statehood depends less on satisfying formal criteria than on the pragmatic willingness of other states to accord recognition to the entity in question. The disparities between the member states of the UN are glaring. But there is no real prospect in the foreseeable future of the state being replaced as the principal unit for the management of international relations. The requirement is rather to take account of its limitations.

Those limitations can, as suggested at the outset of this lecture, be best understood in relation to the concept of sovereignty. The definition of sovereignty mentioned above was 'absolute and independent authority'. There are, however, a range of other meanings of the term. Sovereignty can mean, *inter alia*:

(i)   supremacy or pre-eminence in respect of excellence or efficiency;
(ii)   supremacy in respect of power, domination or rank;
(iii)   supreme domination, authority or rule;
(iv)   the position of a monarch;
(v)   the supreme controlling power in communities not under monarchical government; and
(vi)   a territory under the rule of a sovereign.

Meaning (vi) is of immediate, albeit limited, interest in the present context, since territorial inviolability is naturally regarded as a key attribute of sovereignty. Hence territorial incursion is one of the most obvious sources of infringement of national sovereignty. More generally, however, meaning (v) reflects our prime concern: that is, the exercise of absolute and independent authority by the supreme controlling power in a state. That power may well not be a personal 'sovereign', but rather an elected government, subject to continuous and multifarious public pressures as well as periodic electoral approval. Sovereignty is put in commission.

Meanings (i) to (iv) illuminate attributes of sovereignty which have been associated in the past with monarchs rather than with constitutional governments. The concept of sovereignty of course long predates the nation-state system, and has meant many different things. It can signify not only competence in an administrative sense but also excellence, which has a normative character, more frequently associated with persons than institutions. To that extent it can aspire to command a fuller type of allegiance from the sovereign's subjects. It can mean submission to prevailing force, with the implication that might is right, or that possession, as the saying goes, is nine-tenths of the law. In so far as it implies respect for the status quo, however, it may be a matter of reverence for a personal sovereign rather than of fear of those who wield power. Taken to its logical conclusion, it can mean the divine right of kings. Less than a year after the Peace of Westphalia, the English were cutting off the head of one of their kings who espoused that right not too wisely but too well. His near contemporary in France, Louis XIV, was not unduly worried about divinity. As far as he was concerned, *l'état c'est moi*. The divine right to which European monarchs may have pretended originated in common European Christian tradition. It was, however, subject to moral law emanating from the same source. As a counterpart to the rights deriving from their sovereignty, sovereigns had obligations both to their peers and to those over whom they held sway. The Reformation, and the deep divisions in Christendom which ensued, broke this particular pattern of rights and obligations. We shall revert later in this lecture to the profound implications of that rupture for the management of international relations.[1]

For the moment, however, our prime concern, as noted above, is with meanings (v) and (vi). Sovereignty is exercised in all aspects of the life of the nation, including its international component. But in reality, how much power does the 'sovereign' have, and how will it be exercised in the management of foreign policy? If that power is absolute, then its exercise in the external component of the life of the nation is likely to be a good deal less complicated than if the power is much more subject to democratic control. The processes by which it is exercised will be less complex, the ends to which it is directed may be less diverse, and the degree of public concern and discussion of both substance and process will be less marked. But if society is characterised by concern for representative democracy, respect for human rights and the achievement of good governance, a concern to which those in power cannot but be responsive, the constraints on sovereignty will be much greater. If, moreover, the external component of the life of the nation is large, as it is likely to be in today's interdependent world, then the complexities of good management are compounded by the degree to which the concerns of the electorate are involved with the conditions prevailing beyond the national boundaries, over which the sovereign authority has limited control. The exigencies of the electorate may not be diminished. But the capacity of the sovereign authority to respond to them is clearly reduced. This paradox, to which attention has already been drawn in Lecture 2,[2] goes to the heart of the management of international relations.

There is a growing complaint that, in dealing with many of the problems which assail the international community, the nation-state is either too small or too big to take effective action. In an interdependent world no country is powerful enough to act entirely on its own. International arrangements of a wide variety are required. International machinery is indispensable. Yet such machinery may be ineffectual unless it is given sufficient power. This, however, nation-states may be reluctant to concede. Interdependence at the same time puts pressure on the internal structures of the state, especially where there are significant minorities with strong affinities abroad, ethnic, cultural, linguistic, religious or regional. Even where there are no such minorities, a wide variety of local considerations, combined with a highly articulated popular desire for 'participation', or 'subsidiarity', may exert well-nigh irresistible pressures on central government.

The irony of this state of affairs is that, while until relatively recently it was an engine of modernisation, the state is now being seen increasingly as an impediment to it. The tide is starting to turn in favour of smaller or larger units, as the waves of change already discussed transform the daily lives of ordinary people. The state is more and more under threat. It cannot realistically claim divine right. Nor is constitutional propriety any real long-term defence of pretensions to sovereignty. In the end legitimacy of sovereign power exercised at home or abroad will depend on the capacity of the government to deliver what the voters want. The dilemma was neatly summarised in the (no doubt apocryphal) form of rejection employed by the head of an Oxford college when faced with a prospective undergraduate of whom he did not like the look: 'Young man, I think you would be happier in either a larger or a smaller college.'

SOVEREIGNTY IN RELATION TO OTHER SOVEREIGNS

The 'sovereign' power exercised by a state in the management of its international relations is not a monolith. It is a result of the interaction of all the relevant forces, some of which at least are likely to be in conflict. Sovereignty may in consequence be difficult to locate. But for all its complexities and ambiguities, it is the central feature of international relations, since the state will remain the principal unit of political organisation. Hence relations between sovereigns are still of prime concern. In practical terms, governments recognise that there are internal constraints on their freedom of action in the field of foreign affairs to add to the constraints represented by the activities and interests of other sovereigns. Their room for manoeuvre is thus limited. But the situation is not one of unrelieved gloom. 'Sovereigns' with the capacity to communicate with one another will readily understand the extent to which they face problems in common. The prospects for dealing with them are likely to be improved by tackling them in a spirit of mutual comprehension, even mutual commiseration. One of the merits of the near-ceaseless round of high-level international gatherings characteristic of today's world is the contribution these can make in this regard. Diplomats, solicitous of their own position and prestige, may have been tempted in the past to keep leaders apart, alleging that bringing them together would engender such personal hostility and dislike that disaster would ensue. The days are gone, however, when such an approach could expect to gain much support. The requirement is not to avoid summits but rather to make sure they produce useful results. A key element in this connection is to secure mutual understanding among 'sovereigns' of why they feel impelled to have recourse to particular actions, and of why, if taken, those actions will provoke unfavourable reaction on the part of other 'sovereigns'.

The question of reaction on the part of others to one's own actions is crucial in the diplomatic sphere, as in so many others. Economic theory postulates a 'perfect' market where the actions of individual buyers and sellers have no influence on the actions of other buyers and sellers.

Such perfection is rarely attained in markets. It is unattainable in diplomacy. The situation is characterised rather by oligopoly, where the buyers and sellers are of sufficient size and consequence to affect one another's actions. To gauge the likely reactions of others belongs as much to the realm of instinctive judgement and experience as to that of pure analysis. In view of the consequences of misjudgement, however, recourse even to esoteric analytical methods should not be ignored. The theory of games, first elaborated some 50 years ago,[3] offers exciting, but not inevitably profitable, ideas on how to win at chess or poker, based on predicting the reaction to one's own moves. The applicability of the theory to the fields of business strategy and of diplomacy naturally suggests itself. But perhaps the key element for our purposes is less its analysis of techniques than its description of objectives: whether, for example, the objective is a 'zero sum game', in which the sum of the winnings of all the players is zero at every stage of the game, or a 'positive sum game', in which all the players may aspire to gain, albeit to different degrees.

In international trade theory, the doctrine of comparative advantage is an example of 'positive sum' economics. While one country may be more efficient than another in the production of all goods and services in which they have a mutual interest, and thus have absolute advantage in all of them, it is nevertheless in the interest of both countries for each to sell to the other those goods and services in which it has a comparative advantage and to buy those in which it has a comparative disadvantage. The same considerations broadly apply in the management of international relations. They indeed betoken what has been called a 'mercantile' approach to diplomacy: diplomacy is business and the task of business is to generate more business. Sir Harold Nicolson, writing in the late 1930s,[4] listed the mercantile as one of a number of styles or traditions of diplomacy. He contrasted the styles of four European powers: Britain, Germany, France and Italy. The British, in his view, while hampered by ignorance of conditions abroad and apt to oscillate between the irrational and the realist, nevertheless tended to regard the foundation of diplomacy as 'the same as the foundation of good business – namely credit, confidence, consideration and compromise'.[5]

The German approach, in Nicolson's view, was very different. It was 'heroic' rather than mercantile. German policy was essentially 'power policy', and reflected a warrior of military conception. It attached more importance to inspiring fear than begetting confidence. French policy, Nicolson argued, 'has, for the last sixty years, been governed almost exclusively by fear of her eastern neighbour and is thus more consistent than that of any other Great Power . . . This constant preoccupation is apt to render French policy tense, rigid and inelastic.' This rigidity stood 'in striking contrast to the mobile diplomacy of the Italians'. The Italian system was derived from the tradition of the Italian states of the Renaissance. It was based 'neither on the sound business concept, nor on power-policy, nor on the logical attainment of certain ends. It is more than opportunist, it is based on incessant manoeuvre.'

This comparative survey may seem somewhat bizarre in the 1990s. Nicolson qualified it, however, in two important respects. First, he recognised that what could be regarded as a difference in diplomatic style was really a function of different policies and interests – the inextricable mix, in other words, of our familiar twins, substance and process. Differences in diplomatic theory and practice, Nicolson said, 'arise from variations in national tradition, character and needs. It is these which determine policy; and policy in its turn determines diplomatic methods.'[6] Certainly one can gain from his classification some useful insights into the Europe of the 1930s: British appeasement and wishful thinking; Hitler and Nazi tactics; the weaknesses of the Third Republic in France; and Mussolini's posturing in Italy, the Mediterranean and Africa.

Secondly, Nicolson made it clear that he did not consider his list exhaustive. Rather, its purpose was illustrative. As such it is a valuable point of departure for analysing the range of approaches to the conduct of foreign policy which may characterise certain regimes. The more authoritarian and the more secretive the regime, the more personal, and even psychological, factors can be expected to play a part. What is it, over and above national interest on some general definition, that inspires 'autonomous' moves on the foreign affairs stage? Patriotism? A sense of destiny? Animal spirits (to which the famous British economist John Maynard Keynes attributed at least in part the investment decisions of businessmen)? Caprice? Intuition, a word which has acquired a new and sinister overtone as a result of its association with Hitler? A desire to redress a wrong? Opportunism (a senior British diplomat defined 'defencemanship' as 'the art of winning without actually fighting')? The list is virtually endless. Yet all these motivations can be regarded as 'sovereign', in so far as they recognise no obligation to others, and accept no constraint other than the resistance they encounter. Might, in other words, is right as far as it goes.

It is clear, however, that foreign policy conducted on such a basis is no recipe for world peace and harmony. The more interdependent the world is, the more disruptive such an approach will be. It will be counterproductive, even as regards the countries which adopt it in the belief that it is in their interest to do so. A more logical and effective approach is to work within a framework of obligations and constraints which are acceptable in shaping not only one's own policies but those of others as well. Enlightened self-interest, as distinct from egocentrically focused self-interest, points to some form of system in the management of international relations.

SOVEREIGNTY IN THE INTERNATIONAL SYSTEM

If we take as our point of departure the need for some system of managing international relations in the interest of all concerned, where should we look for guidance as to the construction of that system?

The 'Old Diplomacy', it will be recalled, was the servant of the nation-state system which came into being after the Peace of Westphalia in 1648 and the disastrous Thirty Years War which it brought to an end. The core of the nation-state system is the supremacy of the state, based on the secular doctrine of sovereignty and concerned with establishing law and order primarily in national terms, thus replacing the influence of both feudalism and the Church. The paradox of the situation, however, is that the more emphasis is laid on effective sovereignty at home, and the more sovereignty is regarded as neither moral, nor immoral, but rather amoral, the more doubt is cast on the nature of any authority purporting to govern relations between states. The need for some sort of system, however rudimentary, has been felt whenever communities find it necessary to have dealings with one another. That need was met by reference to such concepts as Natural Law, religious in its origin, and defined by St Thomas Aquinas as that part of the law of God which was discoverable by human reason, in contrast with the part which is directly revealed. Natural Law provides a rationale for control of the behaviour of sovereigns at home and among one another. Once, however, you remove any such restraint on sovereigns, you have another mismatch: that between the unfettered sovereignty claimed by nation-states, on the one hand, and the necessity of arrangements for managing relations between sovereigns, without which it is impossible to achieve their declared objectives, yet which make inroads into that same sovereignty, on the other.

Political theory has supplied a partial answer on the domestic plane: there is a 'contract' between the citizens of a country and the government under which the former concede to the latter very considerable powers of coercion in the pursuit of agreed objectives. This theory, however, cannot easily be transposed to the international scene. The relationships are more obscure. If there is any kind of contract, it is more elusive. It may be stronger on the demand side than on the supply side – that is to say, the need for such a contract may be more clearly perceived than the means of responding effectively to that need. The first approximation, at all events, is the concept of international law. 'The Law of Nations, or International Law', according to a leading British jurist J. L. Brierly in his standard work *The Law of Nations*,[7] 'may be defined as the body of rules and principles of action which are binding upon civilised states in their relations with one another.' This definition is of considerable interest for a number of reasons. First, it complements the definition of diplomacy adopted by the leading British authority, Sir Ernest Satow, which we considered in the first lecture: 'the application of intelligence and tact to the conduct of official relations between the governments of independent states'.[8] Both definitions have their uses as norms of behaviour to which the conduct of foreign policy should aspire. Neither would presume to be a comprehensive description of how governments, and other 'actors' in the field of international relations, in fact behave in their dealings with one another.

Secondly, the use of the word 'binding' implies that there is an obligation to respect the body of rules and principles of action. But the precise nature of that obligation is not stated. The obligation is not 'legal' in the modern sense familiar to us: that is, that it is based on positive law, backed up by the power, vested in some superior authority, to enforce compliance by sovereign states and to punish them for non-compliance. The use of the term 'international law' can be misleading if it suggests close similarity with national law. The term 'law of nations' is more accurate, perhaps, especially in what it suggests about the nature of the obligation expressed by the word 'binding'.

Thirdly, we need to look very carefully at 'the body of rules and principles of action' to which this *nuance* obligation applies. What is involved emerges clearly from Article 38 of the Statute of the International Court of Justice.[9] This provides that the Court, whose function is to decide in accordance with international law such disputes as are submitted to it, shall apply:

(a) international conventions, whether general or particular, establishing rules expressly recognised by the contesting states;

(b)   international custom, as evidence of a general practice accepted as
      law;
(c)   the general principles of law recognised by civilised nations;
(d)   judicial decisions and the teachings of the most highly qualified
      publicists of the various nations, as subsidiary means for the
      determination of the rules of law.

The 1961 Vienna Convention on Diplomatic Relations, which is the
latest and near-universal agreement on 'diplomatic intercourse,
privileges and immunities', affirms at the outset that 'the rules of
customary international law should continue to govern questions not
expressly regulated by the provisions of the present Convention'. This
underlines the point that while sub-paragraph (a) of Article 38 of the
Statute is relatively straightforward, there is inevitably an element of
circularity about paragraphs (b), (c) and (d). Do governments respect
customary law because it is somehow pre-existing, or is the behaviour
of governments, at least of 'civilised nations', the norm which
customary law in fact enshrines? The answer, naturally, is 'both'.
Governments may respect customary law on grounds which are not
legal. Sir Ian Sinclair, a former Legal Adviser to the Foreign and
Commonwealth Office, and a leading expert on international law, put
the matter with characteristic clarity:

> it is indeed because international law is seén to incorporate
> significant elements of international morality and conscience that
> appeals are made so often to its authority; but it is equally because
> there is considerably less than full agreement between states on what
> is the *content* of those international legal rules relevant to a
> particular dispute or situation that the continuing process of
> progressive development and codification of international law
> imposes itself an an imperative.[10]

If the 'body of rules and principles of action' of which the law of
nations is composed is thus a delicate balance between specific
obligations and general norms, the relevance of which has to be
judged in individual circumstances, is this not something of a frail
vessel to contain the hopes of international peace and harmony? There
are those who think that international law could be more realistically
regarded as a branch of ethics rather than of jurisprudence. Others
suggest 'law' should be spelt 'lore'. But that is not an argument for
rejecting it. The requirement is to recognise its limitations and to seek

to remove or diminish them. 'International law' as a form of super sovereignty may be unattainable. As already suggested, it may even be a misnomer. But there is an amalgam of common tradition, common interest, prudence and precedent which can at least be regarded as law *among* nations and which any country capable of taking an enlightened view of its self-interest cannot but uphold and encourage. This law among nations must be fostered, codified and expanded, a task which is rightly seen as a high priority for the United Nations.

A NEW WORLD ETHOS?

If, as suggested above, the constraints which international law imposes upon the exercise of national sovereignty are at least in part a matter of ethics, what role more generally is there for ethics in influencing the behaviour of governments in an interdependent world? Is it feasible to think in terms of an agreed system of ethics to hold the world together? A modern version, for example, of Natural Law? The eminent Catholic theologian Hans Kung believes that our new post-colonialist, polycentric age needs an agreed ethos which only religion can provide. Only religion, in Kung's view, has shown itself capable of leading and influencing whole populations, regardless of background and education. At the same time there would be no peace among the nations without peace among the religions. Dialogue among the latter was essential. Kung expressed his intention of examining the history and theology of Christianity, Judaism and Islam in pursuit of a secure ethical basis for world peace.[11]

This is a more optimistic reading of the international situation than that of Professor Huntington, discussed in Lecture 2,[12] whereby the clash of civilisations will dominate global politics. But it is far from irrelevant to the search for a code of conduct for dealings between sovereign nations. It prompts the question 'How far have we already achieved, *de facto*, if not *de jure*, an agreed ethos?' The United Nations Charter incorporates a degree of enlightenment and morality previously unachieved in international relations. The UN originally consisted of some 50 countries. With its present membership at more than three times that number, it is now effectively universal. Yet its tenets have remained unchanged. They have been expressed in practical form in collective action by the UN and its agencies in virtually every area of human concern. Indeed they have been spelt out in a great many agreed documents, particularly in the field of human rights.

The degree of consensus already achieved in the UN underlies the debate about moral and cultural universalism and moral and cultural relativism. At the United Nations Conference on Human Rights in Vienna in 1993, there was a challenge from a number of African, Asian and Middle Eastern countries as to the universality of the formulations in the 1948 Universal Declaration of Human Rights, the central UN document on the question. There were claims that the Declaration was Western in philosophical content and that the element of conditionality which it encourages in assistance from developed to developing countries constituted external interference in national affairs. In the Bangkok Declaration of April 1993, governments from Asia and the Pacific agreed that human rights needed to be considered in a context which takes account of 'the significance of national and regional particularities and various historical, cultural and religious backgrounds'. It is difficult to contest this proposition. But it does not exonerate governments from respecting the broad thrust of the UN consensus on human rights. Still less does it inhibit international action in pursuit of that consensus.

The record of the UN system is a good illustration of the functionalist approach to international relations associated in particular with the name of David Mitrany.[13] Mitrany's argument was that if states worked together in functional agencies, this would weave a fabric of political co-operation which would progressively promote the peaceful growth of an international society. Once again, there is unlikely to be simple and rapid agreement on any such proposition. But it reinforces the point that the work done by the United Nations, and the agreed formulations which are the basis for that work, are of great importance not only in themselves, but also for what they tell us about how we should conduct our affairs. They form a body of precedent and hence are relevant to customary international law. Brierly stresses that custom in its legal sense means something more than mere habit or usage: it is a usage felt by those who follow it to be an obligatory one.[14] This suggests that functionalism, over and above its political significance, possesses moral and legal significance as well.

While functionalism is a means of encouraging the international co-operation which is an imperative of interdependence, we cannot prudently rely entirely on the momentum which functionalism generates in order to sustain that co-operation. We cannot guarantee that interdependence will provide the necessary degree of enlightened behaviour. Is there then some other foundation upon which we can aspire to build a moral order which will underpin both the United

Nations and international good governance, and the functionalism which serves them?

Once again the answer is indirect. The moral order is desirable in its own right. Its influence resides in its inherent validity rather than in its practical value alone. At the very least we should avoid making the moral order more difficult to achieve. The British Chief Rabbi Dr Jonathan Sacks makes the point that the story of the late twentieth century is one of the displacement of the community by the state and hence of the replacement of morality by politics. What had once been a solution – the 'hyperactive' state – has become a problem.[15] This proposition joins interestingly with the argument, referred to earlier in this lecture, that the state is becoming an impediment to modernisation whereas previously it had been its principal agent.[16] Good governance depends increasingly on non-governmental factors. If, moreover, the greater danger in the future will be war within states rather than war between them, it follows that non-governmental factors will be of greater importance than ever in international relations.

SOVEREIGNTY AND ITS LIMITS

The purpose of this lecture, as explained at the outset, is to consider the limits on the freedom of manoeuvre of the government of states in the exercise of their sovereign responsibilities in the field of international relations. On the internal front, those limits are created by the complexity of the issues and the great variety of pressures and interests within the country which are thereby generated. Far from having a free hand, governments are in most cases subject to the pressure of public opinion and to the expectations of individuals as regards their standard of living and the services they expect from those in authority. Sovereignty is based on democratic legitimacy. The divine right of kings has been replaced by the voice of the people: *vox populi, vox dei.*[17]

On the external front, governments are again hemmed in by the complexity of the issues, of which interdependence is the key feature, as well as by the actions and the reactions of other sovereign governments in relation to them. The result of all these constraints is that life can be very difficult for the sovereigns. 'Uneasy lies the head that wears a crown.'[18] But the difficulties can at least be eased to some extent by effective practical co-operation among sovereign governments, not only on an *ad hoc* basis, but also in a more structured way by means of the promotion of a rule-based system. 'Democracy', it has been observed, 'is a system for counting heads rather than breaking them.'[19] Democracy applied internationally, with the 'New Diplomacy' as its servant, is a means of achieving the prime objectives of foreign policy – promoting the security and prosperity of the realm – not by ignoring the limitations on the sovereignty of governments, but by accepting them in the common interest, and putting them usefully to work.

4 The United Nations

A recurrent theme of these lectures is the mismatch between the inescapable realities of interdependence on the one hand and fierce enduring loyalty to national identity and sovereignty, and to the nation-state system which expresses them, on the other. For the reasons explained in Lecture 1, the mismatch has been growing since the Industrial Revolution in Europe 200 years ago.[1] As long as there is such a mismatch, a wide variety of organisations and arrangements will be required to help manage interdependence. There are indeed thousands of such organisations already in existence, all reflecting in their different ways the need for sovereign nations to act together rather than on their own. At one end of the spectrum these organisations may be concerned solely with regulatory functions in some limited specialist sphere. At the other end of the spectrum stand grand alliances with vital responsibilities for the safeguarding of peace. The organisations may be bilateral, plurilateral or indeed omnilateral; local, sectoral, regional, intersectoral, 'macro' or 'micro'. They all represent a certain national readiness, albeit reluctant, to accord to international bodies a measure of control over national affairs involving some sacrifice of sovereignty.

International organisations were already numerous in the nineteenth century. They have grown in vast profusion in the twentieth. They have also changed in character. In their simplest terms international relations can be thought of for practical purposes as more or less a question of treaties, requiring no follow-up other than observance of their provisions by the governments party to them. But as interdependence increased, a more complicated model of international arrangement was required. Just as on the internal scene self-contained statutory rules, enforced through judicial process, gave way increasingly to a new method by which the statutes merely outlined basic policies, created authorities to administer them, and defined the powers and procedures of those authorities, so in the sphere of international affairs, the self-contained treaty gave way increasingly to the establishment of international organisations with a permanent staff and a continuing existence of their own. The series of 'invasions' of the political foreground referred to in Lecture 1 gave enormous impulse to the building up of international organisations.[2]

The most spectacular development in international machinery was the creation of the League of Nations after the Great War. The League had all the lofty status of a treaty – indeed a covenant – and issued from a peace conference established on familiar 'Old Diplomacy' lines, and using familiar 'Old Diplomacy' terminology, for example, 'High Contracting Parties'. The outcome, however, launched the 'New Diplomacy'. The central feature of the League was the concept of collective security which required a collective enforcement mechanism automatically to respond to aggression regardless of who the aggressors were, a concept which could not but strike Europeans as somewhat utopian.

It is an irony of history that this first great instrument of the 'New Diplomacy' should have been rejected by the US Senate, in spite of the leading contribution to its creation made by Woodrow Wilson. The ensuing 20 years might have been very different if there had been a direct US commitment to the concept of collective security. The League would of course have been far less Euro-centric. There would have been a firmer counterweight to totalitarian ambition – German, Italian, Russian, Japanese. Yet for all its failings in the political and security spheres, the League illustrated the characteristics of the 'New Diplomacy' which have stood the test of time: public content and awareness; concern with democracy and human rights; co-operation in a range of economic and social activities; and priorities far wider than traditional 'political' questions. In the event the League proved more successful in the economic and social spheres than in the political. Its experience was a useful guide to those who set about the construction of a successor organisation at the end of the Second World War.

The name 'United Nations' was first used by President Roosevelt in 1941 to describe the countries fighting against the Axis powers. It was used by the 26 signatory countries of the Washington Declaration of 1 January 1942. They pledged themselves to continue their joint war effort and not to make peace separately. The need for an international organisation to replace the League of Nations was proclaimed in the four-power Moscow Declaration (United States, United Kingdom, China and the Soviet Union) of 30 October 1943. At the Dumbarton Oaks Conference in Washington in the following year those four countries drafted specific proposals. These proposals formed the basis of the discussion at the San Francisco conference in 1945, at which the Charter of the United Nations was adopted.[3]

THE ESSENCE OF THE UNITED NATIONS

The aims and methods of the United Nations are set forth with magisterial succinctness in the Preamble to the Charter, a text which contrives to convey in a mere 200 words the full significance of what was being put in hand.[4] 'The peoples of the United Nations', expressed their determination to save succeeding generations from the scourge of war; to reaffirm faith in fundamental human rights, in the dignity and worth of the human person, in the equal rights of men and women, and of nations large and small; to establish conditions for the maintenance of justice and respect for obligations; and to promote social progress and better standards of life in larger freedom. To these ends, the United Nations further expressed their determination to practise tolerance and to live together in peace; to unite their strength to maintain peace and security; to ensure that the use of armed force should be avoided save in the common interest; and to employ international machinery for the promotion of the economic and social advancement of all peoples.[5]

To give effect to these intentions, the United Nations Organisation was established with six chief components ('the principal organs'):

(i)   the Security Council, with primary responsibility for the maintenance of international peace and security and with mandatory powers to that end. There was to be permanent membership for the five great powers – the United States, the Soviet Union, Britain, France and China – with the right of veto;

(ii) the General Assembly, with overall authority and deliberative responsibilities, but without mandatory powers. Its resolutions contain recommendations to governments rather than impose binding obligations upon them;

(iii) the Economic and Social Council, with responsibility 'under the authority of the General Assembly' for the Charter provisions in the field of economic and social co-operation;

(iv) the Trusteeship Council, with responsibility in the field of some, but not all, non-independent territories;

(v)   the International Court of Justice, which was to function according to a Statute annexed to the Charter. Each member of the United Nations undertakes to comply with the decision of the Court in any case to which it is a party; and

(vi) the Secretariat, under a Secretary-General, who has the right to take the initiative and also, under the terms of Article 100 of the Charter, is to be free from pressure from member governments.

The latter undertake 'to respect the exclusively international character of the responsibilities of the Secretary General and the staff'.

The Charter made provision in three important respects for the operation and elaboration of these principal organs. First, under Article 7, it provided that 'such subsidiary organs as may be found necessary' could be established. Secondly, the Economic and Social Council was empowered, under Article 63, to enter into agreement with the various specialised agencies as to terms on which they should be brought into relationship with the United Nations. The UN was likewise empowered to initiate negotiations among the states concerned for the creation of any new specialised agencies required (Article 59). As a result of these two provisions, an elaborate network of UN bodies has been created, known as the United Nations 'system', as distinct from the United Nations itself. An Organisation Chart of the United Nations system is contained in Annex 1. Thirdly, under Article 71, the Economic and Social Council was authorised to make suitable arrangements for consultation with 'non-governmental organisations which are concerned with matters within its competence'. This provision underlines the point that public opinion and participation are of great importance to the work of the United Nations. It reflects the reference in the Preamble of the Charter to 'peoples' rather than 'governments', or 'High Contracting Parties'.

SIX PRINCIPLES UNDERLYING THE UNITED NATIONS

In the 1990s the provisions of the UN Charter, and the structures designed to give effect to them, may not look particularly radical. It is thus difficult to recapture 50 years later the impact which this great international contract had at the time of its adoption on war-torn nations, hungry for peace and reconstruction. It represented a fulfilment, tempered by inter-war experience, of the Wilsonian approach to the conduct of international relations, an approach very different from the traditional European devotion to *realpolitik* or *raisons d'état*. It epitomises the 'New Diplomacy' in contrast to the 'Old'. There are perhaps six main principles underlying the United Nations. First, it forswears war as an instrument of policy and commits its members instead to the avoidance of the use of force except in the common interest. This was a principle underlying the League of

Nations. But the UN Charter went further by emphasising the sovereign equality of all its members, bringing the concept of democracy into the conduct of international relations as well as of national affairs.

Secondly, it seeks a rule-based international society rather than acquiesence in anarchy or the law of the jungle. The relevant passage in the Preamble to the Charter speaks of the establishment of 'conditions under which justice and respect for the obligations arising from treaties and other sources of international law can be maintained'. This was to be achieved on the one hand by the setting up of the International Court of Justice and on the other by giving the General Assembly responsibility for 'encouraging the progressive development and codification of international law' (Article 13(1)). The International Law Commission was established in 1947 with this end in view. The concept of 'justice' is more elusive than that of respect for obligations, but is fundamental to it, in the sense that such respect will in the end be forthcoming only if the obligations concerned are thought to reflect 'justice'. Equally, respect for obligations will promote justice as well as reflect it.

Thirdly, collective security is addressed in a manner which is practical rather than theoretical. The Wilsonian concept of collective security, as already noted, required a collective enforcement mechanism involving all members automatically to respond to aggression regardless of the identity of the aggressors. The League of Nations appeared at times to operate as if it believed such a mechanism was in place, even though it patently was not. The UN concept is more subtle. It places responsibility where power lies. It requires action from the Security Council, which any of the powers possessed of a veto is able to block. There is thus an element of the *ad hoc* as well as a realisation that if one of the great powers is opposed, for whatever reason, then the mechanism is likely to be ineffective. A prominent British historian described the Charter as 'an Alliance of Great Powers embedded in a universal organisation'.[6] If the alliance is inoperative, which it indeed was for the duration of the Cold War, the Charter cannot be expected to function as intended.

Fourthly, the United Nations is concerned as much with prevention as with cure, as much with crisis avoidance as with crisis management. The causes of war are manifold and are likely to be much more complex than a simple clash of wills between authoritarian leaders controlling homogeneous states. A particular point of attention was the way in which governments treated individual citizens or groups of citizens, including minorities of whatever type – ethnic, linguistic, cultural, religious or regional. Human rights were seen to be a matter of prime international concern. There has in consequence been much discussion of the subject as a whole and the adoption of a large number of texts covering in detail a wide range of subjects. Three instruments may be mentioned as of particular importance: the Universal Declaration of Human Rights of 1948; the International Covenant on Economic and Social Rights of 1966; and the International Covenant on Civil and Political Rights, likewise of 1966. These three instruments, to which the vast majority of member governments have subscribed, together constitute the 'International Bill of Human Rights'.[7]

Fifthly, the logic of concern with the prevention of conflict was seen to lead very wide and very far into economic and social affairs, and the way in which these were handled, both nationally and internationally. Peace and prosperity were recognised as being closely linked. Development is a prime means of building peace. Peace is a prerequisite for sound development. The League of Nations, as already noted, had made some progress in dealing with economic and social issues on an international basis. But action on the scale required became more feasible once governments recognised in a more substantive way their responsibilities at home and, by extension, internationally in these fields, and once the techniques were evolved to follow up this recognition. This issue is examined in more detail in the next lecture on 'The World Economy'.

Sixthly, the United Nations embodied the concept of collective activity far more fully than had been the case previously in international relations. The United Nations is in fact three communities: it is first and foremost a political community, whose sovereign members have legitimate and often divergent interests. These have to be reconciled if the disaster of war is to be avoided. The sources of legitimate concern to the members of this political community are wide, as are the possible sources of conflict. Secondly, the United Nations is a community of management, in the sense that there is now an immense range of business transacted collectively by member governments, or by the Secretariat on their behalf, costing billions of dollars annually. It is thus vital that this business should be transacted effectively, in the sense of achieving the desired results, and efficiently, in the sense of optimal use of the resources required and available. Thirdly, the UN is a community of reflection. In an interdependent world of ever more rapid change, collective willingness to look around and look ahead is essential. Perhaps nothing illustrates this better than our concern with the environment and the need to achieve sustainable lifestyles.

THE 'ESCAPE CLAUSES' IN THE CHARTER

For all its emphasis on peoples rather than on governments, its concern with well-being and human rights, its provision for collective action and expenditure, and its sensitivity to the developments in the sphere of technology and communications which could supersede existing concepts of sovereignty, the UN Charter remains a key source of *governmental* authority and prerogative. This is starkly illustrated in four articles in the Charter which specifically preserve traditional rights of governments. 'Nothing in the present Charter' shall authorise the UN to intervene in matters which are essentially within the jurisdiction of any state (Article 2(7)); shall impair the inherent right of individual or collective self-defence in the event of armed attack (Article 51); precludes the existence of regional arrangements, which are in conformity with its Purposes and Principles, for dealing with such matters relating to the maintenance of international peace and security as are appropriate for regional action (Article 52); or shall prevent UN members from entrusting the solution of their differences to tribunals other than the International Court of Justice (Article 95). With this battery of let-outs, it might seem that there are excessive derogations from the obligations of member governments. There is, however, an inevitable trade-off between the surrender of operational responsibility which governments may be ready to make in the collective interest and in their own interest on the one hand, and the degree to which they are entitled to insist on the right unilaterally to protect what they see as their vital interests on the other.

It can be argued that the United Nations has served to tilt the balance in favour of the role of the state, while in the same breath emphasising citizens' rights, precisely at a time when interdependence has been demonstrating with increasing clarity the limitations on the ability of governments to deal with the problems and priorities of the day. To that extent the working methods and the prevailing ethos of the United Nations could be regarded as a hindrance to the establishment of the arrangements for governance most likely to achieve the full range of objectives of the UN Charter. But the relationship between the rights of individual states and the collective imperatives of peace and prosperity is far from straightforward. We are moving towards a global society, which may increasingly require global regulation. But that is not the same thing as saying we need a world government. Any global regime is likely to emerge from a gradual, and not necessarily orderly, evolution of nation-state arrangements and their reflection on the international scene in the shape of international organisations, especially the United Nations. Paradoxically the greater the safeguards to national sovereignty enshrined in the UN Charter, the more governments may be ready to accept in practical terms the logic of modern interdependence, a point which European federalists tend to forget.[8]

THE FIRST FIFTY YEARS: AN EVALUATION

Fifty years of rapid change is a short period on which to base any definitive evaluation of the role of an organisation as comprehensive as the United Nations. For four-fifths of that time, moreover, the world was blighted by the Cold War. Nevertheless one is entitled to draw up a strongly positive provisional balance sheet. If the scepticism with which the ambitious project was greeted in a number of quarters is taken as a yardstick, simply to have survived is a major achievement. An enterprise with such high aspirations would surely have foundered had it not been soundly conceived. Yet not only has it survived, it has more than tripled its membership, while maintaining a remarkable continuity of purpose and action, and manifesting at the same time the adaptability and flexibility necessary to adjust to radical changes in circumstances. The six principles underlying the United Nations discussed above remain firmly established. The United Nations retains the moral high ground gained at San Francisco in 1945. It was the dictum of Jean Monnet, an early Deputy Secretary-General of the League of Nations, but better known as one of the founding fathers of the European Community, that, while they may not change human nature, institutions can influence the way in which people behave.[9] Anyone looking dispassionately at the manner in which the empires of Europe stumbled into the Great War in 1914 could not but agree that some change in behaviour was desirable.[10] The habit of consultation, the recognition of common interest, the cultivation of common views and the practice of sensible co-operation have become ingrained and are seen for what they are: the servants of international harmony and welfare.

The Preamble to the UN Charter expresses the determination of the peoples of the United Nations 'to save succeeding generations from the scourge of war which twice in our lifetime has brought untold sorrow to mankind'. That determination has succeeded. The world has known many wars and much suffering in the past 50 years. It has been all the more conscious of these agonies because of the enormous growth in communications and media coverage. But it has been spared the catastrophe of war on the scale of the two world wars, let alone the obliteration of civilisation by nuclear holocaust. It would be as foolish to deny the United Nations some of the credit for this blessing as it would be to attribute it wholly to the United Nations. What would be even more foolish is to assume that the international community can dispense with the United Nations in the twenty-first century. This would be to take risks with the future of the human race which no democratically elected government would be entitled to countenance.

The task is rather to assess the performance of the United Nations in the past 50 years and to consider its role in meeting the requirements of the 'New Diplomacy' in the twenty-first century. It can fairly be said to have measured up well, for all its difficulties and shortcomings, to the exigencies of the second half of the twentieth century. It is indeed indispensable. To the extent that the 'Old Diplomacy' can claim to have kept the main peace for 100 years after the Congress of Vienna in 1815, the UN can claim, as already suggested, a similar achievement during the past half-century, in spite of the Cold War, which dominated international relations for most of that period.[11] It can also be credited with having faced, even if it has not solved, the multiplicity of problems short of shooting wars, especially in the areas of 'invasion' described earlier. It has achieved this by virtue of its flexibility and adaptability.

None the less, there are a number of sources of concern about how the United Nations can respond to the exigencies of interdependence today and tomorrow. Three may be mentioned. First, within the field of the maintenance of peace and security, which is the core of the responsibility of the United Nations, it will be necessary to keep under continuous review the extent to which the ban, enshrined in Article 2(7) of the Charter, on intervention in matters 'essentially within the domestic jurisdiction' of states can be realistically maintained in conditions of interdependence.[12] The 'New Diplomacy' is based, as was the 'Old', on the nation-state system. But its key elements of democracy, human rights, responsible government and international co-operation inevitably pose the question of how far legitimacy of government is based, not on the existence of the nation-state system alone, but also on the capacity of the system to deliver the conditions which enable people to lead peaceful and fulfilling lives. The 'New Diplomacy' in this regard points in the long run to the desirability, not simply of good governance in individual states, but also of global governance based on acceptable international authority: in other words, it points to an international civil society in some shape. How to express this, let alone to achieve it, is a task of great difficulty and delicacy.

Secondly, the search for 'social progress and better standards of life in larger freedom' which is at the heart of the UN, is not a matter for the UN alone. The UN can 'promote' – to use the wording of the UN Charter – these objectives. It cannot expect on its own to achieve them. Their promotion is allied to the progress of the world economy and the whole panoply of measures taken by governments to direct and supplement the efforts of individuals and companies in every relevant sphere. Social and economic progress and sustainable development are the products of an enormous variety of forces and of a great dispersal of decision-taking power. To manage the interdependent world we need flexible arrangements, embracing all those, governmental and non-governmental, who have influence in the global economy. These arrangements cannot but be closely linked with the United Nations. It is not essential that they be part of it. This issue is examined further in Lecture 5 on 'The World Economy'.

Thirdly, although the UN has recognised from the outset the significance of regional considerations, and the scope for regional, rather than global, settlement of disputes, the significance of the regional approach to world interdependence has greatly increased since the end of the Cold War. This is particularly true of Europe, not merely in the traditional geographical sense of the area between the Atlantic and the Urals, but also on the *de facto* basis used by the United Nations. As far as the UN is concerned, the European region, as covered by the Economic Commission for Europe (ECE), includes the USA and Canada and the whole of the former USSR. For many purposes Japan has likewise to be regarded as part of the 'ECE region'. Developments within this region, with all their instabilities and unpredictabilities, are crucial not only to its members but also to the whole of the United Nations. Yet its destiny is likely to continue to be worked out to a very great extent within the region rather than within world-wide gatherings. This point is central to the study of 'European Architecture' in Lecture 6.

KEEPING THE PEACE IN CHANGING CONDITIONS

Although the United Nations has two major examples of successful resistance to armed aggression to its credit – in the case of Korea in 1950 and of Kuwait 40 years later – it has been in a less spectacular area that it has become chiefly known, namely that of peace-keeping. Peace-keeping is the maintenance of peace, after hostilities have ceased and with the assent of the parties, by a 'thin blue line' of observers. Peace-keeping was not foreseen in the UN Charter. The elaboration of the techniques evolved has been of very great service to the international community. Since the end of the Cold War peace-keeping has become the largest, if not necessarily the most important, of UN activities with a score of operations in different parts of the world involving more than 50 000 military personnel. The cost of these activities in 1993 was $3 billion, three times the regular UN budget.

But in recent years the character of peace-keeping operations has changed drastically. It is said that 'liberal democracies do not fight each other',[13] a proposition to which post-Second World War experience lends some weight. But a decline in the number of wars between states has been unhappily accompanied by a rise in the number of civil wars, where the conditions inevitably make outside help of any sort more problematical. The thorniest problems with which the UN is now faced fall into this category: Sudan, Rwanda, Somalia, Angola, the former Yugoslavia. Where conflict occurs within states rather than between them, the traditional principles governing peace-keeping do not generally apply: the international character of the dispute; the consent of all the parties involved; impartiality; the non-use of force. What, moreover, is to be the relevance of the principle of non-interference in matters essentially of domestic jurisdiction enshrined in Article 2(7) of the Charter? If there is a complete breakdown of law and order within a country, leading to a situation which is both an affront to the international humanitarian conscience and a threat to neighbouring member countries, is there inevitably a case for moving from Chapter VI of the Charter, providing for peaceful settlement of disputes, to Chapter VII ('Action with respect to threats to the peace, breaches of the peace and acts of aggression'), under which the Security Council may initiate mandatory action? And, by extension of this trend, will the international community wish to intervene where a government, albeit well-entrenched, treats some or all of its citizens in a way which causes general outrage and a clear breach of undertakings as regards human rights? This point has already arisen in the wake of the expulsion of Iraqi forces from Kuwait, and over President Saddam Hussain's treatment of the Kurds and the inhabitants of Southern Iraq.

A NEW DEAL? PREVENTIVE DIPLOMACY, PEACE-MAKING, PEACE-KEEPING AND PEACE-BUILDING

This general approach to the issues of world peace and security has been central to the evolution of discussion about the role of the UN since the end of the Cold War. In January 1992, the Security Council met for the first time at the level of Heads of State and Government. The meeting was held at British initiative and under British chairmanship. While emphasising that 'the world now has the best chance of achieving international peace and security since the foundation of the United Nations', the Security Council undertook 'to address urgently all the other problems, in particular those of economic and social development, requiring the collective response of the international community. They recognise that peace and prosperity are indivisible . . .'.[14] The reference to 'all the other problems' is a reminder of just how wide-ranging is the agenda which the international community has to tackle. As already explained, over the past 20 years or so a range of 'new issues' has forced itself increasingly on our attention: environmental protection; mass forced migration; terrorism; organised crime; drug abuse; HIV/Aids. In addition, a number of social priorities have come into more constructive focus: the role of women in society; the needs of children; measures to help the aged and the handicapped.

The Security Council asked the Secretary-General, who had just taken up his post, to prepare an analysis and make recommendations on the ways of strengthening and making more efficient, within the framework and provisions of the Charter, the capacity of the United Nations for preventive diplomacy, for peace-making and for peace-keeping. Dr Boutros Boutros-Ghali's report was circulated in June 1992, under the title *An Agenda for Peace*.[15] In addition to the categories of preventive diplomacy, peace-making and peace-keeping the Secretary-General added a fourth category of 'post-conflict peace-building'. This is designed to construct a new environment, which should be viewed as the 'counterpart of preventive diplomacy'. There is thus a further link between the promotion of peace and security on the one hand and of economic and social well-being on the other. As the

Secretary-General remarked, 'preventive development is a necessary complement to preventive diplomacy'.

The General Assembly seized on this link when, during its 1992 regular session, it asked the Secretary-General to prepare a report on *An Agenda for Development*.[16] A trawl of member governments was put in hand. The President of the General Assembly held hearings in the summer of 1994 when the Secretary-General's first report was available. Dr Boutros-Ghali's recommendations were submitted to the General Assembly at its regular session in 1994. These are dealt with in Lecture 5 on 'The World Economy'. In the meantime a further summit meeting of the Security Council in January 1995 had been proposed, with the purpose of examining progress since the previous summit meeting. This proposal was not in the event pursued. But the Secretary-General issued on 5 January 1995, *A Supplement to An Agenda for Peace*[17] which laid stress on the practical problems which he was encountering in this area. He emphasised two of these: the difficulty of finding senior people able and willing to serve as Special Representative or Special Envoy of the Secretary-General; and the establishing and financing of small field missions for preventive diplomacy. The availability of troops and equipment had 'palpably declined'. In those circumstances the UN needed 'to give serious thought to the ideal of a rapid reaction force'. In the meantime the UN was unable to undertake peace enforcement operations. Such operations, moreover, were already 'creeping into what are meant to be peace-keeping operations': for example protecting humanitarian activities; protecting civilian populations in 'safe areas'; and 'pressing parties to achieve national reconciliation faster than they are ready to accept'.

It is important that this recital of discontents has not been generally cited as grounds for suggesting that the UN has no role in these difficult and ambiguous situations, still less that there is any other entity to which the responsibilities could be entrusted. Rather, the Secretary-General is challenging the UN membership to find the answers to new and pressing problems.

THE GENERAL ASSEMBLY 50TH ANNIVERSARY DECLARATION

The 50th anniversary of the United Nations was marked by a Special Commemorative Meeting of the General Assembly at the end of October 1995. It brought together a vast number of Heads of State and

Government, who issued a Declaration, the full text of which is reproduced as Annex 2. While its substance may be familiar, the authority and the comprehensiveness of the Declaration give it particular and lasting value to the student of diplomatic practice. It brings together the major international concerns in a manner which reflects both the aspirations which must continue to guide the international community and the attention to practical detail which is essential to fulfilling them. The text aroused little public interest. Its full value as an agenda for the future remains to be recognised.

The Declaration begins by solemnly reaffirming the purposes and principles of the Charter. It expresses gratitude to those who have served the UN so well in the past, especially those who have given their lives in its service. It expresses the determination of the 'Member States and observers of the United Nations, representing the peoples of the world' that the UN of the future will work with renewed vigour and effectiveness. They will equip, finance and structure it to serve effectively the peoples in whose name it was established. Accordingly 'we will be guided by the following with respect to peace, development, equality, justice and the United Nations Organisation'. There then follow detailed desiderata in each of the five fields mentioned. There is, it will be noted, no suggestion that all of this activity is to be pursued solely through the UN system, let alone through the UN itself. Rather, the member states and observers are speaking on behalf of the people of the world in relation to the whole gamut of their activities. Indeed it recalls specifically the pledge in Article 56 of the Charter that members will take both joint and separate action for the achievement of its purposes. The concluding paragraph of the Declaration recognises that common efforts will be the more successful if they are supported 'by all concerned actors of the international community', including non-governmental organisations (NGOs), multilateral financial institutions, regional organisations and 'all actors of civil society'.

Under the heading 'Equality', human rights are given a central position in the Declaration. 'We reiterate the affirmation by the Charter of the dignity and worth of the human person and the equal rights of men and women and reaffirm that all human rights are universal, indivisible, interdependent and interrelated.' The practical achievement of objectives in the field of human rights is seen to be closely linked with the prescriptions under the other substantive headings, namely peace, development and justice. The text of the Declaration illustrates the complexity of the arena in which diplomats have to operate and the need to grasp the institutional means available.

It illustrates the inextricable mix of substance and process. The Declaration is of course a statement of the problem, rather than a blueprint for its solution. The aims are easier to articulate than to achieve.

GOLDEN JUBILEE REFORM

The Declaration recognises that in order to respond effectively to the challenges of the future and to what people expect of the UN, the organisation must be reformed and modernised. It must have adequate resources. Member states should pay their dues promptly. The financial burden should be equitably shared. The Secretariats of the UN system must do a more efficient and effective job of resource management. The member states for their part will pursue and take responsibility for reforming the system.

This is grist to the mill of those who see the Golden Jubilee of the United Nations in 1995 as the context in which to press for reform. A principal area of concern is the role and composition of the Security Council. The preoccupation of the vast majority of member governments with the maintenance of the domestic jurisdiction as provided in Article 2(7) sets narrow limits on the extent of any agreement on increasing the powers of the Security Council to intervene in the affairs of individual countries. In any case the issue, as already suggested, is not one which is likely to be solved by amendment to the Charter. It is more likely to be approached by means of precedents. The United Nations will learn by doing. This in turn puts a premium on the efficiency with which UN operations are conducted, as well as on the clarity of the objectives to which they are directed, and on the maintenance of consensus within the international community, and particularly among the members of the Security Council, during the course of the operations. The achievement of consensus is crucial. It consists not simply of agreed diagnosis of the individual cases and hence of the treatment appropriate to them, but also resides in long-term confidence, established within the membership of the United Nations as a whole, that the Security Council, perhaps appropriately enlarged, is indeed an instrument for the pursuit of the common interest.

Enlargement itself may not be so great a problem in juridical terms, given that the Security Council has already been enlarged from the original membership of 10 to the present 15. Deciding on the terms of membership of the enlarged Security Council would be more difficult. *De facto* permanent membership for Germany and Japan, for example, which seems to be widely regarded as appropriate in view of their size and economic power, and acceptable 50 years after the end of the Second World War, could be achieved by deleting the last sentence of paragraph 2 of Article 23 of the Charter. This provides that a non-permanent member of the Council retiring after election for a period of two years 'shall not be eligible for immediate re-election'. Immediate and automatic re-election would bestow *de facto* permanent membership, without the right of veto. It is in any case unlikely that the General Assembly would agree by the necessary majority – two-thirds – to confer any veto power on new permanent members. Nor would prospective new permanent members be likely to press for it. But which countries other than Germany and Japan should benefit, either on the grounds of their world-wide influence or of their regional significance, from such a change? Indonesia? India? Brazil? Egypt? Nigeria? How far could the Security Council be enlarged without losing its effectiveness? The problem is not one on which the members of the United Nations could be expected easily to agree. Yet it remains a key part of the means of tackling the range of issues of concern to mankind and set forth with such admirable clarity in the Preamble to the Charter. Political consensus is a function of general consensus in the economic and social spheres, a reflection of the extent to which conflict arises from economic and social problems and not from political clashes alone. Crisis avoidance is preferable to crisis management. The focus is on the long, rather than on the short, term. In the longer term, economic issues may well be decisive.

In the UN context, pressure for reform is as great in the economic and social spheres as it is in relation to international security questions. Criticisms levelled at the UN on the economic and social side fall broadly into two categories, which may for convenience be classified as 'macro' and 'micro'. As regards the former, the UN system is regarded as unable to give coherent practical expression to the objectives set forth in the Charter. Hence it is said to require radical reorganisation and consolidation, involving the Secretariat, the General Assembly, the Economic and Social Council, and the structure of the system as a whole. A vast number of ideas have been put forward in this connection. The enduring difficulty about them, however, is that the management of the world economy is both too variegated and too dispersed a business to admit of any single effective controlling body. Even if governments were to agree on the establishment of such machinery, a possibility which is remote, the real world of inter-dependence would defy it. None the less the issue will not go away. It needs to be pursued in tandem with the Secretary-General's two 'agendas'. This again is an issue dealt with in more detail in the next lecture.

As regards the 'micro' category of criticism, the UN is often seen as slow, inefficient, wasteful and corrupt in its operational activities and expensive, unwieldy, over-elaborate and lacking in skill and zeal in its administration. Some of this criticism is the product of prejudice or ignorance. But the UN must follow up with vigour the valid criticisms which have been levelled against it, if it is to maintain confidence in its ability to fulfil the aspirations of the Charter. At the end of the day governments can withhold funds, or threaten to do so, as a means of exerting pressure on UN management. It is apparent that international co-operation in pursuit of the aims of the Charter does not stand or fall by UN activities alone. If it appears in the twenty-first century that there are more effective ways of achieving at least some of the desired ends, UN machinery will find itself at an increasing discount.

THE ULTIMATE RESPONSIBILITY

No organisation is better than its members. Theirs is the ultimate responsibility. The United Nations is neither a panacea nor an alibi. Its possibilities as well as its limitations were recognised from the outset. In the words of the official UK report and commentary on the Charter after its adoption by the conference at San Francisco:

> It is not suggested that all this machinery, however impressive it may be, can by itself preserve the peace or increase the welfare of the peoples of the world. That depends on how governments use such machinery, and their actions in turn will largely depend upon the public opinion of their countries as expressed through their legislative and other bodies. This fact cannot be over-emphasised . . . As it is, a powerful and flexible organisation will shortly be at [members'] disposal. An organisation, moreover, well adapted to the political realities of the modern world.[18]

That clear and sensible verdict has stood the test of time. For the membership collectively, and for members individually, the United Nations represents an opportunity as well as a responsibility. It is an additional dimension to the diplomacy of any country, whatever its size. But a word of warning is appropriate. The renunciation of force does not mean that power, be it military, economic, technological or in the realm of ideas and opinion, no longer matters. I have at times suggested to my students that there should be a further escape clause, to add to those described earlier in this lecture, namely a new Article 112 to conclude the Charter, which might read: 'Nothing in the present Charter should be allowed to foster the illusion that power is no longer of any consequence.' The fact of power cannot be ignored. The same is also true of the principle embodied in the United Nations that self-interest must be enlightened and that enlightened self-interest moderates the use of power, especially as regards the use of force. The 'New Diplomacy' gives scope to the less powerful in a manner conspicuously absent from the 'Old Diplomacy'. Every member country, whatever its size, has something of a handle on world affairs by virtue of its membership. Every diplomat should be familiar with what the UN is and does, and with what it can be induced to do.

5 The World Economy

In the previous lecture we looked at the United Nations as the principal institutional expression of modern interdependence and the leading vehicle of the 'New Diplomacy'. The range of its activities is wide, the range of its deliberations and concerns wider still. It is apparent that the United Nations, however much reformed or restructured, is unable on its own to manage interdependence. There is an enormous amount of business which must be transacted internationally yet which, for one reason or another, cannot be handled by or through the UN. As was explained at the end of Lecture 1, a practical means of assessing this requirement is to look at the reality of the world economy and the arrangements which governments need in tackling it.

As ever, precision is required. What do we mean by 'the world economy', a phrase which has long been in existence? We do not mean simply the internationalising of the economic process *per se*, important though this is. On the other hand, we should be cautious about the use of such all-embracing phrases as 'the Global Village' or 'Planet Earth'. While they have a useful role in stimulating thought and, indeed, aspiration, they may distract attention from the transaction of more detailed, but none the less essential, business at local, national or regional level. What we are concerned with is something in between, which is comprehensive yet specific: namely the ensemble of factors which enter into the international pursuit of economic and social progress, one of the key objectives of mankind, as set forth in the Charter of the United Nations. We pursue this objective, moreover, not only in its own right, but also as a concomitant of the other key objective of foreign policy, namely, ensuring peace and security. The 'world economy', on this definition, extends to virtually the whole range of human concerns in an interdependent world. The 'Old Diplomacy' would be quite unable to cope with such a task. The 'New Diplomacy' needs a variety of mechanisms with which to meet it. It must deal with international society as it is today, as described in Lecture 2. It must accept the limitations on the capacities of governments, as explored in Lecture 3. It must use to the maximum the scope which the UN offers, not only for keeping the peace, but also for advancing human welfare, as discussed in Lecture 4.

'PRIMARY' AND 'SECONDARY' GLOBALISATION

The word 'globalisation' is much in use as an expression of world-wide
interdependence. Once again, it is a word which suffers from
imprecision. By 1914, that is, during the lifetime of the 'Old
Diplomacy', the world had reached an advanced stage of cross-
boundary activity, as measured by standard criteria such as exports as
a percentage of gross national product, the volume of direct foreign
investment, and the scale of migration. International flows of goods,
services, capital and people had been encouraged for centuries, not
least through the classic device of concluding treaties of friendship,
navigation and commerce. Colonial expansion was likewise related to
economic development: 'trade follows the flag'. Two world wars,
separated only by 20 years of troubled peace, caused a sharp set-back
to the process of globalisation. The share of trade in GDP did not
return to 1913 levels until 1970 in the case of OECD countries
generally.[1] In the case of the United States this did not occur until the
late 1980s. For many Latin American and Asian countries the current
share is lower than it was 80 years ago. As regards direct foreign
investment, the total stock was 9 per cent of GDP in 1913, a figure not
regained as late as 1990. There has, however, been a very rapid increase
in direct foreign investment since the mid-1980s. The movement of
people is another story. Migration from Europe to the United States,
Canada, Australia, Argentina and Brazil in the 30 years or so before
1914 was far greater proportionately than it is now. Present controls on
migration stand in stark contrast to the scale and speed in the
international movement of other factors of production.

It is clear that when we look at the 'world economy' as an
institutional feature of diplomacy, it is not 'globalisation' *per se* which
concerns us, but rather the depth and the quality of interaction. The
'world economy' of 1914 was, broadly speaking, commercial and
imperial. The twentieth century, in its multifaceted interdependence,
has produced a far more intricate form of 'globalisation' – 'secondary',
rather than 'primary' globalisation. In Lecture 1 we considered a series
of 'invasions' of the political foreground which explained the transition
from the 'Old Diplomacy' to the 'New'.[2] There has been an
overlapping series of invasions of the commercial and imperial
foreground of the world economy. This series, subject to all the
reservations applying to its predecessor, with which it naturally bears a
close relationship, might be set out as follows:

(a) the onset of the Technological/Information Revolution, super-seding the Industrial Revolution of the eighteenth century, and bringing with it enormous advances in the economic process, including greatly reduced transport costs and increased speed of communication and volume of information;

(b) the rise of the transnational corporation, the principal vehicle of the international transfer of technology and of the globalisation of production, as distinct from trade in goods and services and the movement of the individual factors of production;

(c) a vast increase in international financial flows, representing large multiples of the trade and investment flows which it is their traditional function to lubricate;

(d) the acceptance by governments of much wider responsibilities in the management of the economy, as distinct from the balancing of government expenditure and receipts. Those responsibilities have far-reaching international, as well as national, implications;

(e) the impact of an overriding concern for human welfare and social progress, as distinct from economic growth *per se*, again a concern with wide international ramifications;

(f) the rise of consumer choice as a factor in the world economy, a reflection of the enormous increase in disposable income and personal credit facilities which increased prosperity has brought to the developed countries in particular. Leisure, fashion, entertain-ment, sport and tourism are now potent factors in international affairs;

(g) an abiding awareness of the particular problems and difficulties of the developing countries, which, in the wake of decolonisation, compose the vast majority of the membership of the United Nations;

(h) environmental priorities, which are becoming ever more insistent; and

(i) the security implications of interdependence, reflecting the increasingly complex relationship between the quest for safety and the quest for prosperity to which there is universal commitment.

One can be forgiven for pausing to take a deep breath before tackling the implications of all these 'invasions'. But there is no escape from the task if policy-making is to be effective. Secondary globalisation requires us to be continually on the look-out for relevant facets of interdependence, recognising that, even as we are ready to break new ground in our search, so we must be prepared to rework the old. It has been suggested that a useful indicator of globalisation is the percentage of time taken on national television stations by foreign-produced programmes. Three broad considerations are relevant. In the first place, interdependence advances geometrically rather than arithmetically. Not only is there interdependence *within* categories – countries, or peoples, or issues, or institutions, or channels of communication – there is also interdependence *between* those categories, with the consequent expansion of the phenomena of which we need to take account. To comprehend interdependence you do not add process to substance. You multiply them together.

Secondly, the momentous developments which have changed primary into secondary globalisation are the work not so much of governments as of private enterprise and the market. The main agents of change are non-governmental. The role of government has been to remove impediments to the free play of market forces and human energy and ingenuity. This reflects the philosophy of *laisser faire* that, in order to govern better, it is necessary to govern less. The twentieth century has provided some spectacular illustrations of the truth of this proposition, especially the disasters brought about by socialist planning and interventionism. The collapse of the Soviet Union prompted a former British chancellor of the exchequer to speak of a 'Darwinian' victory of market forces over the command economy.[3]

Thirdly, ensuring maximum scope for private enterprise and market forces does not mean that government can wither away. It is still necessary to hold the ring, a responsibility which governments have to discharge both internally and internationally, at the price of the sacrifice of varying degrees of sovereignty, as discussed in Lecture 3. However little they may directly manage the economic and social affairs of the country, governments are inevitably drawn into an extensive international network of regulation, consultation and co-operative action. The establishment of the network has, however, tended to be tardy. There has been an institutional lag in the way that structure has followed substance.

INSTITUTIONAL TRANSFORMATION: MANAGING THE WORLD ECONOMY

All these developments taken together require a transformation of international economic management. The world, as already noted, has seen a great expansion of international organisations concerned with the various manifestations of interdependence. The network of inter-governmental consultation with which we are now familiar is essential under present and foreseeable conditions, even allowing for the fullest encouragement of 'autonomous', or market-driven, economic activity. The problem is to adapt the machinery to changing requirements.

Perhaps the clearest illustration of this evolution of the world economy is to be found in the content and the context of the Uruguay Round of Multilateral Trade Negotiations, concluded at the end of 1993 under the aegis of the General Agreement on Tariffs and Trade (GATT).[4] The enormous complexity of the discussions and the long drawn-out processes which eventually brought them to a successful conclusion, have combined partially to obscure the magnitude both of what has been achieved, and of what has to be done to take advantage of that achievement. The coverage of the Uruguay Round is far greater than that of previous rounds. The World Trade Organisation (WTO), the body which has been created to succeed the GATT, has much wider responsibilities and greater powers. To examine the current situation, one can usefully start from the achievements of the Uruguay Round, and the related question of the tasks of the newly created WTO; and then survey the context in which arduous agreement was finally reached and in which the WTO will have to work.

THE ACHIEVEMENTS OF THE URUGUAY ROUND AND THE TASKS OF THE WORLD TRADE ORGANISATION

First, the achievements. These are summarised in the Declaration of Marrakesh (Morocco) adopted on 15 April 1994, which brought the Uruguay Round to its formal end:

(a) a stronger and clearer legal framework for the conduct of international trade, including a more effective and reliable dispute settlement mechanism;
(b) global reduction by 40 per cent of tariffs, wider market opening agreements on goods, and increased predictability and security represented by a major expansion in the scope of tariff commitments; and
(c) establishment of a 'multilateral framework of disciplines' in services and trade-related intellectual property rights and 're-inforced' provisions in agriculture and in textiles and clothing.

Ministers at Marrakesh were entitled to claim that the establishment of the World Trade Organisation ushers in a new era of global economic co-operation. But they did not suggest that the issues of trade policy which came within the responsibilities of the WTO were self-contained, still less that the work of the WTO was a comprehensive means of managing the world economy as a whole. Rather, they called for greater global coherence of policies in the field of trade, money and finance, including co-operation between the WTO, the International Monetary Fund and the World Bank. In other words, the world economy is in need of up-to-date management.

The unfinished business of the Uruguay Round, as measured by comparing the actual outcome with the stated intentions at its outset (as set forth in the Declaration of Punta del Este, in Uruguay, on 20 September 1986)[5] is substantial in particular areas, especially services. The world economy, however, is continuously on the move. Conditions have changed in a number of significant respects. The practical requirement now is to list the tasks which the WTO has to perform, some of which arise out of what was not agreed in the Uruguay Round. Without doubt the question of services and new areas of market liberalisation come high in this category. But a first priority is for the WTO to become a truly universal institution: China and Russia are among a score of countries waiting to join. Secondly, the WTO must see to it that the benefits of the Uruguay Round accrue to all its members. Thirdly, it must strengthen the rule of law in international trade, and be seen to be effective in the settlement of the disputes which are bound to arise. Fourthly, it must be able to adapt to the evolving needs and challenges of the world economy and to co-operate effectively with other institutions, especially the IMF and the World Bank. It must also bring its expertise and its authority to bear on trade-related issues which go beyond the concept of market access alone. As a world market gives place to a world economy, international arrangements to regulate and promote trade will penetrate within national borders into the heart of individual national economies and national concerns. These international arrangements may require national legislation. They will certainly be seen by some of the people affected as intrusive.

This international penetration into national economic and social arrangements will profoundly influence the formulation of economic policy, and indeed the development of economic philosophy. There is indeed a certain irony in the fact that while, particularly since the collapse of the Soviet Union, the world has become increasingly market-oriented, faith in the beneficial influence of market forces has come under increasing attack. It is not apparent, for example, that achieving international competitiveness should be the overriding priority, if it has damaging repercussions at home. A number of developed countries, which already face severe unemployment problems, fear that these will be exacerbated by firms shifting production overseas where labour costs are lower. There is a lively academic debate as to which is the greater source of unemployment in the developed world: international low-wage competition or home-produced technological progress. The rapidity of change sharpens this debate. Are robotics indeed a greater danger to the developed world than cheap overseas goods?

To some extent the issue is less important than the need in any case to increase efficiency in the allocation and use of resources. But the danger of increased protectionism which prolonged high levels of unemployment will stimulate needs no emphasis. It is considerations of this general order which may well be decisive as regards the future of the WTO. Are there indeed contradictions inherent in globalisation which will in the end prevent the achievement of the broad objectives of the Uruguay Round? Complete free trade has never existed. 'Managed' trade has never disappeared. The success of the post-war years has been rather in deregulation and liberalisation. But protectionist pressures are built up as the area of managed trade decreases. The sources of protectionism are many, and include security and social, as well as economic, considerations. The more the economy becomes global, the more consumers as well as producers who feel their livelihood or their lifestyle threatened for one reason or another will resist imports, or build regional alliances to counter world pressures. For liberalisation to be sustained, there must be a general confidence that competition is 'fair' as well as conducive to efficiency.

THE INTERNATIONAL CONTEXT OF THE BIRTH OF THE WTO

The international trade agenda facing the WTO is thus crowded. But it cannot be tackled in isolation from the other aspects of interdependence which impact on the world economy in conditions of secondary globalisation. These conditions, already described as a series of 'invasions' of the commercial and imperial foreground,[6] may be classified sectorally. Let us, for convenience, call them 'dimensions':

(a) the economic dimension;
(b) the social dimension, in which the spotlight is on people as beneficiaries of economic development rather than merely its agents;
(c) the migration dimension, that is, the effect of both voluntary and involuntary movement of people across national boundaries;
(d) the developing country dimension, that is, the particular concerns and needs, collective as well as individual, of the less well-off countries which make up the vast majority of the membership of the United Nations, and the need for continuing international assistance to them;
(e) the environmental dimension, namely, the concern for the safeguarding of our planet and our habitat for a worthwhile future for our children and grandchildren; and
(f) the security dimension, that is, the continuous interaction between the quest for safety and the quest for prosperity to which we are all committed.

(a) The Economic Dimension

It is more than 50 years since the Bretton Woods conference brought into existence the International Monetary Fund (IMF) and the International Bank for Reconstruction and Development (IBRD, which, with its affiliates, is now known as the World Bank). It was originally intended that there should be a third institution, the International Trade Organisation (ITO). But its Charter, as drafted at the subsequent conference in Havana, failed to find favour with the United States Congress. However, the commercial policy provisions of the intended ITO were rescued and brought into being in the 'temporary' General Agreement on Tariffs and Trade (GATT). The architects of the Bretton Woods agreements and of the Havana Charter were profoundly influenced by the debilitating and depressing experience of the interwar period, with ultimately self-defeating measures of protection and devaluation adopted individually, and selfishly, by countries in difficulty. John Maynard Keynes was particularly influential in securing acceptance by governments of responsibility for economic management, including the maintenance of a high and stable level of employment.[7] Such policies required international co-operation. Under the Bretton Woods arrangements the objective was to re-establish a world market, with sufficient control on the capital side to prevent the evils of 'hot money' and competitive devaluation. At the same time freedom of international trade and payments (on current, but not necessarily on capital, account) had to be reconciled with the achievement of high levels of domestic employment, and bilateral and regional arrangements had to be reconciled with world-wide arrangements. The IMF was to underpin a system of fixed exchange rates, while the IBRD would finance post-war reconstruction and development. Private capital flows, which were such an important feature of the pre-war scene, were assumed to be a thing of the past. Above all, there was to be a framework for international co-operation to replace the economic nationalism and 'beggar-my-neighbour' policies so prominent in the interwar years.

By any reasonable yardstick the achievement of the Bretton Woods founding fathers was outstanding. The growth in prosperity has been immense. Production and trade have increased enormously in the intervening 50 years. As with the role of the United Nations in the avoidance of world war, it would be as foolish to attribute this economic success wholly to the Bretton Woods institutions as it would be to deny them any credit at all for it. Nor would it be reasonable to suppose that the role and purpose of those institutions should remain unaltered when so much has changed. The system of fixed exchange rates has collapsed, largely because full employment could not be maintained alongside them once capital movements were freed. Nevertheless freedom of capital flows has been the means of providing resources for reconstruction and development on a scale beyond anything envisaged for the World Bank. Private flows have in fact resumed their previous role as a powerful engine for development. Money itself has been transformed by developments in technology and communications. Like information, money is now weightless. The whole of the international monetary system is 'hot' in the sense that daily financial flows represent, as already explained, a large multiple of the trade flows which it is their traditional function to lubricate.[8]

A dramatic illustration of interdependence is the way in which production has become globalised. Goods and services are not simply exchanged across national borders in their finished state. Multinational firms locate their production where the costs of production are lowest. Their capital strength, their technology and their marketing apparatus can be harnessed to production wherever it is most cost-effective. Today a significant percentage of a country's imports and exports may consist of what are called 'intra-company transfers', that is to say, movements across national boundaries of goods at various stages of production within a multinational enterprise. The reality of national economic sovereignty has of course been significantly diminished in consequence.

The fact that the Bretton Woods institutions have failed fully to keep pace with developments on the ground is perhaps of less importance in the long run than the universal recognition they have helped to secure that a continuing framework of consultation is indispensable. Developments in the world economy are more likely to be 'autonomous' rather than the product of established international institutions. The pace of technological change, already rapid, will undoubtedly increase. In response to this, intergovernmental co-operation will need to evolve *ad hoc* as well as to follow existing patterns. But the framework will be there, not only to maintain the rule of law in economic affairs and to monitor what is going on, but also to analyse the phenomena of the global economy, to ventilate and reconcile differing national perceptions, and to think ahead.

(b)   The Social Dimension

The world economy as an institutional feature of concern to diplomats is not confined to economic phenomena, complex though they are. The end-object of economic management is not economic growth alone, but prosperity in the sense of the well-being of the people – 'social progress and better standards of life in larger freedom', to quote again the Preamble to the United Nations Charter. It is a matter of no surprise that the positive approach to economic management, advocated in the 1930s by Keynes[9] in particular, was accompanied by a comprehensive approach to social security, associated in the United Kingdom with the name of William Beveridge. In his famous report on *Social Insurance and Allied Services* published in 1942, Beveridge spoke, in terms almost worthy of John Bunyan, of society's battle against the five 'giants' of idleness, ignorance, disease, squalor and want. His central concern was with enforced idleness or involuntary unemployment, and hence with policies to promote and maintain full employment.[10] He was not alone in this concern. Bitter interwar experience ensured that unemployment would be a focus of attention. It is interesting that the post-war conference in Havana, to which reference has already been made, and of which the purpose was to create an International Trade Organisation, was entitled 'The United Nations Conference on Trade and Employment'.[11]

In the event, unemployment was not a significant problem in the decades immediately after the Second World War. International discussion could in consequence concentrate on economic growth, rather than on unemployment or job creation. But this is no longer the case. The prospect now is that competing pressures for international liberalisation on the one hand, and the safeguarding of employment at home on the other, will be a leading theme of economic discussion and negotiation.

Concentration on the problem of unemployment does not mean that the other four 'giants' targeted by Beveridge are no longer of concern. On the contrary, they are gaining more and more prominence because of increased social awareness and rising expectations. Hence the emphasis on health, education, family structure, the needs of youth, fighting crime and measures to curb drug abuse, to take familiar examples. The relationship between the incidence, or the severity, of social ills and economic growth is of course complex. But the pursuit of economic growth in disregard of social priorities is likely to be counter-productive in the long term.

(c)   The Migration Dimension

One of the curious features of the twentieth century has been the extent to which the mobility of other factors of production – capital and technology – has increased enormously while that of labour has diminished. Migration has been far less 'open' than it was before 1914, except of course within areas of integration such as the European Union. In the nineteenth century the availability of desired destinations in effect exceeded demand. The reverse is now the case. Governments may have been slow to grasp the implications of this change. But a combination of rapid and uneven population growth in the poorer countries and stark contrast between the privations and discontents prevailing in those countries and opportunities known to exist elsewhere, have contrived to put the relatively prosperous areas of the world under great pressure. The most visible aspect of this pressure is of course the flow of refugees perennially seen on television as they flee disasters, man-made or natural. But it exerts itself in other forms. It cannot but be a major factor in the evolution of the world economy. Migration, whether forced or voluntary, will also be of great political and security importance. Ultimately the prosperous areas of the world will have to import either the goods and services or the inhabitants of less prosperous regions.

(d) The Developing Country Dimension

The world has been transformed in the twentieth century by the accession to independence of a large number of previously dependent countries and territories. There are now 185 members of the United Nations, more than three times as many as when the Charter was adopted in 1945. The great majority of these new members are underdeveloped and relatively poor. Some have made spectacular progress. But others will remain in the foreseeable future at a disadvantage. Disadvantage, like advantage, tends to be cumulative.

The international community has long been preoccupied with the problem of underdevelopment and assistance to the needier countries. This preoccupation has passed through a number of phases.[12] At the outset the emphasis was on technical assistance – as witness President Truman's 'Point Four' in 1949 – and on capital for development. But with the rise in the Non-Aligned Movement there was, in a second phase, growing emphasis on the 'rules of the game' in world trade, and on the perceived built-in bias against the newer, developing countries, mainly, of course, primary producers, and in favour of the older, developed countries, mainly industrialised. It is now 30 years since the establishment of the United Nations Conference on Trade and Development (UNCTAD) and 20 years since the proclamation by the United Nations General Assembly of a New International Economic Order (NIEO). The latter represented the apogee of the efforts of the developing countries collectively to restructure international economic relations to their advantage by means of General Assembly resolutions. The sequel to these efforts, generally described as the North–South dialogue, was disappointing for a number of reasons. But perhaps the most important of them was the realisation that excessive concentration on economic discussion tended to exacerbate, rather than to solve, the pressing social problems which it should be the end-object of economic progress to mitigate.

The North–South dialogue, after featuring prominently in the 1970s, gave way to a third phase of world preoccupation with the problems of developing countries. The latter continued to be active collectively in the Non-Aligned Movement and the Group of Seventy-Seven (G77). But the focus shifted. There was greater disaggregation of the study of development issues; more concentration on the benefits to the individual and less on the 'gap' between rich and poor countries; more weight attached both to private capital flows and to non-governmental charitable activities; more emphasis on the policies pursued by developing countries themselves, especially as regards structural adjustment and the encouragement of market forces; and more stress on good governance and respect for human rights. A series of UN conferences was held in the 1970s – on the Human Environment, Population, Food, the Role of Women, Human Settlements (Habitat) and Employment. These have been repeated, broadly speaking, at ten-year intervals. But the 1990s' versions have differed radically from their predecessors by virtue of their size, their scope and the vast numbers of participants, non-governmental as well as governmental. The 1992 Rio de Janeiro Conference on the Environment and Development (the 'Earth Summit') – held 20 years after the first environment conference in Stockholm in 1972 – was an enormous affair.[13] It was novel in that its cost was met by business corporations and foundations as well as by governments. NGOs moreover were active in the preparatory work. The Earth Summit adopted five texts: the Rio Declaration on Environment and Development; Agenda 21, a very wide-ranging programme which recognises the interrelationship between poverty, development and economic issues on the one hand, and environmental protection on the other, and hence the assistance which the South expects from the North as regards the former in the common pursuit of the latter; a Framework Convention on Climate Change, providing *inter alia* for control of the emission of 'greenhouse' gases; and a Convention on Biological Diversity, emphasising the need for the protection and conservation of species. The fifth text established a Commission on Sustainable Development (CSD) to monitor and guide follow-up.

The attendance figures speak for themselves: 178 countries were represented, 117 of them by Heads of State and Government. 1400 NGOs sent observers. In all there were some 35 000 accredited participants. Eight thousand journalists covered the event – indeed, taking into account the accompanying activities, which attracted 18 000 participants, the word 'happening' might be more appropriate than 'event'.

UN conferences would never be the same again.[14] A new phase of the 'New Diplomacy' had been reached. The 1994 Conference on Population, held in Cairo, had 10 757 registered participants, while 4000 people attended the NGO forum alongside the conference. In both substance and organisation the World Summit for Social Development, held in Copenhagen in March 1995, went further in establishing the pattern for this third phase of the international community's concern with the progress of developing countries, after the first phase of emphasis on technical co-operation and capital for development, and the second phase characterised by the 'North–South dialogue'. Social development is a comprehensive concept in that it embraces the environment, inequalities between North and South, population pressures and world tensions as factors in the preoccupation with the quality of life of the individual, in addition to the more immediate constraints of poverty, illiteracy, unemployment and social exclusion. At Copenhagen the specific themes were poverty, employment and social integration. The Declaration and Programme of Action adopted at the Summit were immensely wide-ranging, even while adhering to these priority themes. Two thousand non-governmental organisations were accredited to the Summit and more than 2500 media representatives covered the event.

The Fourth World Conference on Women held in Beijing in September 1995, has been described as the largest international meeting ever convened under United Nations auspices: 17 000 people registered, including 5000 delegates from 189 states and the European Union, 4000 representatives of NGOs and 3200 representatives of the world's media. In addition, an NGO forum was held separately at Huairou, 35 miles from the Chinese capital, which attracted no less than 30 000 participants. The Platform for Action which the conference adopted lists 12 'critical areas of concern': poverty; education; health; violence against women; armed conflict; economic structures; power-sharing and decision-making; national and international mechanisms to promote the advancement of women; human rights; the media; the environment; and the girl child. Summing up the outcome of the conference, Baroness Chalker, the British Minister for Overseas Development, declared that 'at Peking, women's concerns moved up the policy-making agenda. Their relevance to a wide range of economic political and social problems was acknowledged. Much of the inspiration for change has come from thousands of women's groups all over the world. The impact of Peking will depend largely on *their* success in working with men and with governments to turn words into action.'[15]

The next grand event was the Second United Nations Conference on Human Settlements (Habitat II) held in Istanbul in June 1996. It included representatives from cities, the private sector, other local authorities, grassroots organisations and NGOs, as well as from 170 national governments. Some 16 400 people participated in the debates and other sessions. The major theme was that cities are the world's future and they can be made liveable. The Conference adopted the

Istanbul Declaration on Human Settlements, *inter alia* committing governments to the wide-ranging programme contained in the 'Habitat Agenda'.

Each of these UN conferences builds on the work of its predecessors. There has indeed been a continuum of conferences in the present decade. Although they all place considerable emphasis on follow-up, as is to be expected, there is obvious difficulty in securing effective action on such enormously wide-ranging and complex issues. UNCTAD succeeded in establishing comprehensive follow-up machinery 30 years ago. But today's mega-conferences have a somewhat different role, namely, that of drawing attention to issues, facilitating discussion of them among all those concerned, and spurring governments, communities and individuals as well as international agencies, whether governmental or not, to work more effectively on their own and in greater co-ordination with others involved. This broad approach is realistic in that it recognises the degree to which responsibility for taking the action required is so widely dispersed. But it demands a certain patience and persistence about achieving concrete results.

International concern with the social problems of developing countries has become increasingly blended with general preoccupation with social issues, in which the developing countries element is important, but not necessarily predominant. This is an inevitable consequence both of interdependence, and of the wide variations in the economic and social performance of individual developing countries. But it does not remove the need for continuing help for the less well off, the more vulnerable and those afflicted by disaster. Rather, it changes both the context in which help should be sought and offered, and the understanding, in the light of half a century of mixed experience, of what international help can realistically be expected to achieve. There will always be an external dimension of development, including trade, technology, investment, development assistance and general international arrangements. Equally there will always be economists ready to 'prove' that 'aid' is ineffective, if not actually harmful to the recipient. Such assertions are unlikely to appeal to those who take a long-term view of the difficulties which arise in international relations and see the advantages of preventive diplomacy. Nevertheless they are both a useful discipline for the enthusiasm of those who want to help, and a spur to efficient allocation by the poorer countries of the resources available to them. They are also a reminder that aid, however well directed, is of less benefit than trade. In the same way it is the total flow of resources to developing countries which is important, rather than the proportion of these which have a concessional element in them, and can thus be regarded as 'aid'. This total flow of resources is affected by credit-worthiness, including the degree of past indebtedness which developing countries have incurred. For the past decade there has been a great deal of concern about such indebtedness and about the way in which servicing their debt has led some needy countries to be net exporters of capital rather than recipients. The Bretton Woods institutions have incurred some odium, by no means all well-founded, in this context. Mitigation of the effects of indebtedness has led *inter alia* to a number of British initiatives, taken mainly at Commonwealth meetings.[16]

(e) The Environmental Dimension

There are few issues so complex and all-pervasive as the protection of the environment, and few so difficult to handle with the precision required to ensure concrete action. The high profile which environment issues have achieved has in general yet to be matched by effective practical follow-up. Reference has already been made to the 1992 Rio de Janeiro Conference on the Environment and Development (the 'Earth Summit').[17] The documentary outcome of the conference gives some idea of the scope of environmental concerns. Those who negotiated the Uruguay Round, for example, were well aware of the need to safeguard the environment. At Marrakesh[18] trade ministers adopted a Declaration on Trade and Environment, decidedly a new departure for those whose responsibility is commercial. But reconciling awareness of the links between the two with the pressures which international trade negotiations impose on participants is another matter. Nevertheless the world will need to evolve principles for 'greening' trade in the interest, not only of protection of the environment *per se*, but also, of course, of sustainable development, of which protection of the environment is a key element.

(f) The Security Dimension

Finally, the security dimension. This brings us back to the point of departure, namely the interrelationship between the pursuit of security and the pursuit of prosperity as the prime objectives of foreign policy.

The security dimension is as important to the pursuit of economic prosperity as economic factors are to the pursuit of security. Just as the world economy is a great deal more than the exchange of goods and services across frontiers, so world security consists of much more than the avoidance of armed clashes between countries. Security, on its modern broad definition, has been aptly put in context by the United Nations Secretary-General in *An Agenda for Development*, referred to in the previous lecture.[19] We have to wind the security process back from peace-keeping to peace-making; from peace-making to preventive diplomacy; and from preventive diplomacy to peace-building. The causes of war and threats to security lie deep in the economic and social concerns of mankind, as well as in the ambitions and the designs of current leaders. Hence development as an imperative on its own shades inexorably into the removal of causes of discontent and strife. The opening proposition in the Secretary-General's paper is stark: 'development is a fundamental human right. Development is the most secure basis for peace.'[20] Following from this, the Secretary-General lists the dimensions of development in the following terms:

Peace as the foundation.
The economy as the engine of progress.
The environment as a basis for sustainability.
Justice as a pillar of society.
Democracy as good governance.

That is an admirable description of interdependence today, not as a basis for analysis alone, but also as a basis for action. But like the Declaration adopted at the 50th Anniversary Session of the United Nations,[21] it is a conspectus rather than a blueprint. As we have seen in the context of the mega-conferences described in the previous section, the responsibility for action is widespread, going far beyond any intergovernmental programme alone. Governments have to enlighten, encourage, inspire and co-ordinate others, as well as take action themselves, both individually and collectively.

ENSURING EFFECTIVE INTERNATIONAL CO-OPERATION: A RESTATEMENT

We need to restate the requirement: namely, to ensure international economic co-operation, in such a way as to achieve the objectives we hold in common, notably those set out in the Preamble to the United Nations Charter.

First, the world economy needs international (which means intergovernmental) regulation and management, as well as the benefits of market forces and private initiative and enterprise. The World Trade Organisation is the central institutional feature in this regard. It is the key to keeping the world economy rule-based.

Secondly, the work of the WTO has to be seen in relation to a number of other international concerns: it has economic, social, developmental, environmental and security dimensions. It is thus essential for the WTO to co-operate with other international agencies with relevant responsibilities.

Thirdly, the UN family has a central role to play in the management of economic co-operation, as of security co-operation, and in grasping the interaction between them. The question of UN reform is therefore closely linked with that of ensuring effective international co-operation.

Fourthly, this is not a matter which the WTO, the Bretton Woods institutions and the UN can settle between them on an inter-agency basis. It requires the direct and positive involvement of governments, whose ultimate responsibility it is to ensure that all the agencies they have created work appropriately together. Nor is the matter intergovernmental alone. It also requires the participation of all those who have the power of decision. As the Group of Seven – the Heads of State and Government of seven major industrialised nations and the President of the European Commission – put it in the communiqué adopted at their 1995 annual summit, at Halifax in June 1995: 'the major challenge confronting us is to manage [this] increased interdependence while working with the grain of markets, and recognising the growing number of important players. This is especially important in the pursuit of global macroeconomic and financial stability.'[22]

In the UN context the recommendations made by the Secretary-General in *An Agenda for Development* likewise reflect this responsibility. Dr Boutros Boutros-Ghali addresses a wide range of questions: the UN's operational activities; its financial needs; its current financial crises; its machinery of co-ordination, as regards the General Assembly, the Economic and Social Council, the Bretton Woods institutions and the sectoral and technical agencies; and its own managerial responsibility for ensuring inter-agency coherence in the United Nations system through the Administrative Committee on Co-ordination. The Secretary-General is looking to the General Assembly to focus the attention of the international community on forging a new framework for development. The difficulties are formidable. The key to success may be in finding a specific, as distinct from a general, priority which can attract the required authority and support among the membership. It has been suggested that the follow-up to the 1992 'Earth Summit' held in Rio de Janeiro could furnish 'a green knight galloping to the rescue of an ailing international system'.[23] It may be that the Rio process is the most practical hope for institutional reform within the UN system. But, as already suggested, it may also be the case that the pattern of mega-conferences will prove to be the best way in which the UN can hope to achieve the objectives of the Charter, namely, by acting as a forceful development-cum-security lobby on decision-makers, of whatever sort and at whatever level, in the world economy. This would not, of course, be a substitute for action by the UN system itself: but it would be a valuable addition to it.

GLOBAL GOVERNANCE

The most recent of the reports of the major independent commissions which in the last 15 years or so have contributed so much to our understanding of our common problems is entitled *Our Global Neighbourhood*. It was produced by the Commission on Global Governance under the joint chairmanship of Mr Ingvar Carlsson, the Prime Minister of Sweden, and Sir Shridath Ramphal, formerly the Commonwealth Secretary-General.[24] The Report defines governance as:

> the sum of the many ways individuals and institutions, public and private, manage their common affairs . . . It includes formal institutions and regimes empowered to enforce compliance as well as informal arrangements that people have agreed to or perceive to be in their interest.[25]

This definition underlines the comprehensive nature of what is involved in the satisfactory management of the world economy and the number and variety of the 'actors' involved. After setting out 'Values for the Global Neighbourhood', the Commission lists four areas for action:

      Promoting security.
      Managing economic interdependence.
      Reforming the United Nations.
      Strengthening the rule of law world-wide.

It is instructive to compare this formulation with the 'dimensions of development' listed by the UN Secretary-General in his *Agenda for Peace* and the range of concerns of the various summits of the 1990s, beginning with the 'Earth Summit' in Rio de Janeiro. The common message is the interdependence of the issues as well as the inextricable mix of substance and process.

At the risk of failing to do justice to much else in it, one particular recommendation may, in the present context, be picked out of the Report. The Commission says that the time has come to build a global forum to provide leadership in economic, social and environmental fields. Specifically, the Commission proposes the establishment of an Economic Security Council (ESC). The Group of Seven, the Commission comments, is the nearest the world comes to having an 'apex body' concerned with the global economy. But it is 'neither representative of the world's population as a whole nor very effective'.[26] The ESC, the Commission says, would be deliberative only. Its influence would derive from the relevance and quality of its work and the significance of its membership.[27]

It remains to be seen how the United Nations pursue this, and other recommendations made by the Commission. But they would be well advised to heed the Commission's definition of global governance quoted above and of the wide variety of 'actors' involved in it. The management of the world economy is a matter of close intergovernmental concern and needs to be undertaken at least in part on the basis of sovereign equality and democratic procedures which the UN expresses. At the same time, economic and financial realities, even among governments, are reflected in the weighted voting system adopted by the Bretton Woods institutions. To abandon that system would be to marginalise those institutions.

There are inevitably inner groupings. Among the developed countries, the Group of Ten was set up to mobilise additional funds. The Group of Five was involved in particular in financial control and surveillance. When its interests became wider, and it started to meet at Heads of Government level in 1975, the pressure to add first Italy and Canada, and then the European Commission to the original five – the United States, Japan, Germany, France and Britain – became irresistible. Russia's desire to join the Group is manifest. Wider European co-ordination, through the OECD, is substantial and based on the labours of a most competent secretariat. Very useful work is done on the co-ordination of assistance to developing countries. As regards the latter co-ordination among limited groupings has been less significant. Reference has already been made to the Non-Aligned Movement and the Group of 77.[28] The Group of Twenty-Four has been a feature of the Bretton Woods institutions; the Group of Fifteen is a more recent creation. The extent to which they are ready to deploy resources in common, as distinct from adopting policies in common, seems to be limited. Moreover, attempts to manage the world economy on the basis of intergovernmental action alone are doomed to failure. The multiplicity of actors must be taken into account, as noted by the Group of Seven in the passage in their Halifax communiqué quoted above.[29]

6 European Architecture

One of the curious features of our world is the way in which its land surface is concentrated in the northern hemisphere. This disproportion is exaggerated by perhaps the most familiar of traditional world maps – Mercator's projection. On this projection, which has been invaluable for navigational purposes, the lines of longitude and latitude intersect at right angles. However, a degree of longitude shrinks relative to a degree of latitude the further you get away from the Equator and the nearer you get to the Poles. To present a grid of this sort on paper as a rectangle, you have to increase the scale of measurement of latitude as you get nearer the Poles. The effect of this distortion is greatly to increase the apparent size of countries far away from the Equator, thus much reducing the relative size of those countries near it. The distortion is of much less significance in the southern hemisphere as there is little land at higher latitudes. But it is another matter in the northern hemisphere. Anyone looking at a Mercator's projection of the world would not guess that Africa is as large as Canada and Russia combined.

This distortion has its uses as an indicator of the distribution of world political and economic power. It is also a reminder of the way in which the richer, better-endowed countries can be described as the North, and the poorer countries as the South. More recent projections represent land areas in more accurate proportion and so constitute a step away from the Euro-centric geographical and cultural concept of the world.

THE CHANGING NATURE OF EURO-CENTRICITY

The word 'Euro-centric' is of key importance. Europe took some time to emerge from its 'Dark Ages' after the collapse of the Roman Empire. But the past 1000 years have seen a prodigious development of European civilisation, making, after some delay, a profound impact on the rest of the world. The 'Age of Discovery', as the Europeans perceived it, began 500 years ago. In diplomatic terms, Euro-centricity reached its height in the three centuries between the end of the Thirty Years War in 1648 and the outbreak of the Great War in 1914. There is a temptation to see in the wealth, the power and the arrogance of Old

Europe the seeds of its own destruction. At all events, a mere 80 years later it is difficult to reconstruct in one's mind the Europe of 1914. There were six great empires – the Russian, the Turkish, the Austro-Hungarian, the German, the French, the British – and at least five of less political and military consequence: the Spanish, the Italian, the Belgian, the Portuguese and the Dutch. Four years later, much of this imposing apparatus within Europe was in the dust or in the process of disintegration. European sway in other continents was for the time being much less affected. The New World, in the shape of the United States, had been called into existence to redress the balance of the Old.[1] (Japan was scarcely a key factor in the Great War. But its potential was already there for all to see.) The tide of Europe, which had been rising so strongly, had started to recede. The world had come of age.

It was not only American military and economic power which had redressed the balance in the Old World. As already explained, the US President, Woodrow Wilson, brought a new and distinctively American approach to international relations, a 'New Diplomacy' to replace the 'Old'.[2] The contrasting characteristics of the 'New Diplomacy' and the 'Old' have already been described. So has the chequered history of Woodrow Wilson's brainchild, the League of Nations. Whatever their explanation, the political, diplomatic and economic failures of the 20 years after the end of the Great War combined with the Second World War to complete the destruction of the Old Europe and its empires. The issue in the second global conflict was settled not so much by calling in the New World to redress the balance in the Old as by relegating Europe to the role of object rather than subject. European hegemony was replaced by European dependence, and indeed subservience. There emerged two superpowers – the United States and the Soviet Union – and an exhausted and largely prostrate Europe between them. 'Euro-centricity' had taken on a new connotation. It was no longer epitomised by the nineteenth-century high pressure area exerting its imperial influence in the rest of the world, while pursuing with growing imprudence its intra-continental rivalries. It had become the battleground for world powers based outside, a fate from which it could not expect to escape unless it could recover its identity and its sense of purpose, and so play a part in the interdependent world commensurate with its experience and its potential. The opportunity which Allied victory originally offered in 1945 for Europe to reconstitute itself, and build a future less tragic and less fratricidal than its immediate past, was to some extent vitiated by the Cold War, at least as far as the countries of Eastern and Central Europe were concerned. In spite of this, the record of the efforts to rebuild Europe after the destruction of the Second World War justifies a measure of optimism about the awareness of the dangers with which the leaders of today approach their responsibilities. Nevertheless the complexities of the situation, both internal and external, demand an accompanying measure of caution.

Let us begin with the basics. First, Europe in the geographical sense from the eastern shore of the Atlantic to the Urals in Russia, represents a very small part of the Earth's surface. But it accounts for one-third of its GNP and a great part of its intellectual capital. It is the well-spring of the modern world in politics, economics, science, social concerns and culture. It has also accounted for a good deal of the misery inflicted upon the human race in this century in particular.

Secondly, the bitter experience of the twentieth century underlines the point that it is not only Europe on the conventional geographical definition which is at issue in a discussion of 'European architecture'. We are also concerned with the involvement in Europe of other centres of power and influence, especially the United States and Canada to the west, and Russia and Japan to the east. Geography must be flexible enough to reflect the interdependence of economic and political power in the modern world, as these are expressed in such bodies as the Group of Seven and the OECD, and in the North Atlantic Treaty and the Organisation for Security and Co-operation in Europe. Above all the European Union, as it evolves, has vital implications for countries beyond its borders, let alone within them. The Union of Twelve became a Union of Fifteen on 1 January 1995. It may number a score or more at the turn of the century.

The immediate practical relevance in world affairs of all this European machinery is clear. Its full significance on the other hand is much less apparent. It is rooted in the past. In politics nearly everything has a long history. As diplomats we have to weigh the present in the light of the past. Nowhere is this more important than in understanding the bizarre complexities and inconsistencies of 'European architecture' and what these inconsistencies mean for the rest of the world.

REBUILDING EUROPE AFTER TWO WORLD WARS

The approach adopted in this lecture will be to examine, individually but in interaction with the others, the various elements of 'European architecture' which have, in their separate ways, evolved since 1945:

(a) the recovery of *identity*, signalled by the Congress of Europe in the Hague in 1948, and leading notably to the establishment of the Council of Europe;

(b) *economic reconstruction* under US leadership, essentially by means of the Marshall Plan and the OEEC (later transforming itself into the OECD) and the fabric of developed country consultation – G10, G5, G7 – running in parallel with the work of the IMF, the World Bank and the GATT, in which the leading developed countries inevitably played a dominant part;

(c) the search for *security*, in which Germany was gradually integrated into Western defence arrangements, themselves dominated by the Cold War: the Brussels Treaty, the North Atlantic Treaty, the European Defence Community and Western European Union;

(d) moves towards European *integration*: the Common Market, the European Communities, the single market, European Union, 'federalism' and 'subsidiarity';

(e) *the Treaty of Maastricht*;

(f) *enlargement* of the European Community/Union, the membership rising from six to nine, to ten, to twelve, to fifteen; relations with non-members, especially the European Free Trade Association, and the European Economic Area; and the dilemma posed by expanding membership: widening and deepening and the balance to be struck between the two; and

(g) *knitting Europe together after the end of the Cold War*, by adapting and expanding the machinery which had grown up during the course of it, both within the West and between East and West, notably the Conference (now Organisation) on Security and Co-operation in Europe (CSCE/OSCE).

While these elements of European architecture are logically distinct and need to be examined individually, their interdependence is manifest. It will be a test of European statesmanship to keep that interdependence, in all its confusing and conflicting detail, in perspective, and so prevent Europe from again becoming a world powder-keg.[3]

(a) European Identity: The Council of Europe

Dreams of European unity are age-old. But the ferocious rivalries of the end of the nineteenth century and in the first half of the twentieth century, and the fearful destruction wrought in two world wars, gave the quest for European unity fresh impulse. A number of organisations sprang into being after 1945, not least in England, under the inspiration of Winston Churchill, then in opposition after his defeat in the general election of 1945. At a famous speech in Zürich in September 1946, he said, 'My counsel to Europe can be given in a single word: Unite!' An international committee of the 'European Movement' was formed. The Congress of Europe met in The Hague in May 1948, attended by a large number of leading European personalities, including Churchill, who was Honorary President. Those who gathered in The Hague were invited in their individual capacities. Collectively, as they said at the time, they could 'claim to represent with authority every important aspect in the life and opinions of Europe'. The Congress called for the creation of a united Europe, including a European Assembly chosen by the parliaments of the participating nations.

Ministers of the five member countries of the Brussels Treaty Organisation (United Kingdom, France, Belgium, Netherlands and Luxembourg) examined the outcome of the Hague Congress. Subsequently there was a wider meeting of ambassadors resulting in the establishment of the Council of Europe. The Statute was signed in April 1949. The objectives of the Council were: to work for greater European unity; to uphold the principles of parliamentary democracy and human rights; and to improve living conditions and promote human values. The Council was further concerned to develop the common features shared by all peoples of Europe, 'the European dimension'. In essence, therefore, the Council of Europe embodied the recommendations of the Hague Congress, shorn of their supranational and federal elements. The Council was precluded from discussing defence matters, on the grounds that these were dealt with by the North Atlantic Treaty, and economic matters, as coming within the purview of the OEEC. The Council of Europe included in its machinery a Committee of Foreign Ministers, as well as a Consultative Assembly of Parliamentarians from the member countries. The former were determined to keep control firmly in their own hands, the adjective 'consultative' attached to the Assembly being a blunt reminder of the latter's modest status. This had the effect of putting emphasis in the Council's activities on legal and cultural matters, where it has rested ever since. The Council of Europe has become a leading influence in the promotion and protection of human rights. The original members were the five Brussels Treaty Powers, with the addition of Denmark, Ireland, Italy, Norway and Sweden. Subsequently membership rose to 23, including all the countries of 'Western Europe'. In terms of building Europe, the Council of Europe was a start. But enthusiasts for integration had to look elsewhere for giving their ideas practical expression.

(b) Economic Recovery: The Marshall Plan and OEEC

By the end of the Second World War Europe was devastated. The degree of devastation may even have been underestimated. What is certain is that the particularly severe winter of 1946–7 added to Europe's woes to the point where existing recovery efforts were manifestly inadequate.

Europe's plight was succinctly analysed by the United States Secretary of State, George Marshall, in a speech at Harvard University on 5 June 1947. The countries of Europe, he said, needed substantial additional help. But before the United States could proceed much further 'there must be some agreement among the countries of Europe as to the requirements of the situation and the part these countries themselves will take . . . The programme must be a joint one, agreed to by a number, if not all European nations.' The British Foreign Secretary, Ernest Bevin, took the lead in organising a European response to this offer. The Soviet Union chose not to take part and prevented its satellites from doing so. A conference in Paris under Bevin's chairmanship drew up a joint plan for European reconstruction. The conference appointed a Committee for European Economic Co-operation to pursue the discussions with the United States. Sixteen countries were represented on the Committee: the ten original members of the Council of Europe plus Austria, Greece, Iceland, Portugal, Switzerland and Turkey. France and Britain assumed responsibility for Western Germany's participation in the plan. The Committee became the OEEC in 1948. The European Recovery Programme was launched. The scale of the assistance, one-fifth of which took the form of loans and four-fifths of grants, was vast: $12 billion over a period of four years, equivalent to 2 per cent of GNP. On the part not only of the United States, but also of Canada, it was an enterprise of great imagination, administrative effort and generosity. As an act of foreign policy it was an immense success. As far as the European beneficiaries were concerned, the degree of supranationality, in a legal sense, involved in the exercise was limited. But the detailed economic planning co-operation and mutual examination which went into it reflected not only the dire realities of the current situation, but also

awareness of the continuing need for economic co-ordination and
co-operation. The OEEC became the OECD in 1961, a reflection *inter
alia* of its concern with assistance to developing countries. But by this
time integration as the way forward for Europe had become firmly
established within a smaller group of countries – the Six.

(c)   The Search for Security: NATO and WEU

These developments were overshadowed by growing post-war tension
in Europe. As early as March 1946, Churchill had spoken, in a famous
speech at Fulton, Missouri, of an iron curtain descending across
Europe 'from Stettin in the Baltic to Trieste in the Adriatic'. The
wartime alliance between the West and the Soviet Union dissolved into
mutual suspicion and hostility. Classic defence arrangements, already
in being among the countries of Western Europe, were seen to be
inadequate. They had been principally concerned with guarding against
any German military resurgence. The Treaty of Dunkirk between
France and Britain had been signed in 1947. In 1948 the Brussels
Treaty between Britain and France and the Benelux countries (which
had established a Customs Union among themselves in 1945) brought
into being a defence organisation.

The Soviet blockade of Berlin in 1948–9 formed the background to
discussions with the United States leading to the signature of the North
Atlantic Treaty in Washington in May 1949. The United States,
Canada and ten European countries – the Brussels Five plus Denmark,
Iceland, Italy, Norway and Portugal – joined a defence pact whereby
an attack on any one of these would be taken as an attack on all, a
commitment to Europe of incalculable value in the post-war world.
Combined with the Marshall Plan, it represented a United States
contribution without precedent to the security and prosperity of
Western Europe in the aftermath of the Second World War.

The situation of Western Germany became increasingly anomalous.
On the one hand, it was a defeated and occupied ex-enemy, whose
future was regarded with deep misgiving by the former victims with
which it was surrounded. On the other hand, Germany was the front
line in any war, unhappily now no longer beyond the bounds of
contemplation, with the Soviet Union and its satellites. The solution
put forward in 1950 by the French Prime Minister, René Pleven, was
for a supranational European Defence Community (EDC) with the
object of joint control of European military forces within the
framework of Atlantic defence. Under the aegis of the EDC there

would be German contingents in a European army rather than a national German army. The French were unwilling to go through with the EDC unless the British were part of it. The British were, however, determined not to join. Eventually, in 1954, the EDC Treaty, which had been signed in Paris in 1952, was defeated in the French National Assembly.

As a way out of the impasse the British Foreign Secretary, Anthony Eden, proposed instead the expansion of the Brussels Treaty Organisation to include both Western Germany (by now the 'Federal Republic of Germany') and Italy. Italy had been involved in the EDC discussions together with France, Benelux and Germany, that is, the Six. This arrangement would be known as Western European Union (WEU). Eden explained that Britain would, under certain safeguards, station forces on the mainland of Europe, another historic commitment. On this basis it was agreed that the Federal Republic of Germany should become a sovereign state, join the revised Brussels Treaty Organisation and become a member of NATO. A number of limitations were placed on German rearmament. But the militarism which was so greatly feared outside Germany showed very few signs of revival within it.

The issue in institutional terms was how WEU should evolve *pari passu* with European integration in a manner which strengthened rather than weakened the Atlantic Alliance. The principal difficulty in this regard at the outset was that de Gaulle, who had returned to power in France in 1958, insisted on playing an individual role.[4] France's distancing of itself from NATO's integrated structures, as distinct from the North Atlantic Treaty itself, long survived de Gaulle's disappearance. The ambiguity of WEU, as an element in the emerging European Union on the one hand and as the European pillar of Atlantic defence on the other, remains.

(d)   European Integration: The EC and the EU

Reference has already been made to the European Defence Community which foundered in the French Parliament in 1954. Its contemporary, the European Coal and Steel Community (ECSC), fared better. The impulse was the same, namely the need for reconciliation, above all between France and Germany, and, to that end, the creation of supranational institutions, which would not only bind these two countries and others together functionally, but also contribute to the restoration of Western Europe as a factor in world affairs. The idea of a coal and steel community was launched by the Schuman Declaration of 9 May 1950. The words of Robert Schuman, the then Foreign Minister of France, on that occasion had an historic ring to them:

> World peace cannot be safeguarded without the making of creative efforts proportionate to the dangers which threaten it. The contribution which an organised and living Europe can bring to civilisation is indispensable to the maintenance of peaceful relations . . .
>
> Europe will not be made all at once, or according to a single plan. It will be built through concrete achievements which first create a *de facto* solidarity. The reassembling of the nations of Europe requires the elimination of the age-old opposition of France and Germany. Any action taken must in the first place concern these two countries.

France was calling for action on one limited but decisive point, namely the placing of Franco-German production of coal and steel as a whole under a common higher authority. The successful establishment of the ECSC among the Six was indeed a stunning achievement. It marked the breaking of a centuries-old European mould. A similar community was established in the field of atomic energy (EURATOM) in 1957. However, the major step forward towards European integration was taken in 1955, when the foreign ministers of the Six, meeting in Messina in Sicily, decided to extend integration to all branches of the economy.

Britain was not represented at the Messina meeting. It was, however, represented at the preparatory committee which followed, but at a humble level and without significant influence. The general assessment in London was that nothing would come of the venture, an assessment which was rudely disproved when the Six signed the Treaty of Rome in 1957, creating the European Economic Community, better known as the Common Market. The Common Market was essentially a customs union combined with a highly protective Common Agricultural Policy.

The exact degree of integration envisaged, and the speed with which it was to be achieved, were perhaps of less importance than the ultimate objective and the means chosen to reach it. It was stated in the Preamble that the parties were 'determined to lay the foundations of an ever closer union among the peoples of Europe'. They approached their task by 'establishing a common market and progressively approximating the economic policies of Member States' (Article 2). The key element in this task was the European Commission, a supranational secretariat required (Article 155) to ensure the proper functioning and development of the common market. It was given extensive, and indeed monopoly, powers to fulfil its duties. Jean Monnet, the principal founding father of European integration, had for a time been the Deputy Secretary-General of the League of Nations.[5] He had been frustrated by what he saw as the powerlessness of the League of Nations Secretariat. He was determined that the European Commission should have adequate powers both to enforce Community decisions and to take the action necessary to attain its objectives. Monnet had already been the President of the High Authority of the Coal and Steel Community, the supranational precursor of the EEC Commission. But the mandate of the High Authority was not, of course, nearly as wide as that of the Commission. De Gaulle was determined to check the Commission's ambitions.

The UK response to the Treaty of Rome was to propose a European Free Trade Area, encompassing the whole of Europe with the European Economic Community joining as a single unit. De Gaulle scotched this. Britain therefore turned to the alternative of creating a European Free Trade Association (EFTA), with the Scandinavian countries, Austria, Switzerland and Portugal. Agreement was reached in 1960. But its shortcomings were clear to Britain. The Conservative government under Harold Macmillan decided in 1961 to apply for full membership of the EEC. De Gaulle vetoed this application at a famous press conference on 14 January 1963. Britain, he suspected, was too close to the United States, as well as being distracted by the Commonwealth and the sterling area.

The ensuing Labour government under Harold Wilson decided in the autumn of 1967 to reapply. This application suffered a similar fate at de Gaulle's hands a year later. De Gaulle's resignation in the spring of 1969 gave the British an opportunity to press again for membership. De Gaulle's successor, Georges Pompidou, had fewer inhibitions about the British. The application was pursued moreover with particular sincerity and conviction by Edward Heath, who became Prime Minister after the Conservative victory in the general election of 1970. The price Britain had to pay to join was acceptance of the structures and regimes which had by then evolved ('*l'acquis communautaire*') with all the unsuitabilities, especially as regards agriculture and levies on imports from the outside world, which that implied. Failure to be present at the creation was to cost Britain dear.

The United Kingdom, Ireland and Denmark joined the European Economic Community on 1 January 1973. Norway rejected membership in a referendum in 1972 (as it did again 22 years later). Greece acceded in 1981, and Spain and Portugal in 1986. These last three accessions owed rather more to political considerations than to economic inevitability. The need was to cherish democratic growth and resist relapse into militarism and dictatorship. By this time, however, the Community had its eyes on a considerable expansion of the area of common policy and activity. Since 1967 there had been a single Council and a single Commission, exercising all the powers and responsibilities vested in their respective predecessors by the three Community treaties establishing the ECSC, the Common Market and EURATOM. At a summit of the Nine in Paris in October 1972, that is, shortly before the Community was formally enlarged, there was an express decision to move towards monetary union and a more general intention to increase foreign policy co-operation. The European Monetary System (EMS) with its Exchange Rate Mechanism (ERM) was launched in 1979. But the UK refused in the first instance to take part.

The next milestone was the Single European Act of 1986, by which the members of the Community approved a blueprint and a timetable for adopting the measures, numbering some 270, to create a single market by 1 January 1993. The Act also provided for qualified majority voting in certain circumstances, thus bypassing the need for unanimous decision. At the same time the members of the European Communities agreed that they would endeavour jointly to 'formulate and implement a European foreign policy'. To this end, they decided to place European political co-operation on a more solid institutional footing.

(e) The Treaty of Maastricht

At their meeting in Hanover, in Germany, in June 1988,[6] the European Council set about reviving economic and monetary union. An intergovernmental conference was called for in April 1989. At Franco-German behest a separate intergovernmental conference was summoned to deal with political and institutional reform. Both conferences were to open on 14 December 1990. Their respective outcomes were agreed at the meeting of the European Council at Maastricht, in the Netherlands, on 9 and 10 December 1991, in the form of the Treaty on European Union. The Treaty was actually signed at Maastricht on 7 February 1992. There were key British reservations and 'opt-outs', especially in the field of social policy and as regards steps towards economic and monetary union. But these did not affect the central thrust of the Treaty itself. It goes much further than any previous agreement among members of the European Community. It creates a Union – 'a new stage in the process of creating an ever closer union among the peoples of Europe'; it introduces the concept of common citizenship; it sets out a procedure for achieving a single currency as part of an economic and monetary union; it provides for a common foreign and security policy, looking ahead to a common defence policy; and it extends co-operation in the fields of justice and human affairs. It introduces into community law the important but imprecise concept of 'subsidiarity', that is, the principle that action should be taken at Community level only if it cannot be adequately handled by the member states.

There was provision for review, at an Intergovernmental Conference to be convened in 1996, of the elements for the possible revision of which there is provision in the Treaty. On one interpretation of the Treaty and of the circumstances of its adoption, there could be little more to such an Intergovernmental Conference than minor adjustments in the onward march to a federalist Europe. But the realities of Europe may rule otherwise. The history of European integration is replete with instances where intergovernmental agreement has proved empty because intergovernmental discussion has run too far ahead of popular opinion and acceptance. There is a growing feeling that the Treaty of Maastricht is 'a treaty too far'. The text represents the culmination of a process of incrementalism in intergovernmental discussion, whereby European integration has proceeded from one treaty to another, adding to, or subtracting from, previous provisions to the point where even the expert, let alone the uninitiated reader, is baffled as to what precisely is at issue. The sources of legal and political dispute are inexhaustible.[7]

To prepare for the Conference, which opened in Turin on 29 March 1996, European Heads of Government established a 'Reflection Group'. Their report appeared in December 1995. The United Kingdom published a White Paper on 12 March 1996, entitled '"A Partnership of Nations" – the British Approach to the European Union Intergovernmental Conference'. To date there has been little discernible progress. The Conference was inevitably overshadowed by the beef crisis which erupted in the wake of the link suspected between 'mad cow disease' (BSE) and Creutzfeld-Jakob Disease (CJD). Britain's policy of non-cooperation with Europe was not resolved until the European Council meeting in Florence on 21 and 22 June 1996.

As regards the prospects generally, there are two major areas of concern in the post-Maastricht situation. First as regards substance, it can be seen that the detailed provisions for the approach to economic and monetary union are at best highly optimistic. The lessons of the failure of the first bid to achieve economic and monetary union, in the 1970s, have been inadequately absorbed.[8] The world oil crisis swept away the plans of the 1970s. Unemployment within the member countries, and the social malaise it engenders, may be the great stumbling block to Maastricht. The issue of economic and monetary union would be less contentious if there was encouragement to be drawn from the progress made in the other two 'pillars' of Maastricht – a common foreign and security policy and co-operation in the fields of justice and home affairs – which were designed to 'balance' the extension of community powers in the economic and monetary union field. The Bosnian situation has been a notable obstacle in this regard.

Secondly, the question of popular support for European Union has yet to be grasped imaginatively. Just as the Preamble of the United Nations Charter begins with the words 'We the peoples', so the fundamental objective of European integration is to create an ever closer union among the *peoples* of Europe, not among its governments. It is by no means clear that intergovernmental bargaining is the only method of achieving this. One is tempted to suggest that the Eurovision Song Contest or the UEFA Cup may be more effective, as well as less intellectually demanding, for those not directly involved.

The tensions and disagreements among the existing members on 'internal' issues, serious as they are, may be less decisive in determining the future of the European Union than the pressures exerted for enlargement. This pressure comes from the countries of Western Europe aspiring to join and *a fortiori* from the countries of the former Soviet bloc, where interlocking security and economic considerations apply with such force and complexity. It is to these two themes – enlargement of the Union to what inevitably becomes a position of overwhelming predominance to the west of the former Iron Curtain, and admission of countries to the east of it in a manner which will enhance their security rather than diminish it – that we now turn.

(f) Enlargement: The European Economic Area

As already noted, the European Community of Twelve in 1986 has grown to be the European Union of Fifteen with the accession of Austria, Finland and Sweden on 1 January 1995. The implications of a community of this size for the rest of Europe and indeed for the world as a whole, are profound. Indeed the impact of the Twelve, in the perspective not only of forming a single market but also of taking significant further steps towards union enshrined in the Maastricht Treaty, has been a major factor in the international scene for a decade. A Joint Declaration was signed in Luxembourg in April 1984, by the member states of the European Community (then numbering ten) and the EFTA countries – Austria, Finland, Iceland, Norway, Sweden, Switzerland and Liechtenstein. This recognised for the first time that there was need for a European Economic Area (EEA) encompassing both organisations. Official negotiations did not, however, open until June 1990. The text of the 'Main Agreement' of the EEA was signed at Oporto in Portugal on 2 May 1992. It was to enter into force on 1 January 1993, at the same time as the Single Market came into existence. The Agreement recognises the contribution which an EEA 'will bring to the construction of a Europe based on peace, democracy and human rights' and emphasises the 'privileged relationship' between the Community and EFTA 'based on proximity, longstanding common values and European identity'. The agreement provides for the free movement of goods, persons, services and capital. It makes 'horizontal' or flanking provisions relevant to these four freedoms and envisages wider co-operation in matters not specifically covered by the Agreement. Its institutional arrangements include a Council; a Joint Committee to ensure effective implementation and operation of the Agreement; a Joint Parliamentary Committee to contribute, 'through dialogue and debate, to a better understanding between the Community and the EFTA states in the fields covered by this agreement'; and an EEA Consultative Committee to co-operate and comment on 'the economic and social aspects of the growing interdependence of the economies of the Contracting Parties'.

The practical effect of the Agreement was to extend to the EFTA countries the benefits and the obligations of the Single Market without giving them a voice in the evolution of the Community into a Union – economic integration, in fact, without political integration. This arrangement was perceived by the EFTA countries to be inadequate. Applications for Community membership were filed by Austria, Sweden, Finland, Switzerland and Norway. Switzerland rejected the EEA in a referendum in December 1992, but has maintained its application for membership of the European Union. Norway rejected membership of the European Union in a referendum in November 1994. EFTA thus consists of four countries, Norway, Switzerland, Iceland and Liechtenstein.

The EEA must be regarded as a lame duck. Yet the logic of what EEA envisaged cannot but retain its attractions for the anti-federalists within the European Union. The EEA represents a test of the extent to which political and monetary integration are inevitable rather than merely desirable. Is there any inexorable inherent reason why a single market has to be accompanied by economic and monetary union and by a common foreign and security policy, as foreseen in the Maastricht Treaty? The answer for many people is in the negative. The federalist impulse which prompted the moves towards economic and monetary union and to political union is primarily a response to political, security and social, rather than to economic and commercial, criteria. European security since the end of the Second World War has been vouchsafed by the US presence – and, paradoxically, by the stability of the Cold War. The collapse of the Soviet system has injected a significant element of instability into European relations at the same time as it has increased the pressures on the United States to reduce its military presence in Europe. This sea-change in the situation in Europe reinforced the movement which had started in the 1980s to revitalise the European Community, and which was a particular feature of the tenure by Jacques Delors of the presidency of the European Commission, in close association with the Franco-German partnership of President Mitterrand and Chancellor Kohl. France harbours profound misgivings about a reunited Germany unconstrained by strong federal links. Chancellor Kohl wants to put a European roof on Germany rather than a German roof on Europe. He is sometimes referred to as 'Bismarck in a cardigan'. It was a mixture of such considerations and interests, and the need to counter the perceived 'Europessimism' of the mid-1980s, by revitalising the process of European integration, rather than inescapable economic and commercial logic, which produced the Maastricht Treaty.

The problem is sometimes presented in terms of a trade-off between widening and deepening the Union. However desirable it may be on economic grounds or for political reasons, the argument runs, enlargement cannot but risk diluting the Union unless the structures of the latter are strengthened. 'With so many applications for membership on the table or expected in the near future, the Community has no choice but to move further along the road to a union based on the federalist philosophy. Unless it can strengthen its structures and rationalise decision-making to combine efficiency with democracy, the Community cannot hope to develop into a genuine Union.' This observation, from a 1992 official European Community publication,[9] illustrates the confusion which is prevalent among some enthusiasts. While the concept of widening is relatively straightforward

– that is, the question of adding to the membership – 'deepening' has two distinct meanings. On the one hand it can mean making the system, however federalist or non-federalist, work better, by dealing with such issues as the size and the powers of the Commission, the scope for majority voting within the Council of Ministers, the rotation of the presidency of the European Union and the role of the European Parliament, including its relationship with the Council of Ministers and the Commission. This type of deepening, as part of the quest for increased efficiency, is inevitable as the Union increases in size. The structures appropriate for six countries in the 1950s are unlikely to suffice for a score or more countries in the twenty-first century.

On the other hand, 'deepening' can mean increasing the degree of sovereignty surrendered to the Union by the member countries without which, to recall the opinion referred to above, it 'cannot hope to develop into a genuine Union'. It may well be that increase in membership will in fact point in the direction of transfer of further elements of sovereignty to the central institutions on the grounds that the latter could not be expected to do their job without it. But that is not the same thing as an 'autonomous' ceding to Brussels of additional powers covering new areas of competence. 'Deepening' must be seen in context. The purpose of the member countries is to progress towards union, not as an end in itself, but as a means of achieving the wide-ranging purposes set forth in the resolution which forms the Preamble to the Treaty of Maastricht.

(g) Knitting Europe Together after the Cold War

The astonishingly sudden collapse of the Soviet Union and of the Soviet bloc, and the consequent ending of the Cold War, brought in their train a vast array of problems, political, security and economic, for which new European architecture has to be devised. In analytical terms, each of the five aspects of European architecture discussed earlier – European identity; economic reconstruction; the search for security; moves towards integration; and the enlargement of the European Union – has to be looked at afresh in the light of developments in Central and Eastern Europe. This review has to be undertaken, however, not on the basis of starting with a clean slate, but on the basis of what has happened in the last 50 years, both within Western Europe, and in the uneasy relations between the two sides, East and West. It is also vital that the transition from existing structures to modern requirements should take full account of the instabilities unleashed by the transformation in the East. Not least, the transition must be managed in a way which reflects the realities of Russian power and susceptibilities.

At the height of the Cold War it seemed that the most effective piece of machinery for co-operation between East and West, albeit on a modest scale, was the Economic Commission for Europe (ECE), that is, the relevant United Nations Regional Economic Commission. It is significant that both the United States and Canada were members of the ECE, thus emphasising the Atlantic and transatlantic components of the region. A more wide-ranging and high level approach to East–West co-operation was adopted in the convening of the Conference on Security and Co-operation in Europe, which met from 1973 to 1975 and concluded at a Summit in Helsinki with the Final Act of 1 August 1975.[10] This Final Act provided a framework of co-operation in three areas (or 'baskets'): security in Europe; economics, science and technology, and the environment; and 'humanitarian and other fields, especially "human contacts"' (basket three). This programme of co-operation was intended to reinforce, not replace, existing UN machinery, including, of course, the ECE. It was to be supervised by follow-up meetings. The overall objective was to break the ice and encourage *détente*, with consequent benefits in terms of increased contact with the outside world for the citizens of the Soviet bloc. This raised the question of whether it was appropriate for the West to pay the governments of the Soviet Union and of its satellites to behave towards their own people in a manner to which they were in any case already committed by their membership of the United Nations and by their signatures on numerous documents, for example in the field of human rights. As far as the West was concerned, the obligations accepted in this regard under the Final Act were for the most part superfluous. They were already being met. There was thus some fear that the Helsinki Final Act was an asymmetrical arrangement, favouring the East and validating a continuation in strategic terms of the Soviet and American spheres of influence implicit in the Yalta Summit of 1945.

The Soviet invasion of Afghanistan in any case soon put the clock back. President Reagan spoke of the Soviet Union as 'the evil empire'. The 1980s none the less saw a less high profile increase in *ad hoc* East–West co-operation, for example in the Security Council, as well as solid progress in the field of disarmament. The arrival of Gorbachev at the apex of the Soviet hierarchy in the mid-1980s with the slogans of *glasnost* and *perestroika* ('openness' and 'reconstruction') held out promise of new hopes of co-operation with the Soviet Union, in strong contrast to the setback to co-operation with China caused by the Tiananmen Square massacre of June 1989.

By this time, however, the Soviet Empire was beginning to dissolve. The CSCE could clearly represent a key method of dealing with the new situation in all its complexities and uncertainties. A CSCE Summit was held in Paris in November 1990, which was hailed – at least in advance, if not in retrospect – as an event of comparable importance to the Congress of Vienna in 1815. The 35 countries which signed the Helsinki Accords (reduced to 34 by the reunification of Germany) were present. Albania was granted observer status. The Soviet Union reportedly insisted on the exclusion of representatives from the three Baltic republics – Estonia, Latvia and Lithuania – who had been invited by the French government. The 16 NATO countries and the six Warsaw Pact countries signed a Treaty on the Reduction of Conventional Forces in Europe (CFE) which imposed equal ceilings on non-nuclear weapons between the Urals and the Atlantic. A joint declaration affirmed that the signatories were no longer adversaries and that none of their weapons would ever be used except in self-defence. The Hungarian prime minister told delegates that the Warsaw Pact members had agreed to dissolve the Alliance by the beginning of 1992. The Czech representative, the noted playwright and dissident, Vaclav Havel, described the Warsaw Pact as 'a remnant of the past and a typical product of Soviet expansionism'.

The Charter of Paris, likewise adopted at the Paris Summit, spoke of 'a new era of democracy, peace and unity in Europe'. It described the CSCE as 'the central forum for political consultations in the new Europe'. There was extensive provision for follow-up meetings, and negotiations, including annual meetings of Heads of State and Government beginning in 1992. A Secretariat was established in Prague. Declarations by the European Community and the United States, and by the European Community and Canada, on their bilateral relations imparted a West–West character to a fruitful and optimistic Summit mainly concerned with East–West, East–East, and security matters. But there were clouds as well as sunshine. Iraq had invaded and occupied Kuwait a few months earlier. The situation in Yugoslavia was unwinding. The US-led ejection of the Iraqis from Kuwait gave rise to hopes of a 'new world order'. But Yugoslavia came to bedevil not only the 'new era of democracy, peace and unity within Europe', but also intra-Community and transatlantic relations. The CSCE follow-up Summit in Helsinki in 1992 adopted a further admirable document 'The

Challenge of Change'. But it is chiefly known for its failure to make
plans to resolve the crisis in Yugoslavia. The CSCE Budapest Summit
in 1994 was widely held to be a failure because of the well-publicised
disagreement between Presidents Clinton and Yeltsin over the question
of possible enlargement of NATO to cover the countries of Eastern
Europe. A further source of criticism was the impasse over Bosnia, a
subject on which the Summit Declaration, although not erring on the
side of brevity, is silent. But this should not be allowed to obscure the
efforts to come to grips with the post-Cold War situation which CSCE,
now renamed OSCE, is making.

Nevertheless it is clear that cautious development of OSCE will not
suffice to meet imperatives of post-Cold War Europe. The former
Warsaw Pact countries wish to recover not only their European
identity, which Soviet hegemony had for so long effectively denied
them, but also their security and prosperity. If NATO does not expand
eastward, some other mechanism will have to be found. The most likely
means of achieving the security these countries crave would be
enlargement of the European Union, of which they seek membership
in any case for all three reasons – for identity and prosperity, as well as
for security. At the meeting of the European Council in Essen in
December 1994, the German Chancellor made a particular point of
inviting the Heads of State and Government and foreign ministers of
six former Warsaw Pact countries – Poland, the Czech Republic,
Slovakia, Hungary, Bulgaria and Romania – which are already
associated with the European Union through 'Europe' Agreements
to 'hold an exchange of views with them on the strategy for leading
[them] towards the European Union'. The prudence of the language in
this formulation is appropriate. It is evident that the problems of
qualifying for membership, both on economic criteria and in the
prevailing political circumstances, are significant. But the pressures to
secure enlargement in this direction are not less significant. What is
more problematic is how to deal with the aspirations to membership of
the European Union cherished by countries which were previously part
of the Soviet Union itself, rather than members of the Soviet bloc, most
notably the Baltic republics of Estonia, Latvia and Lithuania.

THE EUROPEAN UNION AND THE WORLD

It is inevitable that an entity of the size and consequence of the
European Union should make a great impact on the rest of the world,

in addition to the impact, dealt with earlier in this lecture, on near neighbours and other countries of the European region. That impact is perceived as more direct on the economic rather than on the political side, since it is in relation to the former that Community competence, and hence the conduct in common of external relations, has developed. But as the common foreign and security policy agreed in the Treaty of Maastricht evolves, the impact of the European Union politically will likewise become more direct.

The Union's Mediterranean neighbours were among the first countries to establish economic and trade links with it. Relations with sub-Saharan Africa likewise date back to the Treaty of Rome in 1957, when the overseas territories of certain member countries were accorded associate status. The process of decolonisation which quickened in the early 1960s transformed this link into a new form of association between sovereign countries. Today some 70 countries in Africa, the Carribean and the Pacific (ACP) benefit from special relations with, and help from, the Union under the Lomé Conventions (of which the fourth was renewed in November 1995 to cover the period to 2000). Co-operation with the developing countries of Asia and Latin America is less structured. But the question of evolving relations with regional groupings will become increasingly important. So will relations with the vast emerging economies of China and India. The European Union, as the world's greatest trading entity, will have a major responsibility in securing the establishment and effective operation of the World Trade Organisation.

Politically, all countries are affected to some extent by the existence of the European Union, whatever their size and power, even the largest and most powerful. Perhaps the most instructive comment came from Dr Henry Kissinger in his magisterial study *Diplomacy*: 'geopolitically America is an island off the shores of the large landmass of Eurasia, whose resources and population far exceed those of the United States'.[11]

UNFINISHED BUSINESS

That Kissinger verdict is an encouragement to stand back and look at the wood rather than the trees. We are concerned with European architecture as one of the principal institutional features of which the diplomatic practitioner in today's world has to take account. Judged by the results achieved in the past 50 years, European arrangements have been a great success, despite their occasionally confusing, and even contradictory, elements. European integration is at the core of these arrangements. The big problem in this regard is the follow-up to the Maastricht Treaty, both as regards the deepening of the arrangements among the existing members of the European Union and the path to the widening of its membership.

The business, though vital, is unfinished. Four guiding principles can be offered as to the way ahead. First, integration cannot but be an uneven, perhaps an untidy business, arousing misgivings and reservations as well as enthusiasm and commitment. Any act of faith, based on vision and strong leadership, will evoke scepticism and resistance which the democratic process must comprehend. There will be a tendency for the debate to splinter. There is a temptation to resort to clichés: 'you cannot make an omelette without breaking eggs'; 'if you have to go through a hedge, it may be best to go through it backwards'.

Secondly, creating an ever closer union among the peoples of Europe is not an end in itself. It is primarily a means of avoiding the scourge of war on the European continent. The maintenance of peace in Europe will require continuing United States and Canadian participation. European security has two pillars, one on each side of the Atlantic.

Thirdly, moves to incorporate the countries of Central and Eastern Europe in European security arrangements will be self-defeating if they antagonise Russia. Much patience and skill will be required in establishing a stable situation which both meets the desire for security of the countries of Central and Eastern Europe and respects Russian sensitivities.

Fourthly, the rest of the world has a close interest in the evolution of arrangements within Europe, both on the political and security side and as regards economic co-operation. Absorption in intra-European problems has in the past led to considerable shortcomings in the discharge by the European Union member countries of their responsibilities to the rest of the world, responsibilities which were recognised at the outset of the moves to European integration, for instance in the Schuman Declaration.[12] European architecture, as an institutional feature in today's world, is inextricably mixed with the other two institutional features we have surveyed – the United Nations and the world economy. Speaking to the National Press Club in Washington on 30 April 1952, Jean Monnet put the matter with his habitual incisiveness:

The unification of Europe has a significance for civilisation which goes beyond even security and peace. Europe is at the origin of the progress of which we are all the beneficiaries, and Europeans by their creative spirit are as capable of making a contribution to civilisation as great as in the past. But in order to let that creative spirit flourish again we need to harmonise our institutions and our economy with modern times. It is by unifying Europe that we shall achieve this . . . We are not combining states, we are uniting men.[13]

APPENDIX TO LECTURE 6: THE PEACE AGREEMENT FOR BOSNIA AND HERZEGOVINA

On 21 November 1995, the 'general framework agreement for peace in Bosnia and Herzegovina and the annexes thereto' (collectively 'the peace agreement') was initialled by the Republic of Bosnia and Herzegovina, the Republic of Croatia and the Federal Republic of Yugoslavia at Dayton, Ohio. It was witnessed by the European Union Special Negotiator and by representatives of the member governments of the 'Contact Group', which had played a crucial part in the negotiations: France, Germany, Russia, the United Kingdom and the United States. The peace agreement was signed by Heads of State and Government in Paris on 14 December 1995.

Whether in years to come 14 December 1995 will be regarded as a 'defining moment' which brought not only peace to war-shattered former Yugoslavia, but also relief to the much wider circle of those whose security was threatened, and for the wider circle still of those in an interdependent world whose stability was put at risk, will depend mainly on how the agreement is implemented in practice. But it is also the case that the collective effort, mobilised both to reach the agreement and to provide for its implementation, gives legitimate ground for optimism about the capacity of the international community to tackle complex problems with wide and damaging ramifications. More specifically in the context of these lectures, the peace agreement affords an exceptional opportunity for illustrating the institutional factors affecting foreign policy-making, which we have been studying in Lectures 4, 5 and 6. This appendix accordingly will review first the peace agreement itself and then some relevant considerations as regards European architecture, the world economy and the United Nations respectively.

The Peace Agreement

The text of the peace agreement, in the form circulated to the United Nations,[14] runs to some 150 pages. The annexes to the general framework agreement deal successively with the Military Aspects of the Peace Settlement, including the establishment of the multinational Military Implementation Force (IFOR); Regional Stabilisation, including withdrawal of foreign forces and arms control; the 'Inter-Entity Boundary Line' (that is, the boundary between the Republic of Bosnia and Herzegovina, the Federation of Bosnia and Herzegovina and the Republika Srpska) and Related Issues; Elections; the Constitution of Bosnia and Herzegovina; Arbitration; Human Rights; Refugees and Displaced Persons; the Commission to Preserve National Monuments; Bosnia and Herzegovina Public Corporations; Civilian Implementation; and the International Police Task Force. The mere titles of the various annexes are sufficient to give an idea of the detail and complexity of the agreement and of the number and variety of those internationally involved in its implementation.

An even clearer idea of this international involvement emerges from the conclusions of the Peace Implementation Conference held at Lancaster House in London on 8 and 9 December 1995.[15] The purpose of this conference was 'to mobilise the international community behind a new start for the people of Bosnia and Herzegovina'. The Conference was as good as its word. The Conclusions dealt successively with Military Implementation, including, of course, the vital question of establishing IFOR; Regional Stabilisation, including confidence-building measures on the model of agreements developed successfully elsewhere in Europe under the auspices of the Organisation for Security and Co-operation in Europe (OSCE); Civilian Implementation, particularly as regards re-establishing normal conditions in Sarajevo; the appointment of Mr Carl Bildt, the European Union Special Negotiator, as the 'High Representative' appointed under the terms of the peace agreement to monitor it; Administrative Structures for Civilian Implementation, including a Peace Implementation Council (PIC) (the PIC will have a Steering Board under the chairmanship of the High Representative and composed of representatives of the member countries of the Group of Seven major industrialised countries, Russia, the European Union, the European Commission and the Organisation of the Islamic Conference (OIC)); Humanitarian Assistance, Refugees and Prisoners, involving not only the UN High

Commissioner for Refugees but also other UN agencies and programmes, the International Committee of the Red Cross (ICRC) and a number of non-governmental organisations; Human Rights, the OSCE being entrusted with the preparation and supervision of elections, and also involving the Council of Europe and UN human rights machinery; and Reconstruction, in which the World Bank and the European Commission would take the lead, but with the participation of IMF, the European Bank for Reconstruction and Development (EBRD) and a number of UN bodies as well.

The Peace Agreement and European Architecture

Nothing has proved a greater source of difficulty in building a stable and prosperous Europe after the end of the Cold War than the collapse of the former Yugoslavia and the eruption of a bitter civil war in its territory. Equally, nothing can contribute more significantly to the objective of European stability and prosperity than successful implementation of the peace agreement. Not only will this bring great benefits in itself. It will also inspire confidence in the approach which has been adopted. This approach has been admirably devised. First, the OSCE has been given a clear and important mandate in relation to the political stabilisation of Bosnia and Herzegovina, especially as regards the preparation and supervision of electors. Reference was made earlier to the criticism of OSCE for its failure to deal with the Bosnia situation.[16] There is now more prospect that OSCE can fulfil the role envisaged at the Paris Conference in 1990 of being 'the central forum for political consultations in the new Europe'.[17]

Secondly, the work of the Contact Group and the establishment of IFOR are illustrations of the way in which Russia can be brought into productive co-operation with the West. The difficulties over enlargement of NATO and of the European Union remain. But successful implementation of the peace agreement can help to build confidence between Russia and the West.

Thirdly, NATO has found a massive yet well-defined role. This is a tonic for NATO itself. At its Ministerial Meeting in Brussels on 5 December the North Atlantic Council spoke of its preparations for implementing the military aspects of the peace agreement 'under NATO Command and with the participation of other countries. This confirms the key role of the Alliance in ensuring peace and stability in

Europe . . . The Alliance's cohesion and solidarity . . . are essential to
perform NATO's core functions as well as to undertake an operation
of this kind.'[18]

Fourthly, major US involvement, not only in achieving the peace
agreement but also in supplying forces on the ground, as distinct from
in the air or at sea, as at an earlier stage, has been of great significance
for transatlantic relations generally. The 'New Transatlantic Agenda'
and the 'Joint US–EU Action Plan' signed by President Clinton and
the European Union in Madrid on 3 December[19] cover an immensely
wide range of issues in the political, disarmament, economic, social and
humanitarian fields. They betoken a greater awareness of the extent to
which world problems require transatlantic co-operation. Bosnia-
Herzegovina is a major case in point.

Fifthly, the European Union has managed to put its hesitations and
disagreements over the way forward from the Treaty of Maastricht in a
more positive perspective as a result of the leading part which it will be
called upon to play in implementing the peace agreement. Two
particular aspects of this are the appointment of the European
negotiator, Mr Carl Bildt, as High Representative, and 'the development of a direct and dynamic contractual relationship between Bosnia
and Herzegovina and the European Union within the framework of a
regional approach', to quote the Conclusions of the Peace Implementation Conference in London on 8 and 9 December. The Conclusions
of the Presidency issued after the meeting of the European Council in
Madrid on 15 and 16 December (discussed at the end of Lecture 7)[20]
suggest a degree of confidence and purpose that was absent while the
situation in the former Yugoslavia was the cause of so much dissension
and frustration within the Union.

Sixthly, the peace agreement is of major importance as regards the
evolution of Germany's international role, both individually and as
part of the foreign and security policy of the European Union.
Germany played a very active part in the negotiations leading to the
Dayton Agreement. As part of IFOR German troops will be stationed
abroad for the first time in a role of this nature. They will not in fact be
in Bosnia, but rather in Croatia. And there has been consensus across
the political spectrum in Germany.

Finally, the implications for the conduct of US foreign policy may be
profound. During the presidential election campaign in 1992, President
Clinton laid great emphasis on what he saw as President Bush's undue
concentration on foreign affairs at the expense of domestic problems.
In the event President Clinton has been increasingly involved in foreign

affairs and could not but base his campaign for re-election in 1996 to some extent on his perceived successes in foreign policy. In the end world interdependence will frustrate the attempts of any US administration to reduce its involvement in foreign affairs.

The Peace Agreement and the World Economy

Lecture 5 explained the nature of the world economy today in terms of 'secondary globalisation'.[21] 'Primary globalisation' in the sense of extensive trade in goods and services, migration and overseas investment was a prominent feature of life as early as the beginning of this century. During the course of it, however, the world economy has become an immensely more complicated matter, involving the fusion of traditionally separate economic and political and security issues, with highly complex social, humanitarian, technological, information and environmental priorities. The imperatives of the modern world economy in this secondary stage of globalisation are dramatically illustrated by the ramifications of the Bosnia and Herzegovina peace agreement. They bear out the approach in the UN Secretary-General's twin agendas for peace and for development.[22] They exemplify the approach to world affairs adopted in *Our Global Neighbourhood*, the report of the Commission on Global Governance.[23] Four specific aspects of the peace agreement are worth particular attention: first, the sheer multiplicity of 'actors' – many UN bodies and programmes of other international organisations, the International Committee of the Red Cross (ICRC) and non-governmental organisations in addition to governments – involved in implementing the complicated yet vital provisions of the agreement; secondly, the close relationship between humanitarian assistance and reconstruction, a relationship which is now inevitable in tackling the question of relief of distress and promoting development; thirdly, the requirement for the donors to consult closely in meeting the substantial needs of relief and reconstruction. The World Bank put Bosnia's needs in outside aid at $5 billion over the next three or four years. The Conclusions of the London Conference state that 'frequent aid donors' meetings will be needed to achieve wide and equitable participation in the international aid effort'; finally, and perhaps most interestingly, the Conclusions singled out France as having, by virtue of its chairmanship of the Group of Seven major industrialised countries (G7), 'a specially strong coordinating role in the Peace Implementation Council'. The leaders who devised the G7 20 years ago could scarcely have imagined that it would evolve to the point where it was entrusted by the international community with executive responsibilities of this order.[24] But the logic is inexorable. The stated purpose of the Peace Implementation Conference, as already noted, was 'to mobilise the international community behind a new start for the people of Bosnia and Herzegovina', a purpose which could not but heavily involve the member countries of the G7.

The Peace Agreement and the United Nations

The peace agreement has had far-reaching consequences for the United Nations. The ultimate, and indeed the direct, international authority for concluding the agreement has been reaffirmed as the Security Council, acting under Chapter VII of the United Nations Charter. This emerges with crystal clarity from Security Council Resolution 1031(1995) adopted on 15 December 1995.[25] The UN has in fact provided the framework for the framework agreement. The realities of power have of course been exemplified by the role of the Contact Group under forceful US leadership. It is an illustration of the point made 50 years ago by Sir Charles Webster that the Charter represents 'an Alliance of Great Powers embedded in a universal organisation'.[26] While the great powers can co-operate effectively today after the stalemate of the Cold War, they need the endorsement which a universal organisation alone can provide.

Secondly, the continuing involvement of the UN Secretary-General and of the UN system on a broad basis will be essential on both practical and political grounds.[27] Specifically, the UN will have much to do in relation to police work, human rights reconstruction, and in particular as regards eastern Slavonia and Macedonia. It will also be vital to hold together the political coalition which has made the peace agreement possible. The Security Council will be watching events very closely. It is of interest that half of the contingents composing the IFOR forces will be from non-NATO countries. Nor should the work done by the UN and others in the past, in difficult and often dangerous conditions, be forgotten. Their courage and the sacrifice are part of the background to the present agreement. At the beginning of 1991 the UN had 60 observers in the former Yugoslavia. Its involvement eventually rose to 16 000 troops. IFOR has 60 000 heavily armed troops and they are charged with implementing an agreement to which all the parties have subscribed, rather than trying to keep the peace amid turmoil, which was the fate of UNPROFOR.

Thirdly, the peace agreement emphasises the importance of regional responsibility within the UN framework, a point which has been crucial to the United Nations since the outset. The question of how far the UN will wish to devolve responsibility to regional bodies and coalitions is one which will continue to hold international attention. World-wide interdependence does not necessarily require a universal response. Rather it requires a response which takes account of the universal aspects of interdependence. In the case of Europe, the region includes, as has already been noted, the USA and Canada as well as the whole of Russia. The growing international involvement of Japan makes it increasingly part *de facto* of the European region.

Fourthly, successful implementation of the peace agreement for Bosnia and Herzegovina will be of immense value as a precedent for UN action in situations of conflict within states, as distinct from between them. There are a host of surrounding dilemmas arising from the deeply rooted reluctance to cut across national sovereignty. Article 2(7) of the Charter holds powerful sway. As already noted,[28] the way forward is less likely to be established by amendment of the Charter than by effective precedents. The United Nations will learn by doing and doing well.

From Sarajevo to Sarajevo?

Reference was made earlier to the proposition that the twentieth century could be regarded as having begun and ended in Sarajevo.[29] That is to say, it began on 28 June 1914, with the assassination in Sarajevo of the heir to the Austro-Hungarian throne, which led to the outbreak of the Great War and ended either in April 1992, when the Bosnian Serbs surrounded Sarajevo with the intention of 'strangling' it, or on 14 December 1995, when the peace agreement for Bosnia and Herzegovina was signed in Paris with all that that implied for the capital city of Sarajevo, notably the lifting of a siege which lasted more than three years. Whichever of the two readings events may show to be the more appropriate, it is clear that the break-up of the former Yugoslavia has ushered in a new phase of international relations, carrying the 'New Diplomacy' even further away from the 'Old'. The institutional features of today, which play so important a part in the management of international relations, differ profoundly from those of the nineteenth century.

The sceptics can point with justification to the part which force has played both in the break-up of the former Yugoslavia and in the arrangements which it is hoped will restore peace. Devoutly as it might be wished that changes in the international system in response to changes in international requirements could be brought about promptly and painlessly, history does not suggest that this is a wish likely to be fulfilled. The nation-state system, in which the 'Old Diplomacy' reached its apogee, emerged from a hideously cruel and destructive Thirty Years War. The UN Charter was born of the greatest war in history. Humanity has not yet discovered how to produce the energy, creativeness and co-operation of a post-war phase without having previously undergone the agonies of war. Diplomacy, as the child of its time, should none the less seek the benefits of the former while striving to avoid the latter.

7   Foreign Policy-Making

It is time for a little recapitulation. Our concern is not with analysis of international relations alone, but with the business of diplomacy. At the core of the business of diplomacy is the exercise by governments of power in the international component of the national life. Diplomats must be capable of contributing both to the shaping and to the carrying out of foreign policy. They must be 'foreign policy capable', implying competence on both the advisory and the executive sides of the business. The aim of these lectures is to fashion a framework of thought which will help create this capability. Substance and process are inextricably mixed. We have to think in several dimensions simultaneously. It is necessary to keep a great many things in the front of one's mind, rather than in the back of it.

It serves a useful purpose to distinguish, inevitably somewhat arbitrarily, between various types of component which go into the making of the framework and then to study them separately: analytical elements, to achieve an understanding of what it is that diplomats face; institutional features, to enable them to acquire familiarity with the arena in which they work; and operational factors, to equip them with the skills with which to work effectively, collectively and individually. We have looked so far at the analytical elements in Lectures 1, 2 and 3 and at the institutional features in Lectures 4, 5 and 6. Turning to the operational factors, we need to revisit the subject matter of the six preceding lectures, but approach it from the operational or technical, rather than the analytical or institutional, standpoint. It is convenient to pursue the approach 'hierarchically', that is, in descending order from the factors relevant at the national or governmental level, through those applying to diplomats collectively, when organised in professional diplomatic services, down to those relating to the efficiency and the effectiveness of the individual diplomat. This lecture, accordingly, will deal with foreign policy-making at the national level. Lecture 8 will address Diplomatic Service organisation and Lectures 9 and 10 will concentrate on personal diplomatic skills.

OPERATIONAL AND TECHNICAL FACTORS IN FOREIGN POLICY-MAKING

It is evident that, in an activity such as diplomacy, where substance and process are inextricably mixed, operational and technical factors are of great importance. Useful analysis of them, however, depends on full recognition of the difficulty of isolating those factors from the essence of the events and the policies to which they relate. With our habitual degree of arbitrariness, we shall take seven aspects:

(a) a review of the fundamentals of the national situation on which foreign policy has to be based;

(b) a closer look at the list of 'actors' in the foreign policy-making process;

(c) the role of the media, both as 'actor' and as creator of the 'theatre' in which the action takes place;

(d) public opinion as a factor in the age of the common man and common woman;

(e) how the professional Diplomatic Service fits in (a subject which is treated in greater detail in Lecture 8);

(f) the scope for autonomous action by governments, in spite of all the constraints on their freedom of manoeuvre;

(g) the relationship between policy and strategy.

The lecture concludes with some illustrations of foreign policy drawn from published texts.

(a) Fundamentals of Foreign Policy

The objective of foreign policy, as noted already, is traditionally defined as the promotion of the safety and prosperity of the realm. Of these two qualities – safety and prosperity – it is also recognised that the former must have priority, at least in the short term. The pioneer of British economics, Adam Smith, famously remarked in the *Wealth of Nations* that defence is of more importance than opulence.[1] In Adam Smith's day the distinction was clearer than it is today. In the modern interdependent world both terms need to be defined widely. The overlap between them is considerable.

In conditions of modern interdependence, furthermore, the traditional formulation of the objectives of foreign policy needs some elaboration, not only as regards the complexity of the relationship between security and prosperity, but also because of the great widening of the scope and diversity of overseas involvement. In its latest Departmental Report, prepared as part of the government's expenditure plans for the three financial years ahead, the Foreign and Commonwealth Office lists the basic aims of UK foreign policy as:

(i)   to enhance the security of the United Kingdom and the Dependent Territories;
(ii) to promote their prosperity;
(iii) to promote and protect British interests and influence overseas;
(iv) to protect British nationals abroad.[2]

Implicit in this elaboration is awareness of the international 'porousness' of national existence today. The realities of the world economy are such that, if a country wishes to raise its standard of living, it must involve itself to an ever greater degree in what is going on beyond its borders. This in turn will require an ever greater flexibility and imaginativeness on the part of foreign policy-makers.

The fundamentals of foreign policy are to be found in the basic facts of the national situation: geography; resource endowment, both human and natural; level of economic activity and degree of dependence on overseas sources of supply and export markets; involvement in transactions of whatever type with the rest of the world; vulnerability to external pressures, again of whatever type; intergovernmental contacts and arrangements, bilateral, regional, global; participation in the work of international organisations; formal alliances and contractual obligations. In brief, as was suggested at the outset of these lectures, our concern is with the sum total of the impact which one country makes upon another, indeed which one civilisation makes upon another, extending to cultural relations, sporting contacts, the tourist industry, fashions in consumption, the diverse energies of youth. The list is endless. The message is clear. Foreign policy, if it is to be realistic, must be grounded in the facts of a nation's international involvements, however wide-ranging and elusive they may in some instances prove to be. The response of the country to the facts of its international involvement is the point of departure for shaping foreign policy. The response is not simply automatic or 'objective'. National interest is a more subtle blend of the objective and the subjective. The response will in practice be the resultant of a great many factors and influences within the country.

(b)   The List of 'Actors'

In more leisured and less interdependent days, the government could leave matters of foreign policy largely in the hands of the foreign minister. Those days are now over. A head of government cannot but be heavily involved on a day-to-day basis. *The Economist*[3] reported that Mr John Major's visit to the Hague and Berlin on 7 and 8 September 1994 was his 63rd foreign expedition, excluding holidays, since he became Prime Minister in 1990. He had spent all or part of 164 of his 1381 days in office outside the United Kingdom. To this must be added the time he spent on foreign affairs while in this country, including the entertainment of foreign visitors. Other ministers find that the overseas component of their departmental responsibilities looms large, not only in the obvious portfolios such as trade, finance and defence, but also as regards agriculture, transport, law and order, social affairs and the environment. Beyond this element of direct involvement of individual ministers by virtue of their respective ministerial portfolios is the collective responsibility of governments for external as well as internal affairs and their inescapable interdependence. The scale of this collective involvement is well illustrated by a detailed list of the composition of the British ministerial cabinet committees and sub-committees as at September 1995.[4] There are committees, all of them under the chairmanship of the Prime Minister, on defence and overseas policy; the Intelligence Services; nuclear defence; and Northern Ireland. The Foreign and Commonwealth Secretary is of course a member of all these. In addition he chairs the Sub-Committee on European questions. Foreign Office ministers may be members of other relevant committees or on the sub-committees, or invited to attend their meetings where appropriate.

Parliament likewise cannot but be much involved in foreign policy-making, not only by virtue of its ultimate legislative and electoral authority, but also because of its concern with day-to-day developments. Foreign Affairs committees of national parliaments have a very important role to play, a role which will take different forms according to the constitutional arrangements of the country concerned. A striking case in point is the United States, where the doctrine of the separation of powers finds particular expression in the provision that the president may make treaties only with the advice and consent of the Senate. The saga of the League of Nations in which, as already noted,[5] the Senate rejected the brainchild of President Wilson is a spectacular illustration of the point. As a result of the mid-term elections in November 1994, control of the Congress has passed to the Republicans although the White House is occupied by a Democrat. The effect on the coherence of US foreign policy has already been marked.

The importance of Parliament in the shaping of foreign policy is naturally linked to the way in which Parliament conducts its business. In a number of countries there is a tradition of bipartisanship, or indeed of non-partisanship, in the parliamentary handling of foreign affairs. The tradition is less common in handling home affairs. Parliamentary committees concerned with foreign affairs may enjoy special status in consequence. But in general it must be expected that political parties will play, both through Parliament and more widely, a distinctive role in foreign affairs. Political parties can be of many different sorts. They may reflect religious, social, cultural, sectoral (for example, agricultural), linguistic or ethnic influences. If they are more widely based, they may equally be a coalition of such influences. Their impact on the shaping of foreign policy may well be a reflection of their weight in home affairs, and of the need for the government appropriately to take account of the pressures they exert at home, as much as of any direct concern with, or expertise in, specific foreign policy issues.

Lobbies of all sorts may seek the adoption, or the rejection, of particular items of policy or legislation of concern to them. More generally, they will busy themselves with creating a congenial climate of opinion. They will not be alone in this task. A host of non-governmental organisations, many of them charities, can bring influence collectively or individually to bear on the shaping of foreign policy. Learned bodies, individual consultants and academics may carry great weight. Economic interests may be decisive, not simply because of the views which their spokesmen may advance, but also by the mere fact of their existence and of their international impact. The point has already been made that intra-company transfers account for a large proportion of the visible exports of a number of countries. International financial transactions can sweep away national policies, as witness Britain's undignified exit from the European Exchange Rate Mechanism in September 1992.

(c) The Role of the Media

The revolution in communications and in information technology was bound to have significant impact on the shaping of foreign policy. But that impact does not consist solely of a relentless ever-growing threat to the scope for independent government action. Rather it is a double-edged development, in which developments in technology can either enhance the influence of government or diminish it. A central feature in the very early days of *The Times* was an account of the proceedings in Parliament more speedy, more accurate and fuller than anything hitherto available. But the history of the newspaper is not one of unalloyed deference to those in authority. It commented as well as reported, and its editorials came over the course of time to have the influence on governments, as well as on public opinion, which its nickname 'The Thunderer' would suggest. Other newspapers, less serious but with considerable resources and powers of communication, have occupied positions of great influence without responsibility for the consequences should the policies they advocate be adopted. This state of affairs has been immortalised in a phrase of the poet Rudyard Kipling, used by his kinsman Stanley Baldwin when Prime Minister: 'power without responsibility – the prerogative of the harlot throughout the ages'.[6] Macaulay's less pejorative verdict on reporters and a fourth estate of the realm has already been quoted.[7]

Interdependence in the field of information brought new problems in the sense of concern at the power of the major world-wide news agencies. Even the most factual and politically 'neutral' information may be suspect merely because it comes from overseas, and there is no domestic source against which to measure it. Selection from the vast mass of available information of items for transmission can be held to be a form of pressure. The enunciation of a New International Economic Order at the General Assembly in the 1970s described in Lecture 5[8] was followed by pressure for a New World International Order where the same broad political approach should apply. This proposal did not achieve anything like the same high profile, and contributed to the reservations about the United Nations Educational, Scientific, and Cultural Organisation (Unesco) harboured in certain Anglo-Saxon quarters.

The idea of a new information order in the sense of global regulation of international information flows is very much on the agenda, not so much as a North–South political question as because international telecommunications are in transition from a world of publicly owned national-monopoly utilities to one of privately owned competitive enterprises, transcending national and industrial boundaries. This is one of the new areas of responsibility with which the World Trade Organisation will have to grapple.[9]

Meanwhile the developments of the 1980s and the 1990s have served to put the media in an even more prominent role, not merely as 'actors' but as theatre managers. Satellite television broadcasting has been the means of reporting developments all over the world instantaneously – 'in real time'. When US troops came ashore in Somalia as part of the ill-fated UN operation there, the media, apprised in advance, were waiting for them. Ministers explain that today they are so beset with the question of how to react immediately to television coverage of dramatic new events that this sometimes takes priority over dealing with the events themselves. Reference was made in Lecture 1 to the suggestion that CNN is already *de facto* the sixteenth (and permanent) member of the UN Security Council.[10]

Censorship can provide only a limited defence for governments that wish to avail themselves of it. Newspapers can be banned, radio broadcasts can be jammed, satellite dishes can be proscribed. But at the end of the day the world of communications and computers cannot be kept out. Perhaps nothing precipitated the fall of the Berlin Wall more than television pictures, available in East Berlin thanks to transmission from the West, of vast numbers of East German refugees fleeing to the West. The absurdity of the Wall – known in communist jargon as 'the People's Anti-Fascist Rampart' – could not be disguised any longer.

(d) Public Opinion as a Factor in the Age of the Common Man and the Common Woman

Lectures 1 and 2 stressed that public concern with, and consequent involvement in, international affairs was one of the principal differences between the 'Old Diplomacy' and the 'New'. The growth of communications and the extraordinary developments in information technology have enhanced that involvement. The first approximation in any study of the role of public opinion must be that it is not only a considerable restraint on the freedom of action of governments, but also a source of pressure on them to adopt particular policies. Public opinion will also exercise a similar role in relation to the activities of other 'actors' in foreign policy-making. Governments will need to take account of it, as a barrier to be overcome, as well as a guide, for example, to prospects in the next election. It also has its uses as an alibi for not taking action which governments know to be necessary, but which they also know will be unpopular. In situations where drastic economic remedies are necessary, the exigencies of the International Monetary Fund have been a convenient excuse for governments to take unpopular measures, on the basis that assistance is forthcoming only if IMF prescriptions are followed.

But the argument is not wholly one-sided. The importance of power over opinion has already been discussed. Governments with sufficient clarity of purpose and determination are in no doubt as to the scope the modern world offers for influencing public opinion. It was the German general Clausewitz who gave prominence in the nineteenth century to 'the passions of the people' as a factor in foreign policy and warfare. The potential which exists for mobilising collective will and readiness to make sacrifices is very great, however much this may be the age of the common man and woman. What no longer suffices is the assumption that public opinion is unimportant. One is less apt to hear today than in years gone by the apocryphal allegation that there is no equivalent in such-and-such a language for the phrase 'public opinion' and that the nearest phrase in translation is 'the stupid people'. Seventy years of determined social engineering did the Soviet ideologues little good. In the end the 'stupid people' brushed them aside.

Economic logic suggests that if, as is evidently the case, there is an enormous increase in the supply of information, there must have been an increase in demand to evoke or match that supply. The demand has to come from somewhere, and it is not wholly passive in the sense of merely being induced by skilful marketing. Governments recognise this, as is clear from the extent to which they co-operate in the supply of information. At times it seems as if they believe that any publicity is better than none. The behaviour of the Bosnian Serbs over the taking of hostages which drew universal obloquy down on them, is a case in point. There was also something bizarre to the traditionally minded about the facilities accorded to the Western media in Baghdad by the Saddam regime when the United Nations were expelling the Iraqis from Kuwait and attacking the Iraqi capital as part of the process.

(e)   How the Professional Diplomatic Service Fits In

In the case of 'actors' in the foreign policy-making drama, what is the role of the professional diplomat? A character in Sir Peter Ustinov's play *Romanoff and Juliet* asked what was the difference between an ambassador and a head-waiter. The answer given was that there was none, except that the ambassador was occasionally asked to sit at the table. There may be something of the butler in the position of the professional diplomat, or at least of the inn-keeper, playing host to visiting ministers, parliamentarians and others. But any attempt by ambassadors themselves to minimise their role runs the risk of being misinterpreted as a subterfuge for professional pre-emption of the right of ministers to make policy. The belittling by others, not themselves always disinterested, of the role of ambassadors in modern inter-dependent times is of course commonplace. The facts of diplomatic life give it some validity. Yet it sits oddly with deep suspicions harboured in the same quarters of the power of mandarins in the Foreign Ministry, even though they are so often the same people as the belittled ambassadors but in a different mode. One cannot easily be a ruminant abroad and a carnivore at home.

What is striking however is the shift in the balance of power between diplomats abroad and their colleagues at home. Under the 'Old Diplomacy' professional diplomats abroad may have been executive plenipotentiaries. The advisory role was much less elaborate, even in the case of diplomats at home. Indeed within some foreign ministries, including the British, it was scarcely thought to exist before the twentieth century. Under the 'New Diplomacy' the professional diplomat abroad is many things: public relations expert, salesman (or woman), consultant, analyst, spokesman, journalist, columnist. At home he or she may be many of the same things and at times enjoy willy-nilly a high public profile. But the heart of this miscellany of duties is the confidential relationship with the foreign minister and other ministers, to whom diplomats, unlike other 'actors' in the field of international relations, owe exclusive loyalty. Professional diplomats have no monopoly of wisdom, nor of information, nor of ideas. But they are distinguished from other 'actors' in foreign policy in that they have a supreme duty as regards offering loyal, disinterested, advice to the foreign minister and other ministers and a near unique responsibility when it comes to the execution of policy once adopted.

(f) The Scope for 'Autonomous' Action

The analysis of the distinctive role of professional diplomats in foreign policy-making leads on naturally to the subject of the next lecture, namely Diplomatic Service organisation. But before addressing the latter topic it is necessary to look at two further aspects of foreign policy-making, where the role of the professional diplomat is of peculiar importance: first, the scope which governments have for effective 'autonomous' action, and secondly, the relationship between policy and strategy, efficiency in the latter contributing crucially to the chances of success of the former.

As regards governments' scope for autonomous action, as distinct from reacting to events and pressures, the constraints on freedom of manoeuvre described in previous lectures, especially Lecture 3,[11] are real enough. Just as in national terms the shaping of policy is the resultant of the various forces at work on the national scene, so the state of international relations at any given moment is the result of the activities of members of the international community, a phrase designed to include both the policies pursued by governments and the less structured input of other 'actors'.

A first reaction to the catalogue of constraints could well be pessimism as to the scope for any government but the most powerful to take significant independent action to deal with the situation in which it finds itself. Prudence is indeed essential. But there is room also for ingenuity and determination. Politics is the art of the possible, a phrase which can be interpreted negatively as enjoining caution, but which should rather be thought of positively as a spur to creative activity. This is what 'policy capability' really means. Diplomats who are experts at their job can create opportunities where none might otherwise have been thought to exist. They increase the room for manoeuvre enjoyed by their ministers. However much policy may be the resultant of competing pressures both at home and abroad, the difference between excessive caution and well-judged active pursuit of the national interest abroad may lie in the capacity of the professionals to operate effectively, both as a team and individually.

(g) Policy and Strategy

In no respect is this distinctive professional contribution more important than in the effective execution of policy once adopted. Let us revert to the distinction commonly drawn between foreign policy and diplomacy: foreign policy is about what has to be done and diplomacy is about how to do it. For the reasons explained earlier in these lectures, that distinction can easily be misleading. But it is useful as a warning that it is one thing to have a foreign policy and perhaps quite another to carry it out effectively. Effective policy execution requires a strategy as well as the policy itself. Indeed, the latter without the former is almost a contradiction in terms. The word 'policy', like so many others in use in politics, has a wide variety of meanings. Among them are:

- political sagacity, statecraft or diplomacy;
- a course of action adopted and pursued by a government, party, ruler or statesman;
- a prudent or politic course of action;
- prudent, expedient or advantageous procedure;
- sagacity, shrewdness, artfulness as a quality of an agent;
- a stratagem or trick.

This range of definitions underlines the point that any hard and fast distinction between policy and its execution is unrealistic. Policy implies most careful attention in its formulation not only to analysis and content, but also to the practical considerations of its execution. Once again, substance and process are inextricably mixed. So are foreign policy and diplomacy.

FOREIGN POLICY: FOUR ILLUSTRATIONS

The considerations advanced in this lecture can be illustrated by reference to official documents available publicly. The fact that they were published means that the texts in question may neither set forth the issues in the frankest way nor accurately reflect the true motives of the governments which authorised their publication. Nevertheless, texts are crucial to the understanding, as well as the making of foreign policy. Experience will help the diplomat 'aim off' to compensate for any distortion of the issues, or even concealment of them, which the governments issuing the texts may judge desirable. The basis of interpretation of the actions of other governments is not their words but their interests. The degree of democratic accountability of governments, and hence of obligation upon them to behave responsibly, may vary. But the national interest, let alone the national interest of others, will in the end set limits to any freedom of manoeuvre of governments.

Four texts relating to British foreign policy-making serve to illustrate what is at stake. The first, in chronological order, is a 'Memorandum on the Present State of British Relations with France and Germany', written in 1907 by one of the most illustrious of twentieth-century British diplomats, Eyre Crowe. The second is a speech made by the Foreign and Commonwealth Secretary, Mr Malcolm Rifkind, at Chatham House (the Royal Institute of International Affairs) on

21 September 1995. The third is the Queen's Speech at the State Opening of Parliament on 15 November 1995. The fourth is the Presidency Conclusions issued after the meeting of the European Council at Madrid on 15 and 16 December 1995.

(i) The Eyre Crowe Memorandum

In response to the concern shown by King Edward VII about 'our persistently unfriendly policy towards Germany', Eyre Crowe, then head of the Western Department of the Foreign Office, wrote in 1906 a 'Memorandum on the Present State of British Relations with France and Germany'. Shrewd, informative and well argued, the memorandum, although originally labelled 'secret', was subsequently published and became famous for its analysis of fundamental British foreign policy interests. 'The general character of England's foreign policy is determined by the immutable conditions of her geographical situation on the ocean flank of Europe as an island state with vast oversea colonies and dependencies.' Survival required preponderant sea power. But this would arouse jealousy and hostility in other countries unless exercised with great caution. National policy must therefore be 'directed so as to harmonise with the general desires and ideals common to all mankind', and 'identified with the primary and vital interests of a majority . . . of the other nations'. Those interests Crowe specified as independence and freedom of trade. British policy must support the independence of small nations. Britain must recognise herself as 'the natural enemy of any nation which threatened the independence of smaller countries', which implied opposition to the 'political dictatorship of the strongest single state or group at any given time'.

Crowe was particularly concerned with the growing threat of Imperial Germany, and with the evidence of its hostility to Britain, and hence with the need to foster understanding with France. His concern was very much to the point. The memorandum is a valuable yardstick by which to measure policy 90 years later. Perhaps the most striking aspect of any comparison between 1907 and the mid-1990s is the extent to which the conclusions are the same, even if the starting point as regards the relative power of Britain, imperially, politically and industrially, is so vastly different. Interdependence has replaced hegemony as guiding British policy towards the identification with 'the primary and vital interests of a majority of other nations'.

(ii)   Mr Rifkind's Speech at Chatham House, 21 September 1995

The Foreign and Commonwealth Secretary's speech to the Royal Institute of International Affairs at Chatham House on 21 September 1995, the full text of which is reproduced in Annex 3, is of special interest because it was his first major pronouncement on foreign policy since taking up his appointment two months earlier. It is a profound yet succinct review of British foreign policy and repays close study.

Mr Rifkind's point of departure was the dictum of Lord Palmerston, who was Foreign Secretary and later Prime Minister in the early and middle years of the nineteenth century, and a great exponent of the doctrine of the balance of power at a moment when Britain was reaching the zenith of its relative international power: 'the furtherance of British interests should be the only object of a British Foreign Secretary'. The task was to identify those interests and then to consider how best to further them. As regards British interests, Mr Rifkind gave pride of place to our own territorial security and the maintenance of peace in Europe. Britain's wider interests overseas were substantial: unique ties with 50 Commonwealth countries; particular responsibilities for 14 dependent territories around the world; 8.6 million British citizens living overseas; the great proportion of our production which is exported; total overseas assets in excess of £1.4 trillion; large-scale inward investment; Britain's role as a financial centre. 'These considerations', Mr Rifkind said, in language which echoes Crowe's concern with identifying Britain with 'the primary and vital interests of a majority of the other nations', 'give us an even greater interest than most countries in political stability, freedom of trade and freedom of passage throughout the world . . . Political stability also requires good government and a proper assurance of basic human rights. We have a moral and practical interest in promoting the values of liberal democracy.'

Turning to the question of how best to promote Britain's interests, Mr Rifkind stressed that the nation-state remains the basic building-block of the international system. The conduct of foreign policy must reflect this. But it must also reflect 'new global realities': the electronic media and the necessity for 'an effective public information effort to run in parallel with diplomatic activity'; the protection of the environment to which national boundaries were of limited relevance; and the global market.

In these circumstances, Mr Rifkind commented, no nation, in President Kennedy's words, can build its destiny alone. 'Nations must work together more to defend their security, their prosperity and their environment.' The balance of power was no longer a feasible approach. 'Our common experience of total European war twice this century has convinced us all that we cannot return to the hostility, shifting alliances and regular conflict that has characterised most of our common history.'[12] It was not, however, the case that the only alternative to maintaining the balance of power was a single foreign policy shared with all our neighbours and partners. 'We must not suppress important national interests in order to construct an artificial consensus, a bogus unity, that lacks credibility or conviction.' This, Mr Rifkind commented, was relevant to the debate about the future of the European Union and Britain's role in it. Anxiety was often expressed at the loss of influence that Britain might incur if it did not join an area of integration which our partners in Europe had concluded was desirable. The long delay in the UK joining the European Community was a case in point. But the argument must not be taken too far. While the accretion of influence was the stuff of diplomatic life, it was not an end in itself. Occasionally it might be appropriate to accept a loss of influence if that was the only means to protect one's interests.

Whatever relevance it may have in the immediate Maastricht context, the distinction drawn by Mr Rifkind between influence and interest is often less than clear-cut in the global span of Britain's international involvement. Once one defines a country's interests in terms as broad as those used by Mr Rifkind, it is apparent that the means of promoting them will include persuasion and discussion, and even setting an example, as well as negotiation. To that extent there is no conflict between influence and interest. The two are inextricably mixed. As Mr Rifkind remarks, the accretion of influence is the stuff of diplomatic life. It is not in the interest of Britain to seek to impose, or to be judged to be seeking to impose, its views on others. But it is very much in its interest to convince others of the soundness of its policies. There is a sense in which clear and responsible analysis by a country of its interests and the adoption of policies consistent with that analysis – that is, demonstration of a sound foreign policy capability – will of itself gain influence abroad. Equally, attempts to exert influence in ways unaligned with a realistic assessment of national interest are unlikely to be successful in the shorter, let alone the longer, term.

Mr Rifkind's speech graphically illustrates the range of analytical issues and the institutional features which have been discussed in earlier lectures. It reflects the series of 'invasions' of the political, commercial and imperial foreground with which Crowe was familiar. It faces the reality of international society today and the limits to national sovereignty. It emphasises the central role and the limitations of the United Nations. It is immersed in the world economy, using some illuminating statistics about the scale of Britain's international economic involvement. It stresses the vital importance of European architecture. It is a key point of reference for the discussion in subsequent lectures of professional Diplomatic Service organisation and the acquisition of personal diplomatic skills.

(iii)   The Queen's Speech at the Opening of Parliament, 15 November 1995

Each year the parliamentary session is opened with a speech by the Queen setting out, as it were, the government's stall for the year ahead. The full text of the Queen's Speech on 15 November 1995 is reproduced in Annex 4. The occasion is of considerable interest from at least three points of view: the indications it gives as regards the government's intentions for the coming year; the insight it offers into the prospects which the government sees for getting things done; and the contrast it affords between ceremonial precedence and the realities of power.

First, the indications. More than half of the brief text is concerned with international affairs. It is as useful a summary as one can find of current UK foreign policy. Although couched in general terms, it gives the discerning and well-informed reader a good idea of the specifics which the government will pursue. The absence of reference to any particular topic is an indication that that topic is either unprofitable or inappropriate for priority attention.

The legislative programme set out in the Queen's Speech is based not so much on what the government regards, or believes the public to regard, as of intrinsic importance, as on the realistic prospects of securing the necessary votes and steering the draft legislation to successful completion. The balance to be struck between what one most wants to do and what one is most likely to be able to achieve, referred to at the outset of these lectures,[13] is nowhere more evident. The inextricable mix of substance and process is definitively illustrated. The government's task is dominated by the requirement that the bills which it presents have to be passed in a single session. The nearer the session is to a general election, the more crucial will be the choice of draft legislation. If a general election is called during a parliamentary session, all the government's uncompleted legislation automatically lapses.

The ceremonial itself affords an engaging contrast to the realities which it represents. 'Her Majesty's Most Gracious Speech to Both Houses of Parliament' is of course drafted by the government. The Queen drives to Parliament in a state coach and is conducted to the House of Lords. The lowly Commons are summoned to the Lords and stand respectfully at the entrance to the chamber while the speech is read out to the seated peers. Any acoustic difficulties are mitigated by the familiarity with the text already possessed not only by the government but also by the government's supporters, and by the opposition, thanks to media leaks, if not to advance briefing. Any passage in the Gracious Speech dealing with expenditure is addressed to the Commons only. The Lords have no standing in tax matters. The ceremony all in all is less a reflection of power than a picturesque reminder to those who have been elected that they are not elected in perpetuity.

(iv) Presidency Conclusions Issued at the End of the European Council Meeting in Madrid, 15 and 16 December 1995

Every six months the heads of the state or government of the member states of the European Union meet as the European Council, to review progress and chart the way ahead. The outcome of these meetings is presented to the world in the shape of 'Conclusions of the Presidency', that is, an account delivered by the country which holds the presidency at the time and consequently chairs the meeting. It is textually agreed for the most part by all the member countries. These Presidency Conclusions are often of considerable length, reflecting the great mass of business, some of it very detailed, of which the European Council must be officially cognisant. On the other hand they may be less illuminating as regards the dynamics of the Union, since they tend to conceal rather than highlight differences among the member countries. The most recent meeting of the European Council took place in Florence on 21 and 22 June 1996 under Italian presidency.

The preceding meeting of the European Council had taken place in Madrid on 15 and 16 December 1995, under Spanish presidency. It covered a great deal of ground. The Introduction to Part A of the Conclusions is reproduced in full in Annex 5. (The full conclusions run to 130 pages.) The range of issues covered is very wide, dealing with both internal matters, including the key questions of progress towards economic and monetary union, the future of Europe and the preparations for the Intergovernmental Review Conference, and external questions: the Dayton Agreement on Bosnia; the New Transatlantic Agenda and the 'Joint US–EU Action Plan' agreed between the Union and the USA on 3 December; the Agreement with Mercosur; the Barcelona Declaration concerning the Mediterranean; the signature of the revised Lomé Convention; the Customs Union with Turkey; and enlargement, including a meeting with the foreign ministers of the prospective members: the associate countries from Central and Eastern Europe (CCEE) and Cyprus and Malta.

The UK national perspective on the Presidency Conclusions emerges from the statements made by the Prime Minister to the House of Commons very shortly after meetings of the European Council. There was an informative exchange of views after Mr Major's statement on 18 December.[14] An overall British perspective on European Union affairs is contained in the six-monthly survey of *Developments in the European Union* presented to Parliament by the Foreign and Commonwealth Secretary.[15]

8 Diplomatic Service Organisation

The previous lecture surveyed the national context in which the professional diplomats play their part in the making and carrying out of foreign policy. Policy is the resultant of many forces acting within the country and outside it, of which the Diplomatic Service is only one, albeit one of great importance. Organising a Diplomatic Service to fulfil its tasks requires great care. The fundamentals have already been emphasised. Just as substance and process are inextricably mixed, so the making of policy and its execution are inseparable in practice. Useful as it may be in analytical terms, the familiar distinction between foreign policy, as what has to be done, and diplomacy, as how to do it, will not suffice as the basis for organising the work of a Diplomatic Service. A more reliable guide is the proposition advanced by Lord Strang, the Permanent Under-Secretary at the Foreign Office between 1949 and 1953, as to what it is that diplomats really do:

> essentially they help their Foreign Secretary reach his decisions and then help him carry them out. They help him to settle what to do and then they help him to do it.[1]

Notice the repeated use of the word 'help'. Popular demonology may suggest that the word is a euphemism for 'dominate' (or 'undermine'). But the reality, as the previous lectures have explained, is that the professional diplomats are very far from enjoying a monopoly in the shaping and execution of foreign policy. But they have a distinct and clearly defined role, which it is their responsibility to discharge with the greatest possible efficiency. This lecture will first review some criteria for Diplomatic Service organisation: the scale of professional diplomatic effort; coverage; the balance between home and overseas; priorities in the establishment of missions abroad; and communications. Secondly, we shall look at some relevant management factors: recruitment and training; terms and conditions of service; locally engaged staff; the diplomatic corps; the physical apparatus; information technology; and the family factor. Finally there will be some comment on future trends in Diplomatic Service organisation. Before considering these points generally, and as they may apply especially to the Diplomatic Services of young countries, it is helpful to look at the cost and staffing levels of the British Diplomatic Service, both as a specific case and as an illustration of what is at issue generally.

THE BRITISH DIPLOMATIC SERVICE: COST AND STAFFING LEVELS

What Lord Strang's proposition, quoted above, means in statistical terms is very clearly set out in the annual Departmental Report, referred to in the previous lecture.[2] This publication, apart from the wealth of financial detail which it contains, is a veritable mine of information about the practical work of the British Diplomatic Service. The list of contents summarises what is involved. The tasks of the Diplomatic Service include the disposition of its manpower and other resources at home and overseas; the organisation of its policy work, particularly in the political and economic fields; 'functional services' – commercial, information, consular and immigration; central management and support of all these activities; expenditure on 'other external relations', including subscriptions to international organisations, peace-keeping operations; grants to non-governmental organisations; scholarships for overseas students and military training assistance; support of the work of the BBC World Service and of the British Council; and with the vast area of overseas development assistance, which is managed by a separate Overseas Development Administration.

This is an enormously wide range of activities, which may come as something of a surprise to those not already familiar with the work of Diplomatic Services. Even more surprising, perhaps, is the relative cost of the activities. FCO expenditure is listed under a series of 'Votes', for which the 'estimated outturn' for 1995/96 is the following:

	£ mn
Vote 1 (Overseas Representation)	713
Vote 2 ('Other external relations')	437
Vote 3 (BBC World Service)	178
Vote 4 (British Council)	101
	1429

At the same time the estimated outturn of the external assistance programme administered by the Overseas Development Administration, for which, of course, the Foreign and Commonwealth Secretary is responsible, was £2381 million. This means that out of a total FCO expenditure of £3810 million, less than one-fifth – £713 million – was spent on 'traditional' diplomatic activities under the rubric 'overseas representation'. This small proportion of the total, moreover, includes not only political and economic work, but also functional and managerial work – commercial, information, consular, administration. Political and economic work accounts for approximately one-quarter of overseas costs, and a slightly higher proportion of home costs.

'Policy capability', which we have identified as our chief concern,[3] and of which political and economic work is the core, thus represents a very small fraction of total Diplomatic Service/Overseas Development Administration expenditure. At first sight this may seem to constitute a dissipation of effort, if not a failure to establish priorities. The reality, however, is otherwise. In the first place, the elaboration of the traditional objectives of foreign policy referred to in the previous lecture,[4] which puts emphasis on the promotion of British interests and standing overseas, requires organised activity in a number of different directions. These may at first sight seem ancillary to the more general work of promoting the prosperity of the realm as a whole. But this does not mean that all this activity is unconnected. Rather, it is closely integrated, as the organisation and structure of diplomatic missions demonstrates. The adequate discharge of both the executive function and the advisory function in the core areas of political and economic work, requires a capability in the commercial, information and cultural fields.

A practical test of this effective indivisibility of Diplomatic Service activities is to be found in the personal role of the Head of Mission. Heads of Mission are crucial to policy capability. Their main overall concern, especially at times of international tension, is likely to be with political and economic work. Export promotion, however, will never be far from their thoughts. They also know that their own efforts at any particular moment may be concentrated in any of a number of different directions. They will be unable to forecast with any certainty how much of their time will be taken up with this or that aspect of the mission's work.

Secondly, the emphasis on rigorous economy and on clear management objectives for all aspects of Diplomatic Service expenditure, which is characteristic of the annual Departmental Report, affords some assurance that optional or peripheral activities will be cut to the minimum, where they cannot prudently be discarded. What indeed this integrated range of Diplomatic Service activities underlines is that diplomacy, at least in so far as the role of the Diplomatic Service is concerned, is a business, with the senior officials in the national capital effectively constituting a board of directors.[5] The board of directors, mindful of the constant pressure on resources to which a Diplomatic Service is subject, will naturally have it in mind to monitor the degree of integration of activity which the situation requires. This lecture concludes with some comment on future trends in Diplomatic Service organisation.

COMPARISONS AND OPPORTUNITIES

The principal asset of a diplomatic business is manpower. It is highly labour intensive, and is concerned with 'value added' in the deployment of its resources. The 'value' to be added is admittedly elusive in nature. There is certainly an important prestige or advertisement factor in diplomacy, with the uncertainties and ambiguities which are inherent in expenditure on advertisement.[6] Historical comparisons, and an awareness of what countries with broadly similar international situations do, have their relevance.

The Foreign and Commonwealth Office employs some 6000 UK-based staff, one-fifth less than 15 years ago.[7] Of these, 2472 serve overseas, assisted by 7400 locally engaged staff. All in all, Britain has 221 posts overseas. The comparable figures for France, Germany and Italy are 253, 229 and 265 respectively. It can scarcely be maintained that the British overseas stake is, on any objective measure, less than that of France or Germany or Italy, and hence justifies a smaller number of overseas posts and of home-based Diplomatic Service officers to staff them. The explanation of the difference is many-sided. It lies partly in the efficiency of diplomatic effort and partly in the extent to which governments and taxpayers are ready to finance it, regardless of its merits. It is also a matter of national willingness to create and exploit opportunities. But that willingness depends to a great extent upon the capacity of the Diplomatic Service in the first instance to persuade governments and taxpayers that the opportunities are there. The history of diplomacy, as of fishing, is replete with stories of the one that got away.

SOME CRITERIA FOR DIPLOMATIC SERVICE ORGANISATION

(a)   The Scale of Professional Diplomatic Effort

The question 'How large a diplomatic effort should a country undertake?' may invite the counter-question 'How long is a piece of string?' The considerations referred to earlier in this lecture suggest that there is no simple 'objective' answer. It depends upon a number of factors, some of them measurable by relation to the degree of a country's overseas economic involvement, or of its vulnerability politically, militarily and economically. It will depend also on the response which a country wishes to make to its international circumstances. Some countries seek at times to 'punch above their weight', though this by no means guarantees that they will be ready to devote the additional resources to the diplomatic effort which this entails. Professional servants of the state have perennially bemoaned the unwillingness of governments to accept the resource implications of their policy decisions. Diplomatic Services face this unwillingness in a particularly acute form, since their activities tend to be regarded by others as expensive as well as esoteric. The value of what they do has at best to be taken largely on trust by the taxpayer. They are thus attractive targets for cuts in government expenditure. But the disruption and loss of efficiency caused by such cuts are more than proportional, since manpower represents a very high percentage of the cost of diplomacy. Diplomats, moreover, are spread around the world in penny packets. There is in consequence an inevitable measure of defensiveness about the priority to be accorded to expenditure on diplomatic effort. Perhaps the crucial question Diplomatic Service managers are driven to ask is 'What harm will be done to the national interest by failure to be represented in a particular country or at a particular international gathering?' The basic answer, as the French put it, is '*les absents ont toujours tort*': those absent are always wrong. But that is no absolute guide. The key is to be able to distinguish between when one cannot afford to be present, and when one cannot afford not to be present.

(b)   Coverage

There is a temptation to conclude from rigorous analysis of the role of a Diplomatic Service that it must be capable of dealing with virtually any range of subject matter which enters into the country's foreign relations. In the case of the United Kingdom, the 1943 White Paper 'Proposals for Reform of the Foreign Service'[8] took the line that the general level and ability of diplomats would hopefully be such that no aspect of foreign relations should be regarded as 'the exclusive province of experts'. But Heads of Mission should have expert advice and assistance on various issues 'when this is in the public interest'. Experience, on the other hand, suggests that such an approach is over-ambitious. It is not a matter of diplomats being omnicompetent with experts at their elbow only as required. The content of international affairs permits no such over-simplification The most recent comprehensive inquiry into British diplomacy, the *Review of Overseas Representation*, conducted in 1977 by the Central Policy Review Staff (also known as the 'Think Tank'),[9] suggested that there should be much more interchange between the Home Civil Service and the Diplomatic Service, indeed that there might be a merger of the two, with the creation of a combined 'Foreign Service Group' to handle the bulk of diplomatic functions. This idea found little favour. But it was a sign of interdependent times following British accession to the European Community.[10]

Perhaps the most interesting aspect of the question of the coverage to be expected of a Diplomatic Service is the way in which 'political and economic' work is regarded as a unitary affair. It was not always so. Reference was made in Lecture 1 to a particularly far-sighted British diplomat, Sir Victor Wellesley, who was Deputy Under-Secretary of State at the Foreign Office between 1925 and 1936.[11] His thesis, it will be recalled, was that diplomats thought far too much in conventional 'political' terms and took insufficient account of economic factors. No such criticism could be levelled at diplomats today. The latter might, if they wished to be provocative, echo the view of an anonymous United States ambassador that 'economics is politics studied seriously'.[12]

(c) The Balance Between Effort at Home and Effort Abroad

A Diplomatic Service seeking taxpayers' money to conduct its operations must be able to deploy a convincing case. The preceding section dealt with the scale of operations as a whole. A consideration no less important is the division of effort between home and abroad. It is implicit in conditions of modern interdependence that very few issues of international concern will be susceptible of management on an exclusively bilateral basis, or even by means of a network of bilateral arrangements. Diplomacy will tend increasingly to be conducted multilaterally, and much of bilateral discussion will relate to issues which are handled multilaterally. This affects not only the balance of effort between multilateral and bilateral posts, but also the balance between home and abroad, since the home content tends to be larger in multilateral than in bilateral business and is often of direct and continuing concern to a number of different ministries. The case for effective representation at major multilateral diplomatic centres is thus very strong. It is otherwise with bilateral relations. In general there must be strong reason for establishing bilateral missions in countries where there is no significant political or economic interest. There may, however, be strong commercial or consular grounds for doing so. It is important to note that the establishment of diplomatic relations with another country does not of itself require the setting up of a post in that country. There are several alternative possibilities to permanent physical presence. An ambassador may be non-resident. Multiple accreditation is common, with the ambassador residing overseas, but in only one of the countries to which he or she is accredited. Sometimes the non-resident ambassador is based at headquarters.

Contact can of course be maintained without the use of ambassadors or resident bilateral missions. Foreign ministers can and do visit one another without benefit of permanent local representation. It is also easy to arrange meetings at multilateral diplomatic centres such as New York and Geneva. Indeed the scale of bilateral contacts in the margins is one of the more prominent features of large international gatherings. At the opening of the regular session of the UN General Assembly in New York, the contacts in the margins of the Assembly itself are unquestionably of greater importance than the stately procession of foreign ministers to the rostrum to deliver their worthy monologues as part of what is somewhat whimsically described as the 'General Debate'.

The criteria for the establishment of bilateral missions are to be found in the formulation of the basic aims of foreign policy referred to in the previous lecture. How directly, in other words, does the promotion of national security and prosperity, of national interest and of standing overseas, depend upon a permanent diplomatic presence in any particular country? If the dependence is direct, then failure to have a permanent diplomatic presence in the country concerned will cause the national interest to suffer, perhaps cumulatively. But where the relationship is more tenuous, scarcity of resources, human and financial, militate against the establishment of a mission. Other things being equal, it costs much less to employ a Diplomatic Service officer at home than abroad. Resources can thus be more effectively deployed at home, provided that contacts with other countries are adequately maintained by the alternative methods referred to above.

A price for keeping down the number of posts abroad will probably have to be paid in terms of impairment of both the advisory and the executive functions. This, in turn, puts a premium on efficiency at headquarters. Continuity of staffing is crucial, especially to the organisation of the advisory function. A sound advisory capability is indispensable to the proper discharge of the role of the Diplomatic Service in helping the foreign minister to shape policy. In smaller ministries of foreign affairs there may be no planning staff as such. But the concept, implied in the existence of planners, of a co-ordinated approach to current activities, based on analysis of national requirements and circumstances, on the one hand, and developments abroad, on the other, remains valid. Even if in the world of today elaborate foreign policy planning may be an unattainable goal, imparting a measure of coherence to the conduct of a mass of variegated daily business is not merely desirable. It is essential.

As with other questions of the allocation of scarce resources to competing uses, a balance has to struck. After safeguarding the efficiency of its headquarters operations, a Diplomatic Service can approach the setting of priorities in the establishment of posts abroad on the basis of some such criteria as the following:

1   major multilateral diplomatic centres, especially New York and Geneva;
2   capitals of major countries with which there are strong political, economic, cultural or military ties, especially where these contain in addition the headquarters of major multilateral bodies – Washington, Brussels, Paris, London, Rome, Vienna;
3   capitals of countries which are major export markets or sources of inward investment and development assistance;
4   regional centres, for example, Addis Ababa, the headquarters of the Organisation of African Unity;
5   capitals and major cities of neighbouring states, especially those with significant relevant ethnic minorities.

The list is, of course, indicative rather than definitive. The circumstances in which a country finds itself are, if not unique, at least highly individual. This will suggest a different order of priorities in each case.

Moreover, there is obviously some overlap between the five suggested categories.

(d) Communications

Communications between headquarters and posts abroad, both in the sense of the technical apparatus available and of the substantive use made of that apparatus – the means of communication and the subject matter communicated – are central to the work of a Diplomatic Service. It is apparent that accuracy and security are indispensable and that speed is highly desirable. As ever, substance and process are inextricably mixed. The more accurate, secure and rapid communications are, the less the ambassador abroad will feel isolated from his or her government, and the more the latter will wish to know about what is going on, with a view to giving the ambassador instructions. Increasing sophistication in diplomatic communication is not an isolated phenomenon. It is part of the 'information technology invasion' described in Lecture 1.[13] It is apparent that in our globalised life today, sources of information about what is going on are far more voluminous, speedy and sophisticated than before, and governments need to react to a far greater range of events. The media rather than the events set the parameters. Governments' need of their own network of information is reduced, as is the scope for effective independent action of their representatives abroad. None of this is surprising, let alone distressing. Diplomatic communications are designed to supplement world information flows, not to supplant them. Diplomatic action is designed to take account of those flows, not to ignore them. Diplomacy is a child of its time, not of bygone ages.

It is none the less only to be expected that, the more rapid and sophisticated communications become, the greater will be the question-mark hanging in the public mind over the usefulness of the diplomatic mission abroad. Ever since the invention of the telegraph each new development has encouraged assertions that ambassadors matter much less than they used to, and that foreign relations can be conducted without an elaborate network of missions. Reporting on conditions abroad, the argument runs, can be left to the media. Negotiation can be entrusted to ministers or officials sent from headquarters as the need arises. Ubiquity of air travel and the ceaseless peregrinations of foreign ministers underline the point.[14] There is undoubtedly a measure of truth in this line of reasoning. But it is also highly misleading. It is not the innumerable details of developments abroad, which are essential to the formulation of foreign policy, so much as the interpretation of the way in which they affect the interests of the nation. Likewise it is not the glitter of an occasional summit, so much as diligent preparation of the ground beforehand and shrewd follow-up, which will ensure the successful execution of foreign policy. Humankind has not so far found a satisfactory substitute for face-to-face advocacy. It is of interest to note that one mid-nineteenth-century British Foreign Secretary, Lord John Russell, took a very different view of the significance of the telegraph. He pointed out that, in former days, the foreign secretary wrote a long despatch which formed the ambassador's instructions (or the minister's: in earlier days missions abroad were graded in importance; the less significant were headed by ministers rather than ambassadors). The latter could speak only from his brief. Now, however, owing to the brevity inspired by the use of the telegraph, the ambassador was obliged to supply a large proportion of the argument himself.[15] Lord John Russell's line of argument cuts both ways. It is indeed a familiar experience for ambassadors to receive succinct instructions which may make admirable sense to those at headquarters who send them, but are beset with difficulty as perceived by those who are deputed to carry them out. The traditional caveat in the instructions 'unless you see objection' is more than a formality. If matters go wrong when the instructions are carried out, the opprobrium could well fall on the head of the ambassador rather than that of their originator.

Any ambassador worth his or her salt feels grateful for, rather than threatened by, extensive media coverage of his or her sphere of responsibility. Ministerial visits, far from sidelining or replacing the ambassador's work, in fact enrich it. Ambassadors in the main are deterred from pleading for more ministerial attention not by anxiety about putting themselves out of work, so much as by acute awareness of the horrendous demands on the foreign minister's time. The latter point tends to be overlooked by those anxious to stress the superfluousness of ambassadors in the world of modern communications. Sir Edward Grey, who was Foreign Secretary in the years before, and during the early part of, the Great War, and whom one tends to associate with the last golden days of peace before 'the lamps went out all over Europe',[16] once said that during his term of office he was so pressed that he could not remember having taken any step that was not of immediate urgency and for the solving of a problem directly in front of him. The pressure has of course greatly increased since then. When he returned to the Foreign Office in 1951 Mr Anthony Eden (as he then was) told his immediate predecessor, Lord Morrison of Lambeth, that he found that the work had doubled as compared with 1945 when he had last been foreign secretary.[17] What either would have made of the hideously burdened life of the foreign secretary today is a matter of speculation.

MANAGEMENT FACTORS

(e) Recruitment and Training

Management, in the sense of the direction and control of collective effort deployed in the shaping and execution of foreign policy, is essential. Indeed, it is the central theme of these lectures. But there is a no less important aspect of management on the input rather than the output side: namely, the development and utilisation of resources in a business which is highly specialised and demands considerable flexibility and imagination.

As already noted, the resources of a Diplomatic Service are mainly human. There is a premium on getting hold of the right people; training them, not only at the outset of their careers, but also during the whole course of their service; and providing them with the infrastructure which will ensure that they are in a position to do the job. Recruitment must, in a democracy, be seen to be both effective and fair. Under the 'Old Diplomacy' there was a good deal of unpublicised patronage. Today patronage would be much more difficult to conceal, while the likely inadequacies resulting from it would be all too apparent. Diplomacy is an exacting profession and its varied tasks and responsibilities seem to have encouraged a certain amount of narcissism among those authorities who expatiate on what is required. The ultimate example of this can be found in a comment, tongue no doubt well in cheek, by Sir Harold Nicolson:

> These then are the qualities of my ideal diplomatist. Truth, accuracy, calm, patience, good temper, modesty and loyalty. They are also the qualities of an ideal diplomacy.
>
> 'But', the reader may object, 'you have forgotten intelligence, knowledge, discernment, prudence, hospitality, charm, industry, courage and even tact'. I have not forgotten them. I have taken them for granted.[18]

A Diplomatic Service composed exclusively of such paragons would, to put it mildly, lack appeal. It would also discourage people of less attainment but who would none the less do a very good job. It is fortunate that, in the case of the United Kingdom for example, there is in general no shortage of applicants, since job satisfaction is high. But it is not always easy to detect in people in their twenties the capacity to grow to the job over the period of their working lives, which, of course, may last another 40 years. Perhaps the key qualities are those of receptiveness and adaptability which will enable the diplomat throughout his or her career to deal with changing requirements and circumstances and develop the personal skills which will yield effective action in response to these. As already indicated, training is a career-long affair rather than the acquisition at the outset of a corpus of knowledge and expertise of permanent validity. 'Training' as a concept must include career development. Individual officers are encouraged by some Diplomatic Services to devise their own training plans which they can fulfil as circumstances permit. As noted at the outset of these lectures, the acquisition of what might be regarded as 'vocational' skills, such as proficiency in languages and expertise in consular or immigration work are allied to, rather than opposed to, the skills which are required in developing policy capability in the more traditional areas of political and economic work.

(f)   Terms and Conditions of Service

Personnel management presents particular problems for an organisation which is spread thinly over a great number of scattered locations, as is the case with a Diplomatic Service. The members of the service will need to be paid overall at a rate which bears comparison with that for comparable jobs. But it will also have to include elements to take account of the degree of mobility and unpredictability of the job and the discomfort, or even danger, which may be a feature of life at certain posts. It will have to take account of morale problems which stem from the peripatetic nature of the job. It is most important to reassure those furthest or longest away from headquarters that they are not forgotten. Equality of opportunity is of cardinal importance. The regular reports which senior members of the service make on those who work for them are essential in this regard. Quality is vital, and legitimate ambition and competitiveness are essential to maintaining it. But nothing is more destructive of morale, and indeed of enjoyment of the job and of the life that goes with it, than the feeling that some people never get a chance and that others are shown favouritism.

(g) Locally Engaged Staff

On grounds of cost alone, there is a strong case for employing locally engaged staff in preference to home-based staff in a mission abroad, wherever this is possible. Considerations of confidentiality or security may preclude it in a number of instances. On the other hand, expert knowledge of the local situation is essential not only to the efficiency of the work of the mission – particularly in commercial or consular work – but also to the welfare and safety and hence the efficiency of the home-based officers who staff it. Where administrative talent at home is scarce, the grounds for employing locally engaged staff are even stronger. The same consideration applies to the use of local consultants and local expert services of various kinds, especially perhaps in the legal field. Those who work for you need not do so full time.

(h) The Diplomatic Corps

Foreign diplomats in any particular national capital are known collectively as the 'Diplomatic Corps', a phrase which may occasion suppressed laughter among the irreverent, but which nevertheless has its uses. Legally, the Corps is composed of those to whom the host government grants, under the terms of relevant international under-standings – principally the Vienna Convention[19] – certain privileges and immunities. The Corps includes the members of recognised international organisations which have their headquarters or branch offices in the capital concerned. A Diplomatic List containing all these details is an extremely handy document, not simply for the current factual information which it yields, but also for the insight it gives into the judgement which individual countries or organisations make as to the scale of their representation at the diplomatic centre in question.

The *London Diplomatic List* of December 1995,[20] shows that some 160 countries have diplomatic missions accredited to the UK government, of which 15 or so are non-resident, being actually based in Paris, Brussels or The Hague. The scale of representation varies greatly. Some countries have well over 50, or even as many as 100, diplomatic staff. Others may have only two or three. The diplomatic staff of the International Maritime Organisation (IMO), the UN specialised agency based in London, and of the Commonwealth Secretariat are likewise substantial. There is, of course, no simple correlation between the size of a country, as measured by population or GNP, and the size of its mission in any particular place. As already noted,[21] the scale of representation depends upon the individual circumstances of the sending country and on the extent to which its interests are bound up with the host country. Some countries are lavish with the ranks they bestow on their diplomats: their missions are weighed down with ministers and counsellors to assist the ambassador. Others, more austere, put their trust in attachés or even assistant attachés.

In multilateral posts the members of the Diplomatic Corps see a great deal of one another, since their responsibilities may in theory, if not in practice, be confined to the international organisations based there. In the larger bilateral capitals the diplomats will probably be dispersed and see relatively little of one another. But in smaller posts, especially where conditions are difficult and information perhaps hard to come by, diplomats may be greatly dependent upon one another for professional support and social relaxation. Diplomats are for the most part agreeable companions, so agreeable, in fact, that they may at times represent a distraction from the job, which is contact with the country or the international organisation to which you are accredited. The essential point, however, is that the Diplomatic Corps is an important asset to a professional Diplomatic Service in the discharge of its responsibilities, at home or abroad.

(i) The Physical Apparatus

Office accommodation and living quarters abroad are of great importance, not only from the point of view of the efficiency and security of the work and the health and well-being of the staff, but also from the point of view of the image of the country which they project. The representational factor is difficult to evaluate, as has already been noted. But it is there. On all these grounds it is of advantage to own outright or occupy on long lease the office accommodation and a substantial proportion of the living accommodation abroad. The United Kingdom has some 3900 properties abroad of which 258 are offices, 221 are houses for Heads of Mission and 3250 are staff houses or flats. 40 per cent of the offices, 65 per cent of the residences and 40 per cent of the staff accommodation are owned freehold. The maintenance of such a vast amount of property spread all over the world is a major task, especially where the buildings are well known for architectural or historical reasons, or occupy a prominent site. Any Diplomatic Service establishing a post abroad needs to consider location very carefully with an eye to the factors mentioned above. At the same time, these factors have to be measured against the usual financial constraints, which will probably stand in the way of securing the really desirable, and require instead acceptance of something less than optimal.

Office equipment and decoration likewise have their representational, as well as their security and efficiency criteria. But here again imagination and resourcefulness can do a good deal to overcome financial stringency. It is heartening to see how such good use is made of limited facilities. The art of living has a direct bearing on diplomacy.

(j) Information Technology

Looked at in managerial terms, information technology is a means of helping a Diplomatic Service to discharge its responsibilities more thoroughly, more quickly, more securely and more cheaply. Until recently the most significant developments have been in communications, specifically the combining of the hitherto separate functions of processing information and transmitting it – for example, in the encrypting and transmission of telegraphic messages. Developments in this regard were not accompanied by parallel progress in information storage and retrieval, or in dissemination. The combined effect of rapid development in all these spheres simultaneously is cumulative – a matter of geometrical rather than arithmetical progression.

Reference has already been made to a monograph by a member of the British Diplomatic Service, Stewart Eldon, entitled *From Quill Pen to Satellite*.[22] This contains invaluable practical advice on the introduction of information systems into diplomatic work. Eldon suggests four 'stages of organisational learning with IT': technology identification and investment; technological learning and adaptation; rationalisation management control; and 'maturity'. These stages see a Diplomatic Service through the initial task of finding the technology appropriate to its requirements, and finding a pilot project, to the introduction to the wonders of IT of the staff as a whole, to the point where the latter understand it, and appropriate support systems and controls can be devised to ensure that it is used efficiently.

All of this will introduce change into accepted diplomatic practice. The most significant developments could well be a 'flattening out' of the hierarchies in Diplomatic Services and greater problems of control for those responsible for the work of a mission as a whole, given the facilities for direct communication with headquarters by such means as E-mail from each 'work station' (formerly 'desk').[23] It must be said that conventional diplomatic hierarchies owe at least as much to the traditions of the 'Old Diplomacy' as to the requirements of the 'New'. It is to the Australian Foreign Service, for example, that we are indebted for the definition of the role of Second Secretaries: it is 'to assist First Secretaries and to direct Third Secretaries'. Policy capability is in general a levelling influence within Diplomatic Services. Management, moreover, must take in its stride the scope of developments in technology in fields other than information for achieving greater efficiency.

(k) The Family Factor

Politics and diplomacy are among the careers in which there is particularly rich scope for partnership between spouses. The extent to which statesmen are indebted to their wives has been clear throughout history. Only more recently, with the emancipation of women and their growing role in public life, has the reverse proposition become equally clear. The role of the diplomatic wife likewise has been chronicled entertainingly on a number of occasions.[24] But it is still all too easy to underestimate.

The increasing part played by women diplomats is rightly attracting attention, not least from the family point of view. When women were at first admitted to the British Foreign Service (as it then was) they were obliged by the regulations to resign on marriage. The cynics suggested that those opposed to the whole idea saw to it that only those women were selected who were of such outstanding beauty, charm and ability that their marriage would be instant. Today the situation is different. There are many married women diplomats. Husband and wife partnerships in the diplomatic career are common. Gone are the days when it was assumed that a wife would have no professional career of her own and that her husband's peripatetic career would pose no problems for her in that regard. Today, when both spouses are likely to have careers, mobility creates difficulties and pressures for the one or the other which need to be taken carefully into account. The basic value of the family team remains undiminished. The difficulties of realising it to full effect are much enhanced.

Family life is, of course, complicated by a peripatetic existence. The plus is the stimulus which it gives to the development of the children.

The minus is the unpleasant choice it may pose between children's separation from their parents in the interest of continuity of their education at home, and disrupted or fractured education as the price of their remaining with their parents as the latter move from post to post. The British public school system provides a palliative of sorts in that it makes boarding school education less unusual, even in the case of stationary families. The French *lycée* system is a boon because of the uniformity of day-school education which it provides world-wide, and can thus offer continuity even to families on the move. There is no fully satisfactory answer. Children of diplomats are apt to draw their own varied, and not always respectful, conclusions. Many of them acquire, and retain, a formidable expertise in air travel.

FUTURE TRENDS IN DIPLOMATIC SERVICE ORGANISATION

One of the qualities most demanded of diplomats, individually and collectively, is adaptability. They have of necessity to be ready to uproot themselves, mentally as well as physically, as successive postings take them from one country to another. The way in which Diplomatic Services are organised has changed greatly since the end of the Second World War. There is no reason to suppose that the rate of change will diminish. Growing world interdependence will prompt changed responses to the circumstances which the country faces. Four possible trends suggest themselves. First, the emergence since 1945 of a very large number of new members of the United Nations may have encouraged an excessive growth in the network of bilateral diplomatic missions. There may have been some tendency in the past for emerging countries to regard elaborate diplomatic representation overseas as an essential attribute of their newly acquired sovereignty. Hard economic facts have put any such tendency under increasing pressure. In any case the growth of international diplomatic centres, and of the volume of business transacted multilaterally rather than bilaterally, call in question the validity of the network on its past generous scale. While multilateral diplomacy may be a growth industry, the prospects for bilateral diplomacy are more problematic.

Secondly, the trend towards the multilateralisation of diplomatic business may encourage the search for activities which can be hived off from the main political and diplomatic work. Commercial, consular and information services were separate from 'core' diplomacy until the recent past, as has already been explained.[25] The grounds for integrating them, within the comprehensive approach to policy capability which these lectures have stressed, may become less persuasive with the passage of time. In practical terms, we may see a tendency for bilateral diplomacy to concentrate increasingly on commercial, cultural, information and consular work, while political and economic work reflects the growing multilateralisation of diplomacy. This could lead to a situation where bilateral posts are managed more and more by locally engaged staff. But if this occurs it will be nothing new. The consular function, for example, flourished in the days before the rise of organised Diplomatic Services. Foreign communities would appoint one of their number to be their representative in the capital or country in which they resided. To this day a special type of document is furnished to consuls-general or consuls validating their appointment: it is known as an *exequatur*.[26]

Thirdly, any hiving off of diplomatic function for performance by locally engaged staff overseas or by non-governmental agencies would encourage the interchange between the Diplomatic Service, increasingly home-based and concentrating on 'core' political and economic work, on the one side, and the Home Civil Service, increasingly involved in questions with overseas ramifications on the other. Reference was made earlier to the ideas expressed in this regard in the 1977 Report of the Central Policy Review Staff.[27] It could well be that moves towards increased integration within the European Union will revive the issue.

Fourthly, there could well be a trend towards collective diplomatic activity. The European Union has not yet developed to the point where member governments feel they can entrust their overseas representation to the European Commission's own network of missions. But there is scope for pooling facilities and for the saving of resources, both human and financial. There has been some exchange of diplomats at desk level, for example, between the German, French and British foreign ministries.

The essential point is that the professional diplomatic apparatus should display the adaptability and the imaginativeness necessary to the efficient discharge of its responsibilities on both the advisory and executive sides. This is not only a matter of managerial firmness and clarity. It is also a function of the calibre of the individual diplomat. It is to this question that these lectures now turn.

9 The Acquisition of Diplomatic Skills: Drafting

Any organisation, however well designed and managed, will depend ultimately for its effectiveness on the quality of the individuals who work in it. Hence the importance of recruitment, training and career development, which, *inter alia*, were considered in the previous lecture. At the same time, a profession relies heavily on the capacity of its members to train themselves and to develop their personal skills. It is a recurrent theme of these lectures that the skills of a diplomat can in the main be acquired only by dint of long practice and experience, including watching others at work. But initial training can help. The point is well illustrated in the use in diplomacy of the written word.

ADVOCACY AND THE WRITTEN WORD

In essence the business of diplomacy is advocacy. In whatever sphere people interact, advocacy is at the heart of the interaction. The more important and complex the subject of interaction, and the greater the lack of mutual familiarity of those who interact, the more delicate will be the task of advocacy. Diplomacy must rank as one of the higher forms of persuasion. People may be persuaded by reason or by emotion, or, in all probability, by a combination of both. They may be convinced, cajoled, flattered, inspired. They can be misled. The impact which one person makes upon another is an amalgam of many factors: intellectual, moral, physical, personal. That amalgam is, moreover, a matter partly of nature and partly of art.

At the end of the day advocacy in the case of a diplomat comes down to the preparation and finalisation of texts for use orally or in written form. The word 'advocacy' carries with it the connotation of legal form and procedure, which underlines the point that diplomatic texts have distinctive characteristics.

'Diplomacy', Sir Harold Nicolson insists, 'is not the art of amicable conversation, but the technique of exchanging documents in ratifiable

154

form . . . an agreement which is committed to writing is likely to prove more dependable in future than any agreement which rests upon the variable interpretation of spoken assent.'[1] Diplomacy therefore cannot but be much concerned with texts: what they say; what they do not say; how they say what they say; why they say it. There is much to be learned from all of these. This is not only vital in the short term, in the conduct of current business. It is vital also in the long term. There is some truth in the proposition that the lesson of history is that statesmen do not learn from history: they are too busy making it to have the time to study it. As diplomats we have a responsibility not to fall into that error. Good archives, and effective use of them, are essential to our work.

The basic elements of diplomatic drafting are no different from those of drafting generally. The definition of the verb 'to draft' is 'to draw up in a preliminary form'. That is to say, we are concerned with the sort of text where we do not expect to achieve the final version at the first attempt. If we imagined we were going to get it right first time, we should not be talking about drafting. The implication, moreover, of drawing a text up in preliminary form is that the process of getting it right may ultimately be collective rather than individual. It is convenient to pursue the art of diplomatic drafting under four headings: content; form; style; and collective effort.

CONTENT

At the outset the questions to be answered are: 'What is the message you desire to convey, and to whom do you wish to convey it?' The answers must, if they are to be useful, be precise. No less precise an answer is required to the consequential question: 'What sort of message?' Are we for example concerned with conveying information, not, of course, for information's sake alone, but as a means of helping to persuade? Are we emphasising a conclusion, again not just as a conclusion in its own right, but as the basis for agreement and follow-up action? Are we aiming at leaving a conclusion to be drawn by the recipient of the message, on the grounds that people may prefer to persuade themselves than allow themselves to be seen to be persuaded by others? (Devotees of the television series *Yes Minister* will have seen this particular approach used to great effect by civil servants with ministers). The likelihood is that the desired message will be a mixture of all these elements, since they are closely interrelated, a point which is summed up in the numerous meanings of the word 'argument'. Argument can mean a statement of fact advanced to influence the mind and hence support a proposition. It can mean a connected series of statements intended to establish (or subvert) a position, and hence a process of reasoning. It can mean a statement of the pros and cons of a proposition and hence discussion or debate. And it can mean the summary of the subject matter of a book or play and hence its contents.

The next question to consider is what it is that must be included in the message. I repeat 'must', because anything of which the inclusion is desirable rather than essential will probably best be omitted. Our job is to deal with the essential and to convey it in its most coherent, concise and persuasive form. And this, like so much else in diplomacy, requires considerable effort. You must assume that both the willingness of the recipient to concentrate on your message and his or her capacity to absorb it are limited. Hence a summary of the argument always helps the reader or listener. You can with advantage think in terms of beginning, middle and end. You say at the outset what you are going to do; then you do it; and then you finish by saying what you have done. This technique also concentrates your own mind. Francis Bacon, the English statesman, essayist, philosopher and systematic thinker, used to say that reading makes a 'full man' and conference (or speech) a 'ready man', but writing makes an 'exact man'. How often, when you try to put something on paper, do you realise that your thought is insufficiently precise? Writing concentrates the mind. It helps to show when a message is best left unsent. Some of the best letters you write are those you do not send.

The other side of the coin is the question 'What can be left out?' It is a never-ending source of surprise how much can be left out, not only without damaging the message, but actually with advantage to its effectiveness. Playwrights know about this. So do the writers of detective stories and advertisement copy. I was delighted with a recent Eagle Star Insurance Company advertisement (Annex 6) as an object lesson in what can be deleted without losing the force of the message. My other illustration (Annex 7), for which anonymous long-suffering delegates to GATT negotiations are to be thanked, is an example of how to speak at length without saying anything.

If you are known not to waste a word, you are likely to be read or listened to. But brevity does not come easily. Blaise Pascal, a famous seventeenth-century French mathematician, theologian and author, made the now familiar point that it takes longer to write a short letter than a long one: *'je n'ai fait celle-ci plus longue que parce que je n'ai pas eu le loisir de la faire plus courte'*.[2]

But a word of warning has to be added. Do not sacrifice clarity to brevity. Brevity is a great courtesy to the recipient of your message. Clarity, however, is an essential, and the greatest courtesy of all.

Let us assume that the message is orderly, accurate and complete – no easy achievement. Let us further assume that as a result it will strike the recipient as balanced, which is not the same thing as saying that it expresses no firm views. All of that is a necessary condition, but it is not a sufficient condition. The message must also have the quality of magnetism to draw the recipient to its essence. The writer, after all, has the great advantage over the reader of choosing the terrain. He or she will therefore need to ensure that the reader is started off down the right path and encouraged to keep on it. The first sentence may be crucial in this respect. What follows must keep a sense of priorities, a temporal sequence and a grouping of related ideas and thoughts. It can be strengthened by illustration, description, addition, development and variation. The message may also be strengthened by playing devil's advocate and then demolishing the devil's arguments. But the core of the message should never be out of focus. Finally, remember that at this stage our message is a draft. You might almost say that, if you think you have got it right first time, that really means you do not understand the matter. An exaggeration perhaps, but not a grotesque exaggeration.

FORM

In any activity or walk of life one finds that certain conventions are observed which have established themselves as useful or appropriate. One may wonder why they exist. It will always be rewarding to examine the rationale of these conventions, without of course incurring automatically any obligation to accept them. Usually one finds good reason for them. I am attracted by the definition of a conservative (with a small 'c') as someone who does not think his father was a fool. Conventions are not, moreover, simply a matter of convenience. They are related to the easing of tension and even to the avoidance of war. At a more prosaic level, norms of behaviour are important. 'Only fools laugh at etiquette: it simplifies life', said a wise Frenchman. As usual, Shakespeare had something profound to say on the subject:

Take but degree away, untune that string
And hark what discord follows.[3]

It is important to address your remarks to the chair, and to use the
courtesy form 'Your Excellency' when talking to ambassadors, unless
they prefer to be addressed as '(Mr/Madam) Ambassador', just as it is
important to observe the customary niceties, even in the case of those
whom one may have good reason to regard as not morally entitled to
them. The same justification exists for respecting unusual and
seemingly quaint forms of diplomatic converse. Because it is for the
most part a matter of dealings between governments and official
agencies, and may involve formal undertakings and understandings,
there is a tendency in diplomatic language towards the archaic and
stereotyped, if not to the solemn and pompous. This can be defended
partly on grounds of precision in relation to previous texts and to other
forms of precedent. It is true that, just as substance is affected by
process, so content is affected by form. But this does not mean that
form necessarily constrains content. Artistic expression bears witness
to the point that mastery of form can often stimulate creativity rather
than stifle it, and by the same token enhance the impact of the message
you wish to convey rather than blunt it. Mastery of form gives scope
for originality of expression, and for individuality of expression. A
clever use of familiar form, or of an eye-catching variation of it, can
add to the effect. Judicious exploitation of form can turn a bludgeon
into a rapier. There was the taxpayer who used to end his letters to the
internal revenue authorities with an inversion of the customary official
salutation of the time: 'You are, Sir', he would write, 'my obedient
servant'. I doubt if it reduced his tax bills. But it must have contributed
to his sense of well-being. It is of interest that at the end of the Second
World War the Foreign Office considered whether to change the
system of drafting despatches, but reported that 'we have come down
against any change because it is a fallacy to think that the writing of a
despatch precludes terse and pithy expression'.

In this lecture I shall not deal in any detail with the more exotic
forms of diplomatic communication, such as first-person notes
addressed by Heads of Mission to one another or to the government
to which they are accredited, or third-person official communications
which are also common in diplomacy. At times their respect for
protocol outruns their sincerity. The authors, for example, may declare
that they cannot refrain from expressing their confidence in continued
friendly relations between two countries which everyone knows to be at

daggers drawn. But if such niceties serve to lower the temperature and open the way to a meeting of minds rather than a clash of arms, there is no reason to spurn them. Rather I intend to concentrate on four less romantic and more workaday types of text which, while subordinating content to form to some extent, are none the less chiefly of interest because of their content: resolutions; communiqués and declarations; minutes of meetings; and reports on meetings or events.

(a) Resolutions

The normal way in which gatherings of many sorts record their decisions is by means of a resolution. The United Nations, both the organisation itself and the system as a whole, have frequent recourse to this type of text. It has developed a standard form. The preambular paragraphs rehearse the background to the issue under discussion and make mention as necessary of previous discussions and decisions: 'recalling' this, 'noting' that, or 'deeply concerned at' the other. The operative paragraphs record the outcome of the discussion. They may state the conclusion of the participants; make recommendations to governments or to other interested parties; decide on action to be taken, for example by the Secretariat; establish procedures and funding for whatever action it has decided to take; and make administrative provision for keeping the issue under review and reverting to it at a later date. As we noted in Lecture 4,[4] resolutions of the General Assembly have no binding effect on members of the United Nations. (Resolutions of the Security Council, as was illustrated in the case of the recent Gulf crisis, may be mandatory if they are adopted under the aegis of Chapter VII of the Charter.) But even where they have no binding effect, General Assembly Resolutions, especially if adopted without a vote, have some moral force as the expression of world opinion, a collective verdict on a major topic. The study of resolutions is thus of some significance in gauging world opinion. And the art of framing them and securing their acceptance is an important part of the diplomat's armoury.

(b) Communiqués and Declarations

Heads of governments and other ministers meet now so frequently that it is desirable to record the sense of their discussions in a communiqué which they could all sign. Such a text requires considerable negotiation among the delegations so as to get the balance right. All too often the complexity of the subject matter, the need to satisfy all parties and the pressure of time – you cannot really draft the communiqué until the ministers have discussed the issues, and they do not want to wait very long after they have done so before adopting it – take priority over the literary merit of the text. Communiqués are not usually quoted as the finest examples of prose available. But they afford an insight into what went on, even if they require some decoding. In the case of regular meetings of established organisations – the European Council, or the OECD or the World Bank and International Monetary Fund, for example – comparison with the communiqués issued after the previous meetings will indicate what may have changed.

Declarations are less hasty, and hence likely to be of greater literary merit than communiqués. They usually cover one subject rather than the agenda of the meeting as a whole. They will in all probability have been the subject of careful preparation beforehand by officials acting on behalf of their ministerial champions. And, if that preparation has been successful, the texts will be correspondingly more positive and more decisive. Meetings of the Group of Seven, of the European Council, or Commonwealth Heads of Government afford good examples of the practice of selecting a particular subject for the issue of a declaration which is separate from the text of the general communiqué.

(c) Minutes of Meetings

At some important meetings verbatim records may be provided. Even where this is not the case, there may be summary records and some form of tape-recording to be consulted if necessary. But such records may be of limited use in extracting the essence of a meeting for future enlightenment and guidance. Where a text has been adopted, of course, you know more or less what transpired, though you need to study closely the terms in which delegates may subsequently explain their vote. In the United Nations explanation of vote is the means of squaring troublesome circles. A delegate may explain for example that, although he or she has just voted for a resolution affirming that chalk is different from cheese, his or her government really believes that in certain circumstances they may in fact be identical. Where the outcome is hazy, the record of the discussion contained in the minutes of a meeting, if well kept, can help. But often the discussion may be so diffuse and so inconclusive that no useful purpose would be served by recording it in the terms in which it actually took place. For this reason administrators insist that a record of a meeting, if it is to be of service, must bring out whatever decisions were reached (or half-reached) and, if necessary, set out the decisions which the sense of the meeting would have suggested, and which some of the participants may fancy had been reached. The chairman, in other words, can secure, by virtue of the minutes subsequently circulated, a decisiveness not achieved at the meeting itself and leave it to those present, when they see the minutes in draft, to object if they so desire.[5]

The scope for creative minute-writing is thus considerable, as recorded in the following lines:

> And now while the great ones depart to their dinner,
> The Secretary sits, growing thinner and thinner,
> Racking his brains to record and report
> What he thinks they think
> That they ought to have thought.[6]

(d) Records

A talent for writing minutes serves well in the wider area of recording conversations and interviews generally. Another key area is reporting on developments, the stock-in-trade of diplomats abroad whose job it is to keep their colleagues at home informed. Accuracy is paramount. So is speed. So is selectivity. Both factual reporting and comment are essential. But it must be absolutely clear which is which. If the facts are obscure, you can promise to elucidate further at a later stage. If the source of the information is doubtful, say so. If you are not sure that you understand what you have been told, do not be afraid to ask. There are obvious difficulties in operating in a language which is not your own. Be careful not to get out of your depth. It is better to underestimate, or allow others to underestimate, your knowledge of another language, than to create the impression that you have a greater mastery of it than is in fact the case.

Reverting to reports, make these as clear as possible. Keep the paragraphs short. Use side headings if it helps. Avoid complicated sentences. If you cannot easily read your reports aloud, they are probably not as clear as they should be.

If you want a good guide in preparing your reports, you have but to read articles in the reputable press. I am lost in admiration for the way in which top-class journalists do their job. They go out and get the information direct from the horse's mouth. They assess it. They report in a way which distinguishes between fact and opinion or interpretation. And they do it all to very tight deadlines. Diplomats are not in competition with journalists. But they can learn much from them.

STYLE

'Style' is another flexible word: it can mean distinction, excellence, originality and character in any form of literary or artistic expression. Its essence is individuality. It is an 'extra', and I put it third after content and form, because ultimately there is something optional about it.

Gilding a text just for the sake of gilding it is not what is at issue. The concern is to enhance the favourable impact of a text by imparting to it a quality, a dimension even, which strikes the recipient as instinctive and natural, rather than added and contrived.

Do not go overboard in pursuit of style. Plain cooking may be best. If content and form are right, style will to a certain extent look after itself. Once again, this aspect of drafting is of particular importance when you are working in a language which is not your own. Precision and clarity are naturally more difficult to achieve in a foreign language than in your native tongue. Those for whom English falls into the latter category have an advantage over their colleagues which cannot but seem unfair. It has occurred to me to suggest at United Nations gatherings that no delegate should be allowed to use his or her own language. This could well shorten the debates and thus have the additional advantage of saving time and money. I doubt if it would enjoy much support. It is of interest that there has grown up in the United Nations what is known as 'Conference English', a form of communication with a limited vocabulary. This helps to achieve precision without frills, but it does not necessarily add to the pleasure of listening or reading.

Even where you are using your own language, accuracy is of more importance than elegance. The spelling checks furnished by word processors can be a mixed blessing. The word 'libretto' was rejected by the spelling check on one occasion within my experience and replaced by the word 'liberalism'. This gave the sentence in question a somewhat mysterious character.

Humour has its place in drafting. One can be serious without being unduly solemn. But jokes are likewise a serious matter, especially if more than one language is involved. They often do not translate easily. Puns by definition fall flat when translated.

Punctuation can be a matter of choice as well as of accepted rules. Rumour has it that young French diplomats are instructed on joining the Quai d'Orsay only rarely to use question marks in their drafting and never to use exclamation marks. This means, the cynics say, that the Quai d'Orsay asks itself few questions and is never surprised.

COLLECTIVE EFFORT

Drafting, to repeat, is the act of drawing up a text in a preliminary form. That implies, first, that we do not expect to get the final version at the first attempt, and secondly, that the process of getting it right is likely to be collective rather than individual. In the case of any major document the process will certainly be collective and may be lengthy and arduous. Younger diplomats are likely to start the process off. It is crucial that they acquire the habit of asking themselves how their first draft will look to their superiors, especially if the final version will bear someone else's name. Will it go out under the name of the ambassador or of the foreign minister? How will that affect the drafting? How can you combine the official content of the draft with the type of approach or personal style that you may know the ambassador or minister to favour? If the text is impersonal, can it none the less combine persuasiveness with authority and accuracy?

If you are asked to do the first draft, make it easy for others to see how you have approached your task and hence easy for them to see whether they agree or disagree with you. A covering word of explanation as the draft is submitted can help. The more space you leave for others to comment, the less likely they are to use it. Conversely, a closely packed draft may irk subsequent readers and spur them to comment where there is no real need to do so. Again, the more accurately you can foresee the likely reactions of your superiors, the greater the possibility that your draft will survive unscathed.

But there is no need to despair if the final version differs greatly from your original. Francis Bacon emphasised that, just as 'ashes are more regenerative than dust', so a particular line of argument can be more helpful in stimulating thought than a neutral draft. Sherlock Holmes, the great sleuth of fiction, put the point more pungently to his much maltreated assistant, Dr Watson: 'in noting your errors I am occasionally guided towards the truth. Some men, though not themselves luminous, can none the less be conductors of light.'

The phrase 'the inverted sieve' is used to describe the system whereby papers filter up from the junior levels of the hierarchy to the senior, thus enabling the former to prevent the latter from being troubled with trivial questions. But matters do not always work that way. Sir Henry Taylor, a distinguished and eminently practical Colonial Office official of the middle of the nineteenth century, took a different view. His opinion was that:

> official criticism is chiefly valuable when exercised by the inferior functionary upon the work of the superior, who will be enabled to weigh the comment undisturbed by deference for the authority of the commentator.[7]

That is fair comment. But it should not be taken as open season for the 'inferior functionaries'. For while superior functionaries slightly less robust than Sir Henry Taylor might be undisturbed by deference for the authority of junior commentators, they might still take amiss undue frankness on the part of the latter, especially if it is absolutely on target. You have been warned.

10   A Diplomat's Decade

On almost any subject you care to think of, you can buy a book or read an article full of hints on how to do the job or do it better. The maxims often stand by themselves and can be easily remembered with the help of illustrations or mnemonics. But they are more likely to be of lasting value if they are accompanied by an explanation of what lies behind them. To this extent they relate practice to theory and so complement bolder (or more foolhardy) attempts to set out the theory and relate it to practice. Diplomacy is no exception to this state of affairs. So I finish with a few 'precepts' which hark back to the more formal sequence of analysis and prescription attempted in the earlier lectures. I call these precepts a 'Diplomat's Decade'. A decade is not necessarily a period of ten years. It can be any group or series of ten. The group or series can change if circumstances change. The precepts which follow may, or may not, commend themselves. 'These are my principles', the proverbial politician is supposed to have said, 'if you do not like them, I have others.' The right to offer good advice is one of the most fundamental of human rights. An equally fundamental human right is the right to reject that good advice.

(1)   IT TAKES TWO TO NEGOTIATE

Critics are apt to suggest that diplomats believe that everything can be solved by negotiation, whereas statesmen are able to accept situations in which differences are irreconcilable. This is, at best, an over-simplification. Any experienced diplomat knows that at times there is no future in trying to negotiate. The task is to recognise such occasions and hence not to raise false hopes by continuing the search for accommodation. It is not the case that 'every problem has a solution'. Rather it is the case that 'every situation has an outcome'. There is no point in offering a concession, if, far from evoking a counter-concession on the part of your interlocutor, the latter interprets it as a sign of weakness on your part to be exploited by the making of further demands. But – and it is a big 'but' – diplomats know only too well that apparently irreconcilable differences can often be settled, given time, patience, understanding and imagination. Mutual suspicion, personal antipathies, political vulnerability, imperfect health, even simple physical exhaustion, can at times be more important causes of international stalemate than divergence of 'objective' national interest. It is not only an understanding of the manifold subjective causes of dispute and disagreement which prompts the diplomat to seek to bridge gaps. It is also an awareness of the horrendous consequences of hostilities engendered by supposedly irreconcilable differences, an awareness which insists that no stone should be left unturned in the search for accord. If the painstaking turning of stones leaves those engaged in the process open to the accusation of being naive, or of asking to be cheated, so be it. 'Nothing ventured nothing win'.

The proposition that it takes two to negotiate has to be looked at dynamically rather than just statically. It is not a matter of whether or not at any particular moment all parties are ready to negotiate. It is also a matter of creating the conditions in which a seemingly no-hope situation can be changed into one in which all the parties can see advantage in negotiation. The task is to recognise the possibility of creating those conditions, to act on that possibility, and to encourage others to do likewise. This, of course, is part and parcel of the general job of a diplomat. Patiently making and developing contact helps foster attitudes which lead towards the search for agreement rather than away from it.

(2)   A PROBLEM POSTPONED CAN BE A PROBLEM SOLVED

A diplomat has only to advance such a proposition as this to arouse indignation in certain quarters. In everyday life we are frequently tempted to 'have it out' with someone, or to insist that a particular issue must not be 'fudged'. Emotionally satisfying as such an attitude may be, it is often likely to be mistaken. In politics or in diplomacy it can be disastrous. A sense of frustration is a dangerous basis for policy-making. The cause of frustration may be a horns-locked difference between the parties to a dispute, of which there is no immediate prospect of a resolution. But, as we are often reminded, 'a week is a long time in politics'. Personalities change. Governments change. Perceptions change. Priorities change. Acute differences may become differences. Differences may cease to matter. If one has to choose between the Micawber wishful-thinking approach of waiting for something to turn up on the one hand, and resorting to trial by ordeal to decide between two opponents aroused as much by circumstance as by substance, on the other, then Mr Micawber should be preferred.[1] To contain a difference may at times be as much as can be achieved. That may be an unheroic achievement. But its value can be enormous.

Containing differences is not of course simply a matter of rushing around with a fire-extinguisher once those differences have become acute. The task is rather to look for signs of trouble and find ways of preventing the problem in question from arising. Preventive diplomacy is the most economical and efficient branch of the profession. But it is not necessarily that which brings the greatest rewards in career terms. One senior British diplomat complained that, in the British national scale of values, one is apt to get far more credit for extricating the country from difficult situations than for preventing it from falling into them in the first place. The priority for a diplomat must none the less be to contain a problem in the sense of trying to prevent it from becoming acute, as distinct from trying to solve it when it has reached the point of crisis.

It may well be that the essentials for settling a dispute on a basis which respects the interests of the parties become clear, even at an early stage, at least to outsiders. An intermediary may be necessary to help bring this home to the parties. In that sense it may sometimes take three to negotiate, namely the go-between and the two parties. It may also be the case that the way of settling a dispute is clear to the parties themselves, but that they are precluded for one reason or another from embracing it. Sir Anthony Parsons, the well-known former British Ambassador to the United Nations, evolved 'the Parsons theorem', which states that a dispute may be solved when, for their independent reasons, the parties to it simultaneously conclude that the time has come to settle on the basis of terms long since available. The corollary to this proposition is that the international community, by such means as a contact group, for example, should pursue the settlement of disputes and keep the basis of agreement ready to hand for the time when the parties each feel disposed to settle. This may not be a direct illustration of the precept that a problem consciously postponed may be a problem solved. It is, however, a reminder that the element of timing may be more elusive than the substance. A familiar dictum in government is that everything takes far longer than could be reasonably expected. It is not necessarily defeatist to heed the warning that dictum conveys.

(3) EVERYTHING HAS A LONG HISTORY

Reference has already been made to the assertion that statesmen are so busy making history that they have no time to learn from it. But diplomats can be allowed no such shortcoming. It is not simply that the facts of any particular situation are rooted in the complexities and the difficulties of the past. It is also that perceptions of the past powerfully affect attitudes to the present. One of the more imaginative definitions of a nation is that it is 'a community of memory'.[2] 'Memory', moreover, is not synonymous in this connection with accuracy of recollection. Collective consciousness of past wrongs, or difficulties, and the consequent nursing of grievances, may not be any the weaker for being ill-founded. The opposite may often be the case. We have to understand why it is that people think and act as they do. That does not mean we need acquiesce in others' mistaken and disruptive reading of the past. Our slogan is not '*tout comprendre c'est tout pardonner*': to understand everything is to forgive everything. But a firm grasp of the antecedents in any particular case is essential to wise action in relation to it.

In bureaucratic terms, we need to be sure of our facts and dates and quotations. We need to assemble the reference papers in such a way as to bring out the difficulties and point the way to solutions. It is easy to underestimate the influence which junior members of a diplomatic hierarchy can have on the making of policy where they present the background material in a coherent and helpful form. Sir Henry Taylor, whom we encountered at the end of the previous lecture, emphasised the importance of summaries, of 'abridgements', as he called them, and added that 'he who makes [them] must have the hand of a master and should be called a statesman rather than a precis writer. . . He who has the statement of a question after this manner will, generally speaking, have the decision of it.'[3]

Just as case law is important in jurisprudence, precedent is important in diplomatic practice. Its importance in drafting was discussed in the preceding lecture.[4] As regards substance, reference was made in Lecture 3 to the factors which the International Court of Justice should take into account in dealing with the disputes referred to it.[5] These include 'international custom, as evidence of a general practice accepted as law' and 'judicial decisions and the teachings of the most highly qualified publicists of various nations'. It is clear therefore that a detailed knowledge of the past history of any issue is relevant to understanding not only its substance, but also the process applicable to it. However, there comes a point beyond which precedent may cease to be useful. It is reported that at a US consular post in a particular African country, the number of US career officials had fallen from the usual complement of three to one. The sole US-based official in due course wished to go on leave. His application was refused on the understandable grounds that there was no precedent for leaving a post without a US-based official on duty at it. Shortly after rejecting the leave application, the State Department received a brief telegram from the solitary gentleman in question. 'Precedent established', the telegram said.

(4) THE CONFUSION THEORY OF POLITICS IS GENERALLY A BETTER GUIDE THAN THE CONSPIRACY THEORY

Every diplomat should remember the warning given by the eminent seventeenth-century Swedish statesman and administrator Count Axel Oxenstierna to his son, who was one of his country's representatives at the negotiations leading to the Peace of Westphalia in 1648: 'Dost thou not know, my son, with how little wisdom the world is governed?' The actions of governments may be rationalised after the event. But that does not necessarily mean that decisions were rationally taken at the time. Memoirs, biographies and more general histories may seek to explain with careful research and logic the factors which combined to bring about a particular policy or act. Yet in so far as they assume total rationality on the part of decision-takers, these works are indulging in the abstract rather than adhering to the concrete. *Homo diplomaticus* is no more real than *homo economicus*. The role played by chance, coincidence, internecine rivalry, distraction, ignorance, fatigue, illness and at times even caprice, may have been decisive, difficult as this can be to evaluate and unsatisfactory to accept as an explanation of events.

This is not simply a matter of historical refinement. Its practical significance lies in assessing the current policies of governments. When the Cold War was at its height, it was a regular temptation to attribute to the government of the Soviet Union an omniscient, omnicompetent cohesion in its conduct of policy, both overt and covert. Thanks to *glasnost*, we can now see the reality to be very different. This is only a particularly stark example of the mistake of attributing superhuman conspiratorial powers to a government, the real explanation of whose actions lies in ignorance, suspicion, corruption and incompetence. The world does not overflow with Machiavellis. Rather it needs the best possible channels of communication of information between those who have interacting responsibilities. 'Our relations', the saying goes, 'are built on trust and understanding. You don't trust me and I don't understand you.' That is a situation which diplomats must play their full part in avoiding.

Even if you do not understand the position of your interlocutor, you should leave him or her in no doubt where you stand (or wish to be thought to stand: there is no denying the role which constructive ambiguity or creative tension can sometimes play). It is a good idea to offer a text – a *bout de papier*, or a more formal *aide mémoire* – so that your position is accurately set out, and understanding of it in the upper reaches of your interlocutor's government is not dependent upon the comprehension or the reliability of your interlocutor alone.

(5)   THINK ROUND A PROBLEM AS WELL AS THROUGH IT

The 'precepts' discussed so far in this lecture constitute a collective warning against an over-rational approach to diplomacy. The concept of policy capability is based on rigorous analysis and prescription. But effective action also depends on flair, imagination and patience, as well as experience. Time and again the wise course is oblique rather than direct. Many years ago the Cambridge philosopher Alfred North Whitehead drew a distinction between 'intelligence' and 'ability'. He described 'intelligence' as quickness of apprehension, whereas 'ability' was the capacity to act wisely on the thing apprehended. Whitehead held that ability on this definition was rarer than intelligence. If that is true of human beings, how much truer is it of governments and of large corporate bodies, in an age when our quickness of apprehension is increased by a flood of information and our ability hampered by the difficulty of processing it. Wisdom is not derived from logic alone. We have to think round our problems as well as through them.

Let us revert to the familiar inextricable mix of substance and process. As regards substance, it is vital to examine the assumptions, implicit perhaps even more than explicit, on which an issue is being addressed. All too often those assumptions do not stand up to rigorous examination. Alternative assumptions may yield different lines of enquiry. The more clearly you can bring out the different possibilities and the relative merits of the lines of action they indicate, the greater help you will be to your superiors.

The context in which a recommendation may be made or a decision taken is vital. Long-term considerations may well be at variance with those of the short term. Obstacles may increase or decrease with time. Personalities may make all the difference. They change. Pointing out the snags to some favoured course of action is perhaps unheroic or even unpopular. 'A bureaucrat is someone who has a difficulty for every solution.' But the fact remains that a straightforward 'linear' approach to an apparently clear-cut issue may be unfruitful, or even unwise.

As regards process, the extent to which it is necessary to think round a problem, as well as through it, no doubt explains the appearance of a sizeable and entertaining literature on how to achieve your objective by indirect means. Expertise in procedure implies mastery of both the straightforward and the more roundabout approaches. It may be an exaggeration to say that these procedural devices and gambits are essential to the conduct of business. But it is unrealistic to imagine that agreement is reached between nations on the basis of direct and 'rational' discussion alone. At a more practical level it is useful to be able to recognise when others with whom you are in discussion are resorting to procedural devices and gambits. Forewarned is forearmed.

There is no more delightful example of procedural advice than a slim volume entitled *Microcosmographia Academica, being a guide for the young academic politician*, written in 1908 by F. M. Cornford, a distinguished classical scholar at Cambridge University. Cornford's point of departure was that the object of university politics was to prevent action from being taken, at least until everyone was agreed that it should be taken (which would probably be too late). He therefore produced a series of stratagems with which to oppose any innovation. I can personally testify to the use of Cornford's stratagems in much discussion of foreign affairs, but very rarely with attribution and not always with adequate competence.

(6) DIPLOMACY IS HUMAN, NOT JUST CEREBRAL

Diplomacy demands a good deal of the brain. But it does not stop there. It also demands the exercise of virtually all the personal qualities. You are dealing with human beings: you are one yourself. Your interaction with others will bring into play all the skills and attributes which you possess and which they possess. Orators, preachers, advocates, actors and musicians know that the impact which they make on their audiences is the result of many factors, not least the sincerity, conviction and warmth which they display. The same is true in diplomacy. Your human qualities may be decisive. If you have no genuine interest in other people, other people will soon recognise it. Your power to persuade other people is a function of the respect which they believe you to feel for them.

The capacity to inspire respect, and affection, in others is built up gradually rather than achieved overnight. The justification for continuity of diplomatic representation in another country or at a large multilateral organisation is the increase in effectiveness which can be achieved by influencing one's interlocutors on the human as well as the intellectual plane. This is not a one-way affair. It is not a sign of weakness to be influenced by others. Rather, it is part of a mutually beneficial process which enables the interests of different countries to be harmonised.

Participation in joint endeavour, which is characteristic of the work of missions to major organisations, can do a great deal to build up the necessary degree of confidence and trust. The work of embassies accredited to governments in capitals is slightly different in that there is a contrasting functional relationship. The representatives of the sending state are inherently the *demandeurs*. But they also have the advantage of being foreigners, of being distinctive. This gives them added scope for making an impression on those with whom they come into contact. At the same time, the more they can identify in one way or another with the country to which they are posted, without, of course, forgetting which government it is that they serve, and which country's interests it is their duty to promote, the more effective as diplomats they will be, and the more they will enjoy their posting.

Official entertainment is often the target of public derision. But its efficacy, as a means of doing business, will ensure its survival. In modern diplomacy the medium of entertainment is more likely to be a reception or a buffet, where a great deal of personal contact can be made quickly and relatively inexpensively, than a luncheon or dinner giving scope for more leisurely conversation with a smaller number. Yet the proposition that 'dining is the soul of diplomacy' retains its essential truth. There is no substitute for talking to fellow diplomats on their home ground. It can build mutual comprehension and respect. It affords new insights into what motivates them. 'Tell me what you eat', said the great French gastronome Brillat-Savarin, 'and I will tell you what you are.' The same could be said about a person's books, even more about his or her home.

(7) YOU MUST BE READY TO SUBSTITUTE DETACHMENT FOR COMMITMENT

To some extent this precept may seem to be a contradiction of its immediate predecessor. If a diplomat's effectiveness is a function of his or her ability to identify, and to be seen to identify, with the country in which he or she is serving, is it not demanding too much of human nature to insist at the same time on the importance of detachment? The answer is that it is indeed demanding a great deal. But it is inescapable, given the nature of diplomatic work. The logic of the analysis in these lectures is not only that there are limits to useful diplomatic activity in any particular circumstances, but also that there may be changes in those circumstances as a result of which the whole of one's effort may seem to have been wasted. A breach of diplomatic relations, involving the closing of diplomatic missions, is a spectacular case in point. A change of government in either the receiving or the sending state may be followed by fundamental policy changes, with significant effect on the general conduct of relations between the two countries. The individual diplomat may be obliged to make an adjustment overnight from absorption in an endeavour to the limits of his or her talents to abandonment of that endeavour without looking back.

This juxtaposition of detachment and commitment is not simply a matter of stoicism in the face of misfortune if or when it arises. It affects the balance which a diplomat has to strike. Diplomacy, as is often stressed, is a way of life rather than simply a job. In this respect it has much in common with other professions. But it often differs from the latter in the degree of 'limited liability' which it may require of its practitioners. A diplomat at a post abroad is in a highly artificial situation, dependent upon specific intergovernmental agreement and on convention and precedent. That artificiality may not seem relevant much of the time. But it is always there. At times it can be crucial.

A professional Diplomatic Service requires of its members a readiness to change posts, or countries, or areas of expertise, at regular or irregular intervals. Such changes are unlikely to be governed by the intrinsic demands of the issues or circumstances in which the diplomat happens to be immersed at the time. It will be in response to the requirements of the Diplomatic Service, and to the vagaries of which it has to take account. The life of a diplomat abroad is governed by priorities and preoccupations at headquarters which may be a source of mystification at a distance. One must resign oneself to occasional receipt of instructions which seem restrictive or likely to lead to the loss of opportunities. But there is no way round this. One should be grateful for the chance to make a useful contribution, rather than bewail what seems to be denial of the opportunity personally to bring some endeavour to a successful conclusion. We may in the course of our careers achieve something in the latter regard. But it is not the central objective of our profession. Sir Ernest Satow, it will be recalled, defined diplomacy as 'the application of intelligence and tact to the conduct of official relations between governments of independent states',[6] a dispassionate and anonymous affair, demanding of our best at all times, even if it leads but rarely to the visible award of large export contracts, or to the conclusion of treaties to the accompaniment of public rejoicing.

(8) LIKE WHAT YOU GET RATHER THAN ALWAYS STRIVE TO GET WHAT YOU LIKE

Those of exceptional talent and application may, on entering a particular field of endeavour, not only fix their eyes on the highest position obtainable within it, but also successfully chart their course to its achievement. The great majority of us are better advised to look on this as a high-risk policy more likely to bring heartache than satisfaction. Of no career perhaps is that more clearly true than diplomacy, with all its uncertainties and unpredictabilities. A proper measure of ambition is what a Diplomatic Service expects of its new recruits. But that ambition is better pursued in general than specific terms. It is common experience that a post long sought after proves on eventual achievement to be a disappointment or an anticlimax. By contrast another post, coming out of the blue, proves to have attractions and interests which were quite unforeseen. The recipe for a happy and a fruitful career for most of us is to have no great preconceptions about the jobs we should try and secure, but rather to set about whatever task we are allotted in a positive frame of mind. Absorption in the question of where you may go next can deflect you from putting your best into where you are now. Opportunity knocks in the most unusual ways. Those who draw the seeming short straw may end up the winners. I recall the circumstances of an autumn visit to the UK some years ago by the United States Vice-President. The Vice-Presidential aircraft was due to land at Heathrow. The great and the good of the American embassy in their numbers went to await its arrival. It being the mellow season of mist and fog, a junior embassy official was sent to Gatwick on a contingency basis. He cursed his luck. Sure enough, the Vice-Presidential aircraft was diverted from Heathrow to Gatwick. The junior official had the pleasure of a happy *tête-à-tête* with the Vice-President on the train to Victoria, while his superiors at the embassy rushed back disconsolate from Heathrow. His career never looked back.

Some plants thrive if occasionally you dig them up, root-prune them and replant them somewhere else. To other plants such treatment can be fatal. Diplomats, if they are to be happy, should belong to the former, rather than to the latter, category. So should diplomats' spouses and families. Not only is this true as regards current enjoyment of life. It is also a key to the building of a diplomatic career. The upheavals and disruptions fall into perspective later. The trouble we share with other human beings is that we can understand our lives only when we look back on them. But we have to live them forwards, not backwards.

(9)   DO NOT GET CARRIED AWAY BY THE TRAPPINGS OF DIPLOMATIC LIFE

'Take your job, but not yourself, seriously.' There is a great deal of truth in that proposition. Necessary self-respect – and ambition – must be accompanied by a sense of humour and an absence of vanity. Vanity in others can easily be exploited. It is a weakness against which one should be constantly on one's guard. In the distinction which has rightly grown up between the roles of elected ministers and appointed officials, the publicity, the glory and the plaudits are customarily accepted by the former and kept from the latter. This is a useful discipline for the latter. I will not speculate on what it does for the former.

Even though it may be less glamorous now than in times past, diplomacy still does its senior practitioners a great deal of honour. 'Your Excellency' is a form of address which one should accept as a mark of respect for one's country rather than as an estimate of one's personal worth. I confess I took a little time to get used to it. I found myself looking round the room to see who it was to whom the gracious epithet was being applied. You may find yourself tricked out in an improbable uniform and feel that your place should be in the ranks of an amateur operatic and dramatic society. You may also find yourself, as you go about your representational duties, subject to a wide variety of treatment, some of it due to the hesitancies and nervousness of those receiving or entertaining you. Do not stand on ceremony. The important thing is to put your hosts at their ease. When it is a sit-down occasion do not bother about *placement*: 'where the [British] Ambassador sits *is* the head of the table'.

One's family is a great help in this regard. There is nothing like healthy teenage scepticism for putting the niceties of diplomacy into proper perspective. 'Tell me, Daddy, what do you actually *do*?' My stock reply – 'I try to make the world a less dangerous place for you to live in' – at least used to give me a breathing space in which to try and concoct a slightly less general answer.

Retirement likewise puts it all into perspective. In a moment, in the twinkling of an eye, car, driver, secretary, staff and establishment vanish and give place to a modest pension and do-it-yourself. 'From mink to sink in one bound' was the slogan in less environmentally conscious days. For statesmen the change can be even more abrupt. A general election may bring about a change of tenant at No. 10 Downing Street literally overnight. Polling day in Britain is usually a Thursday. The new incumbent moves in on Friday. One lot of household goods moves in at the front door as another consignment exits at the back.

(10) 'THIS ABOVE ALL, TO THINE OWN SELF BE TRUE'

Polonius is not generally regarded as the hero of Shakespeare's *Hamlet*. But the 'few precepts' which he offered to his departing son Laertes bear examination.[7] Their peroration is comprehensive: 'This above all, to thine own self be true, and it must follow, as the night the day, thou canst not then be false to any man.' There is no better watchword for a diplomat. Our effectiveness, to repeat, is a function of the total impact which we make upon those with whom we come in contact. Being true to one's self is the guarantee of integrity which validates and enhances one's powers of advocacy. It is the characteristic which in the end carries most weight.

Earlier in these lectures I referred to the tendency of experts on diplomacy to draw up long and narcissistic lists of the essential qualities of diplomats.[8] These lists can be usefully pruned. But there is one quality which cannot be omitted: integrity. It has been rightly said that there is no greater diplomatic asset available to a government than the 'word of an honest man' (or woman).[9] 'Word' does not signify simply the utterances of the speaker. It also includes the character and commitment which lie behind them. The whole is greater than the sum of the parts. 'Word' expresses the great sum of human aspiration and effort. In our profession it is harnessed to the world's greatest task: building a just, prosperous and sustainable peace.

Annex 1
The United Nations System: principal organs of the United Nations

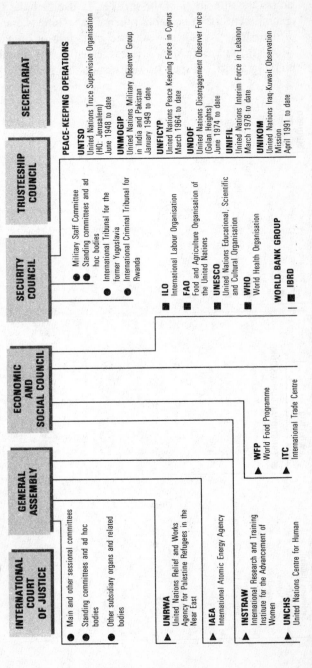

INTERNATIONAL COURT OF JUSTICE

GENERAL ASSEMBLY

ECONOMIC AND SOCIAL COUNCIL

SECURITY COUNCIL

TRUSTEESHIP COUNCIL

SECRETARIAT

- Main and other sessional committees
- Standing committees and ad hoc bodies
- Other subsidiary organs and related bodies

▲ **UNRWA** United Nations Relief and Works Agency for Palestine Refugees in the Near East

▲ **IAEA** International Atomic Energy Agency

▲ **INSTRAW** International Research and Training Institute for the Advancement of Women

▲ **UNCHS** United Nations Centre for Human

▲ **WFP** World Food Programme

▲ **ITC** International Trade Centre

● Military Staff Committee
● Standing committees and ad hoc bodies
● International Tribunal for the former Yugoslavia
● International Criminal Tribunal for Rwanda

■ **ILO** International Labour Organisation

■ **FAO** Food and Agriculture Organisation of the United Nations

■ **UNESCO** United Nations Educational, Scientific and Cultural Organisation

■ **WHO** World Health Organisation

WORLD BANK GROUP
■ **IBRD**

PEACE-KEEPING OPERATIONS

UNTSO United Nations Truce Supervision Organisation (HQ: Jerusalem) June 1948 to date

UNMOGIP United Nations Military Observer Group in India and Pakistan January 1949 to date

UNFICYP United Nations Peace Keeping Force in Cyprus March 1964 to date

UNDOF United Nations Disengagement Observer Force (Golan Heights) June 1974 to date

UNIFIL United Nations Interim Force in Lebanon March 1978 to date

UNIKOM United Nations Iraq Kuwait Observation Mission April 1991 to date

Settlements (Habitat)

▲ **UNCTAD**
United Nations Conference on Trade and Development

▲ **UNDCP**
United Nations International Drug Control Programme

▲ **UNDP**
United Nations Development Programme

▲ **UNEP**
United Nations Environment Programme

▲ **UNFPA**
United Nations Population Fund

▲ **UNHCR**
Office of the United Nations High Commissioner for Refugees

▲ **UNICEF**
United Nations Children's Fund

▲ **UNIFEM**
United Nations Development Fund for Women

▲ **UNITAR**
United Nations Institute for Training and Research

▲ **UNU**
United Nations University

UNCTAD/WTO

● **FUNCTIONAL COMMISSIONS**
Commission for Social Development
Commission on Crime Prevention and Criminal Justice
Commission on Human Rights
Commission on Narcotic Drugs
Commission on Science and Technology for Development
Commission on Sustainable Development
Commission on the Status of Women
Commission on Population and Development
Statistical Commission

● **REGIONAL COMMISSIONS**
Economic Commission for Africa (ECA)
Economic Commission for Europe (ECE)
Economic Commission for Latin America and the Caribbean (ECLAC)
Economic and Social Commission for Asia and the Pacific (ESCAP)
Economic and Social Commission for Western Asia (ESCWA)

● **SESSIONAL AND STANDING COMMITTEES**

● **EXPERT, AD HOC AND RELATED BODIES**

International Bank for Reconstruction and Development

■ **IDA**
International Development Association

■ **IFC**
International Finance Corporation

■ **MIGA**
Multilateral Investment Guarantee Agency

■ **IMF**
International Monetary Fund

■ **ICAO**
International Civil Aviation Organisation

■ **UPU**
Universal Postal Union

■ **ITU**
International Telecommunication Union

■ **WMO**
World Meteorological Organisation

■ **IMO**
International Maritime Organisation

■ **WIPO**
World Intellectual Property Organisation

■ **IFAD**
International Fund for Agricultural Development

■ **UNIDO**
United Nations Industrial Development Organisation

• **WTO**
World Trade Organisation

MINURSO
United Nations Mission for the Referendum in Western Sahara
April 1991 to date

UNOMIG
United Nations Observer Mission in Georgia
August 1993 to date

UNOMIL
United Nations Observer Mission in Liberia
September 1993 to date

UNMOT
United Nations Mission of Observers in Tajikistan
December 1994 to date

UNAVEM III
United Nations Angola Verification Mission III
February 1995 to date

UNPREDEP
United Nations Preventive Deployment Force (The former Yugoslav Republic of Macedonia)
March 1995 to date

UNMIBH
United Nations Mission in Bosnia and Herzegovina
December 1995 to date

UNTAES
United Nations Transitional Administration for Eastern Slavonia, Baranja and Western Sirmium
January 1996 to date

UNMOP
United Nations Mission of Observers in Prevlaka
January 1996 to date

UNSMIH
United Nations Support Mission in Haiti
July 1996 to date

▲■ United Nations programmes and organs (representative list only)
■ Specialised agencies and other autonomous organisations within the system
● Other Commissions, committees and *ad hoc* and related bodies

* Co-operative arrangements between the UN and WTO are under discussion

Published by the United Nations Department of Public Information – DPI/1857 – October 1996

Annex 2
Declaration on the Occasion of the Fiftieth Anniversary of the UN

Fiftieth session
Agenda item 29

RESOLUTION ADOPTED BY THE GENERAL ASSEMBLY

[without reference to a Main Committee (A/50/48)]

50/6. Declaration on the Occasion of the Fiftieth
Anniversary of the United Nations

The General Assembly
Adopts the following Declaration:

DECLARATION ON THE OCCASION OF THE
FIFTIETH ANNIVERSARY OF THE UNITED NATIONS

Fifty years ago the United Nations was born out of the sufferings caused by the Second World War. The determination, enshrined in the Charter of the United Nations, "to save succeeding generations from the scourge of war" is as vital today as it was fifty years ago. In this, as in other respects, the Charter gives expression to the common values and aspirations of humankind.

The United Nations has been tested by conflict, humanitarian crisis and turbulent change, yet it has survived and played an important role in preventing another global conflict and has achieved much for people all over the world. The United Nations has helped to shape the very structure of relations between nations in the modern age. Through the process of decolonization and the elimination of apartheid, hundreds of millions of human beings have been and are assured the exercise of the fundamental right of self-determination.

At this time, following the end of the cold war, and as the end of the century approaches, we must create new opportunities for peace, development, democracy and cooperation. The speed and extent of change in today's world point to a future of great complexity and challenge and to a sharp increase in the level of expectations of the United Nations.

Our resolve on this historic occasion is clear. The commemoration of the fiftieth anniversary of the United Nations must be seized as an opportunity to redirect it to greater service to humankind, especially to those who are suffering and are deeply deprived. This is the practical and moral challenge of our time. Our obligation to this end is found in the Charter. The need for it is manifest in the condition of humankind.

On the occasion of the fiftieth anniversary of the United Nations, we, the Member States and observers of the United Nations, representing the peoples of the world:

- Solemnly reaffirm the Purposes and Principles of the Charter of the United Nations and our commitments to them;

- Express our gratitude to all men and women who have made the United Nations possible, done its work and served its ideals, particularly those who have given their lives during service to the United Nations;

- Are determined that the United Nations of the future will work with renewed vigour and effectiveness in promoting peace, development, equality and justice and understanding among the peoples of the world;

- Will give to the twenty-first century a United Nations equipped, financed and structured to serve effectively the peoples in whose name it was established.

In fulfilment of these commitments we will be guided in our future cooperation by the following, with respect to peace, development, equality, justice and the United Nations Organization:

PEACE

1.   To meet these challenges, and while recognizing that action to secure global peace, security and stability will be futile unless the economic and social needs of people are addressed, we will:

- Promote methods and means for the peaceful settlement of disputes in accordance with the Charter of the United Nations and enhance the capabilities of the United Nations in conflict prevention, preventive diplomacy, peace-keeping and peace-building;

- Strongly support United Nations, regional and national efforts on arms control, limitation and disarmament and the non-proliferation of nuclear weapons, in all aspects, and other weapons of mass destruction, including biological and chemical weapons and other forms of particularly excessively injurious or indiscriminate weapons, in pursuit of our common commitment to a world free of all these weapons;

–   Continue to reaffirm the right of self-determination of all peoples, taking into account the particular situation of peoples under colonial or other forms of alien domination or foreign occupation, and recognize the right of peoples to take legitimate action in accordance with the Charter of the United Nations to realize their inalienable right of self-determination. This shall not be construed as authorizing or encouraging any action that would dismember or impair, totally or in part, the territorial integrity or political unity of sovereign and independent States conducting themselves in compliance with the principle of equal rights and self-determination of peoples and thus possessed of a Government representing the whole people belonging to the territory without distinction of any kind;

–   Act together to defeat the threats to States and people posed by terrorism, in all its forms and manifestations, and transnational organized crime and the illicit trade in arms and the production and consumption of and trafficking in illicit drugs;

–   Strengthen consultation and cooperation between regional arrangements or agencies and the United Nations in the maintenance of international peace and security.

DEVELOPMENT

2.   A dynamic, vigorous, free and equitable international economic environment is essential to the well-being of humankind and to international peace, security and stability. This objective must be addressed, in greater measure and more effectively, by the United Nations system.

3.   The United Nations has played an important role in the promotion of economic and social development and has, over the years, provided life-saving assistance to women, children and men around the world. But the pledge recorded in the Charter that all Members of the United Nations shall take joint and separate action in cooperation with the Organization for the achievement of higher standards of living, full employment and conditions of economic and social progress and development has not been adequately implemented.

4.   It must be recognized that notwithstanding past efforts, the gap between the developed and developing countries remains unacceptably wide. The specific problems of countries with economies in transition with respect to their twofold transition to democracy and a market economy should also be recognized. In addition, accelerating globalization and interdependence in the

world economy call for policy measures designed to ensure the maximization of the benefits from and the minimization of the negative effects of these trends for all countries.

5.   Of greatest concern is that one fifth of the world's 5.7 billion people live in extreme poverty. Extraordinary measures by all countries, including strengthened international cooperation, are needed to address this and related problems.

6.   In response to these facts and circumstances, the United Nations has convened a number of specifically focused global conferences in the last five years. From these conferences, a consensus has emerged, *inter alia*, that economic development, social development and environmental protection are interdependent and mutually reinforcing components of sustainable development, which is the framework of our efforts to achieve a higher quality of life for all people. At the core of this consensus is the recognition that the human person is the central subject of development and that people must be at the centre of our actions towards and concerns for sustainable development.

7.   In this context, we reaffirm that democracy, development and respect for human rights and fundamental freedoms, including the right to development, are interdependent and mutually reinforcing.

8.   In order to foster sustained economic growth, social development, environmental protection and social justice in fulfilment of the commitments we have made on international cooperation for development, we will:

–   Promote an open and equitable, rule-based, predictable and non-discriminatory multilateral trading system and a framework for investment, transfers of technology and knowledge, as well as enhanced cooperation in the areas of development, finance and debt as critical conditions for development;

–   Give particular attention to national and international action to enhance the benefits of the process of globalization for all countries and to avoid the marginalization from and promote the integration of the least developed countries and countries in Africa into the world economy;

–   Improve the effectiveness and efficiency of the United Nations system for development and strengthen its role in all relevant fields of international economic cooperation;

–   Invigorate the dialogue and partnership between all countries in order to secure the existence of a favourable political and economic environment for the promotion of international cooperation for development based on the imperatives of mutual benefit and interest and genuine interdependence, while recognizing that each country is ultimately responsible for its own development but reaffirming that the international community must create a supportive international environment for such development;

– Promote social development through decisive national and international action aimed at the eradication of poverty as an ethical, social, political and economic imperative of humankind and the promotion of full employment and social integration;

– Recognize that the empowerment and the full and equal participation of women is central to all efforts to achieve development;

– Reduce and eliminate unsustainable patterns of production and consumption and promote appropriate demographic policies in order to meet the needs of current generations without compromising the ability of future generations to meet their own needs, recognizing that environmental sustainability constitutes an integral part of the development process;

– Intensify cooperation on natural disaster reduction and major technological and man-made disasters, disaster relief, post-disaster rehabilitation and humanitarian assistance in order to enhance the capabilities of affected countries to cope with such situations.

EQUALITY

9. We reiterate the affirmation by the Charter of the dignity and worth of the human person and the equal rights of men and women and reaffirm that all human rights are universal, indivisible, interdependent and interrelated.

10. While the significance of national and regional particularities and various historical, cultural and religious backgrounds must be borne in mind, it is the duty of all States, regardless of their political, economic and cultural systems, to promote and protect all human rights and fundamental freedoms, the universal nature of which is beyond question. It is also important for all States to ensure the universality, objectivity and non-selectivity of the consideration of human rights issues.

11. We will therefore:

– Promote and protect all human rights and fundamental freedoms, which are inherent to all human beings;

– Strengthen laws, policies and programmes that would ensure the full and equal participation of women in all spheres of political, civil, economic, social and cultural life as equal partners and the full realization of all human rights and fundamental freedoms for all women;

- Promote and protect the rights of the child;

- Ensure that the rights of persons who can be particularly vulnerable to abuse or neglect, including youth, persons with disabilities, the elderly and migrant workers, are protected;

- Promote and protect the rights of indigenous people;

- Ensure the protection of the rights of refugees and of displaced persons;

- Ensure that the rights of persons belonging to national, ethnic and other minorities are protected, and that such persons are able to pursue economic and social development and live in circumstances of full respect for their identity, traditions, forms of social organization and cultural and religious values.

JUSTICE

12.   The Charter of the United Nations has provided a durable framework for the promotion and development of international law. The continued promotion and development of international law must be pursued with a view to ensuring that relations between States are based on the principles of justice, sovereign equality, universally recognized principles of international law and respect for the rule of law. Such action should take account of developments under way in such areas as technology, transport, information and resource-related fields and international financial markets, as well as the growing complexity of the work of the United Nations in the humanitarian and refugee assistance fields.

13.   We are determined to:

- Build and maintain justice among all States in accordance with the principles of the sovereign equality and territorial integrity of States;

- Promote full respect for and implementation of international law;

- Settle international disputes by peaceful means;

- Encourage the widest possible ratification of international treaties and ensure compliance with the obligations arising from them;

- Promote respect for and the implementation of international humanitarian law;

- Promote the progressive development of international law in the field of development, including that which would foster economic and social progress;

-   Promote respect for and implementation of international law in the field of human rights and fundamental freedoms and encourage ratification of or accession to international human rights instruments;

-   Promote the further codification and progressive development of international law.

UNITED NATIONS ORGANIZATION

14.   In order to be able to respond effectively to the challenges of the future and the expectations of the United Nations held by peoples around the world, it is essential that the United Nations itself be reformed and modernized. The work of the General Assembly, the universal organ of the States Members of the United Nations, should be revitalized. The Security Council should, *inter alia*, be expanded and its working methods continue to be reviewed in a way that will further strengthen its capacity and effectiveness, enhance its representative character and improve its working efficiency and transparency; as important differences on key issues continue to exist, further in-depth consideration of these issues is required. The role of the Economic and Social Council should be strengthened to enable it to carry out effectively, in the modern age, the tasks it has been assigned with respect to the well-being and standards of life of all people. These and other changes, within the United Nations system, should be made if we are to ensure that the United Nations of the future serves well the peoples in whose name it was established.

15.   In order to carry out its work effectively, the United Nations must have adequate resources. Member States must meet, in full and on time, their obligation to bear the expenses of the Organization, as apportioned by the General Assembly. That apportionment should be established on the basis of criteria agreed to and considered to be fair by Member States.

16.   The secretariats of the United Nations system must improve significantly their efficiency and effectiveness in administering and managing the resources allocated to them. For their part, Member States will pursue and take responsibility for reforming that system.

17.   We recognize that our common work will be the more successful if it is supported by all concerned actors of the international community, including non-governmental organizations, multilateral financial institutions, regional organizations and all actors of civil society. We will welcome and facilitate such support, as appropriate.

40th plenary meeting
24 October 1995

Annex 3
Speech Delivered by the Foreign and Commonwealth Secretary, Mr Malcolm Rifkind, 21 September 1995

PRINCIPLES AND PRACTICE OF BRITISH FOREIGN POLICY

Introduction

Let me start by thanking Sir Laurence Martin for inviting me to speak at Chatham House so soon after my return to King Charles Street. There is no better place for a new Foreign Secretary to set out his thinking and objectives.

Let me also offer my congratulations on its 75th anniversary. It has become a favourite meeting-place of foreign policy-makers and analysts. 75 years ago, it should be admitted, the prospect of a new institute was viewed by some with suspicion. It was an eminent Foreign Office Under-Secretary who perceived a subtle but insidious threat:

> Outside opinion will seek opportunities ... to influence the judgement and attitude of officials ... [This] may be healthy and may remain harmless. There is however a distinct danger the reverse may happen ... No Service is without its faddists.

I am glad that a different view prevailed. The Foreign Office today welcomes informed outside opinion as a contribution to policy-making. The conference that was held in March on the theme of Britain in the World was an excellent example of the fruitful dialogue Chatham House stimulates.

To be appointed Foreign Secretary is a formidable challenge. There is a slight sense of trepidation, perhaps not confined to the new Minister. One of my predecessors, the Earl of Malmesbury, wrote of his first day in the Office in 1852:

> All the staff were kindly disposed, but I could see that they expected me to give them much trouble and to ask their advice.

187

Other nineteenth-century diplomats learnt to avoid making such taxing demands. In Washington Thomas Jefferson wrote one day to his Secretary of State:

> We have not heard anything from our Ambassador to France for three years. If we do not hear from him this year – let us write him a letter.

The machine that I have inherited operates at an entirely different pace. Last year the British Ambassador to France sent well over 2000 telegrams to London, and we sent quite a lot to Paris.

So the engine is turning fast, generating plenty of heat and light. The question for me today is what use to make of this high-powered organisation? What should be the objectives of British foreign policy in the late-twentieth century?

Britain's Interests

Let us start with first principles. I am not pre-occupied with agonised soul-searching about Britain's historical vocation. Are we a Great or Medium Power; are we Good or Bad Europeans; are our bilateral relations still special: these labels are distractions. They are prisms which distort our vision. They do not throw much light on our real needs and policy choices.

The best starting-point is Lord Palmerston's dictum:

> the furtherance of British interests should be the only object of a British Foreign Secretary.

Thus we must identify first what interests do we have as a nation, and second, how do we best further them.

The answer to the first question is clear. Our most important interest is our own territorial security and the maintenance of peace in Europe. For some countries that might constitute a complete answer. For us it is only part. Britain's interests overseas are substantial and they are wide. In part that is the legacy of an imperial past. History has bequeathed us unique ties with 50 Commonwealth members. It has left us with particular responsibilities for 14 dependent territories around the world. Britain has duties to fulfil. A rumbling volcano in Montserrat; oil exploration in the South Atlantic; securing a stable, prosperous future for Hong Kong.

But our internationalism is more than the residue of history. Modern Britain remains pre-eminently a nation of traders and travellers. 8.6 million British citizens live overseas. Three in five of our people travel abroad each year. And we live by commerce. We export one quarter of all we produce; a greater share than Japan or the United States, more than Germany or France. We are the world's third largest outward investor: the biggest foreign investor in the US; the third largest source of private capital to the developing world. Last year our total assets abroad exceeded 1.4 trillion pounds. We had a net income of over 10 billion pounds from our investments overseas.

Britain's economy is open and international. Only the US attracts more foreign investment. There is more US investment here than in the whole Pacific region, more than in Germany, France, the Netherlands and Italy combined. We are the number one choice in Europe for Japanese and Korean investors. Britain is the world's leading centre for international bank lending, foreign exchange, aviation and marine insurance.

So Britain's interests spread across the globe. These considerations give us an even greater interest than most other countries in political stability, freedom of trade and freedom of passage throughout the world, not just in our own continent. Political stability also requires good government and a proper assurance of basic human rights. We have a moral and practical interest in promoting the values of liberal democracy. It follows that our foreign policy must be global.

It is why we have a permanent voice in the Security Council. It is why a strong, effective United Nations matters to us. Not because we cherish dreams of being a world power. Not because we want to be a big player for its own sake. But because we must be active wherever our national interests are at stake; and they are at stake throughout the world. Furthermore the world needs, and is desperately short of, countries with a long experience of political stability, a tradition of moderation and a global perspective. Only a handful of states meet the criteria. Britain is one of them.

These principles underpinning British policy would be familiar to our predecessors of a century ago. What of the modern setting, the context within which we must work today? How do we best promote our interests, the second question I posed in my earlier remarks?

Most importantly, the nation state remains the basic building block of the international system. It is nation states to which most people feel their first allegiance. International relations are still principally about dealings between states. The conduct of foreign policy must reflect this.

But it must also reflect new global realities.

The electronic media, both instant and multinational, serves as a powerful focus for bringing public opinion immediately to bear on policy-makers. It demands their attention, making policy formulation more complex and multinational. The media spotlight requires governments to be open and accessible. An effective public information effort must run in parallel with diplomatic activity, and be an integral part of it.

Take the environment. The squandering of natural resources has become a matter of immense public concern. But national boundaries are of limited relevance to controlling fish stocks, preserving clean air, or providing fresh water. So countries have to work together to protect their common interest.

Or take the global market. In commerce and the media we are near the end of geography. What matters in high finance and broadcasting today is not location but speed of access to information. International capital flows and multinational corporations operate freely across the frontiers of nation states.

So even the most powerful sovereign states have lost some of their freedom of action. Nations are not the only actors in the modern system. We live in a less controllable, more interdependent world. As President Kennedy put it more than three decades ago: 'No nation can build its destiny alone.'

That does not mean the end of sovereignty. It does not make policy-making futile. It does demand new approaches. It means accepting the limits on what governments can do by themselves and working within them. Above all, it means nations must work together more to defend their security, their prosperity and their environment. It means building alliances wherever we have common interests, in NATO and the European Union, across a wider Europe, in the United Nations, in order to enhance the prospect of securing our objectives.

Co-operation in Europe

For centuries the affairs of our continent were marked by wars between states with global interests. Through shifting alliances we sought to contain the frictions of such rivalry. Maintaining a balance of power in Europe was our objective and often realised, most successfully during the nineteenth century after the Congress of Vienna.

Such a strategy did not eradicate distrust or suspicion between European states. One recalls Metternich's remark on learning that the Russian ambassador had died, 'Really, I wonder what his motive can have been.'

Nor did it provide an assurance of stability. Europe collapsed frequently into conflict. In the first half of this century combat finally erupted on a world scale.

In the nuclear age and with Western Europe no longer able to take world supremacy for granted, the classic concepts of the balance of power within Europe have lost much of their relevance. There is no strategic threat to the safety of the United Kingdom that would not also be a similar threat to France or to Germany. The interests that bind Europe together have become far greater than the interests that occasionally divide us.

The furtherance of these common interests have been bolstered by the institutions of the post-war world. NATO has protected Western Europe from the threat of war from the old Soviet Union and the Warsaw Pact. It has been the fundamental achievement of the European Union that it has reconciled the peoples of Western Europe and made war between them inconceivable. Our common experience of total European war twice this century has convinced us all that we cannot return to the hostility, shifting alliances and regular conflict that has characterised most of our common history.

But if maintaining the 'balance of power' is not and cannot be any longer the basis of our foreign policy in Europe, it is not the case that the only alternative is a single foreign policy shared with all our neighbours and partners. That may evolve one day but we have not got it yet nor are we likely to in the foreseeable future.

A common foreign and security policy implies an identity of interests, and although we do have much in common we have a long way to go. The current controversy over French nuclear tests, the residual colonial obligations of the United Kingdom and France, the differences between Greece and Turkey, the self-imposed constraints on Germany's contribution to peacekeeping, are examples of a continuing diversity of interests and, therefore, of policy.

This need not depress us nor should it lead us to reject those many areas where our interests are the same and where the pursuit of them will be strengthened by a common approach. Where there is a genuine identity of interests British objectives can be furthered by being part of a European consensus with the weight and influence that that provides. What we must not do is suppress important national interests in order to construct an artificial consensus, a bogus unity, that lacks credibility or conviction.

It is not the case, as is often argued, that failure to obtain a single foreign policy would lead us back to a diplomacy in Europe based on the balance of power. Rather, modern Europe will see close cooperation as its primary feature. The conflict of the past replaced by a willing and natural cooperation will be the basis on which we build security, prosperity and freedom.

Britain in the European Union

These considerations are relevant to the debate about the future of the European Union and Britain's role in it. Let me say at once, that the European Union has made an enormous contribution to prosperity and security in our continent. While it may sometimes produce ideas that are inimical to our interests, it is not a conspiracy against Britain. It will not be a super-state. Europe is a diverse construction and will remain so.

As Chesterton once remarked, 'The golden age of the good European is like the heaven of the Christian; it is a place where people will love each other; not like the heaven of the Hindu, a place where they will be each other.'

Variable geometry is already well-established. Some members of the Union cherish their neutral status. Others have shared their defence for years in NATO and the Western European Union. Some members take part in the Schengen Agreement. For others, like Britain, monitoring border controls remains an effective way to counter the risks of drug traffic and illegal immigration. It is clear that full economic and monetary union will not be a sensible option for all members in the foreseeable future.

Sometimes one hears this described as a potential two-speed Europe. But that is unwise. It implies a common destination arrived at in different timescales. That is certainly relevant to enlargement but may not be appropriate to social policy or to a Single Currency. There may be some areas of integration that even in the long-term will not be attractive or acceptable to a number of member states. As the European Union increases from 15 to 20 and then, perhaps, to 25 states that is bound to become more and more likely.

If this reflects the reality of different interests, then the European Union will need to respond in a sensitive and flexible manner. Europe has such a rich tapestry of culture, history and language that it would be extraordinary if each country was as comfortable as every other with a given degree of integration.

There is often anxiety expressed at the loss of influence that Britain might incur if it did not join an area of integration which our partners in Europe had concluded was desirable. One has heard this argument with regard to the Social Chapter and the Schengen Agreement. It is relevant to the future debates over a Single Currency and other matters. It is not an unreasonable point. If one is not part of an organisation one does lose influence and this can inhibit us in the pursuit of our national objectives. Our long delay in joining the European Community is a good example. But one must not take this argument too far. While the accretion of influence is the stuff of diplomatic life and particularly important to a power like Britain, we must constantly remind ourselves that influence is a means not an end in itself. Occasionally it may be appropriate to accept a loss of influence if that is the only way we can protect our interests.

Other countries have had to face this dilemma. The French, since de Gaulle, have been in NATO but outside the integrated military structure. This may have irritated their allies but it has not undermined the Alliance nor severely damaged the French where it really matters to them. Their influence in certain areas has been reduced but they judge that is a sacrifice they are willing to make to protect their interests.

Likewise, the Swiss have undoubtedly reduced their influence by declining to join the United Nations or the European Union but they have concluded that to be necessary in order to protect their national interests. Whether we agree with the French or the Swiss is irrelevant. They are the best judges of their own national interests just as we must be of ours. In some areas it may be sensible to accept a reduction in our influence in order to protect our interests. Influence can never be an end in itself and we should not be obsessed by it.

How then should Britain respond to proposals for further integration in the European Union? It should, in my view, do so by a cool assessment of the British interest. The criterion we should apply is the net effect of integration as opposed to cooperation in that particular area of policy. Would there be a significant benefit to the prosperity, security, or quality of life of the people of the United Kingdom that would justify the loss of national control over decision-making in that area? If harmonisation would be harmful to the United Kingdom, or if it were being pursued for ideological rather than practical reasons, we should oppose it with courtesy, courage and conviction.

In the case of the single market the net benefit of harmonisation was clear. That is why we championed this major reform. We have reached the same conclusion in many other cases. In these areas, we take the lead in insisting that the rules must be properly obeyed – by all.

But, as with other countries, there will undoubtedly be occasions when integration is not acceptable. For example, as far as the social chapter is concerned or the removal of frontier controls, the balance for Britain would be a significant disadvantage. Hence the British opt-out negotiated by the Prime Minister.

This pragmatic approach should not be interpreted as implying a lack of enthusiasm or commitment to the European Union. We are as committed as France or Germany or the Netherlands to our membership of the Union. It has brought and will continue to bring major benefits to all the peoples of Europe. It was a French statesman who called for a 'Europe des patries' and that is close to our vision.

A Revived Transatlantic Partnership

A further challenge for Europe is its relationship with the United States and Canada. We must build a new partnership between Europe and North America. The common heritage and values we enjoy in Europe extend across the Atlantic. We should build on them now a revived transatlantic partnership.

We know already the rewards such partnership can bring. Thanks to NATO we have enjoyed its fruits in war and peace for fifty years and continue to do so. But we would be rash to take those blessings for granted today. Harold Nicolson wrote of Europe after the Congress of Vienna:

History teaches us, and invariably we disregard her lesson, that Coalitions begin to disintegrate from the moment the common danger is removed.

In the late twentieth century one common danger has been removed, but many common interests remain. Europe and North America share an interest in a stable world where democracy and commerce can flourish. We face together the risks posed by terrorism and drugs, regional instability and weapons of mass destruction. Domestic or regional pressures must not distract us from global challenges. Renewed cooperation is as much an interest of the United States and Canada as of Europe.

Britain, because it shares its history and cultural values with the United States, is in a special position to promote closer and more productive ties across the Atlantic. We will work hard to revive and enrich the transatlantic partnership. One vital area is trade. First, because our economies are already closely enmeshed. Investment between Europe and the United States accounts for 3 million jobs on each side of the Atlantic. One sixth of our exports go to each other's market. Second, because the size of our markets, our shared faith in an open system, make us the natural motor for the development of a wider multilateral trading system. If the World Trade Organisation is to be effective, if we are to achieve further global liberalisation, Europe and North America must lead the way. There will need to be much analysis, but transatlantic free trade should be our clear goal.

Our renewed partnership must go beyond commerce. We need a much closer dialogue between Congress and the parliaments of Western Europe. As we all know the US Congress plays its own part in determining the United States' foreign policy. We have all benefited from the close and constant dialogue between American and European administrations; between the US military and our own armed forces; between the diplomats on both sides of the Atlantic. That experience needs to be applied to our legislatures and parliamentarians if occasional differences are to be reduced and resolved. We must work together to tackle nuclear proliferation and organised crime. We must coordinate our efforts to secure peace in the Middle East, to help the developing world exploit its resources. All these should be the themes of closer dialogue and common action.

Europe Reunited

Of course Europe is not just Western Europe or the European Union. We have a fresh challenge. After the last war we built a new Union from Europe's rubble. After the Cold War we must build a wider Europe from the debris of Communism.

With the fall of the Soviet Empire Europe can begin to realise its full potential. The West must welcome back the countries of Central Europe and the Baltic States forcibly separated from their natural heritage, first by Hitler then by Stalin. We must help nurture and stabilise the identities of new countries like Moldova and Belarus. We must support the emergence as independent states of ancient nations like Armenia, Georgia and, above all, Ukraine.

Most of all we must establish a new relationship with Russia, that respects her special character but is founded on the values and aspirations we now share in common. There will be differences between us – as there can be between Britain and France, or Britain and the United States. But they can be resolved by cooperation and the search for understanding. We must prove the advantages of cooperation. We must show that political and economic exchange can benefit each side without destroying the best traditions of either. We must show that Western institutions, most importantly NATO and the European Union, are not instruments of exclusion but part of a wider framework to enhance the indivisible security of all European states. We want to proceed with enlargement of both at a measured pace which will foster stability, prosperity and security, not create new divisions. We must respect Russia as a major power with an ancient history and a noble future.

Earlier this month I went to Kiev and Moscow. I wanted to see for myself the progress of reform, to ask how Britain and the West could continue to help. I came back with two overriding impressions. First, the enormous energy and courage being displayed by the people of Eastern Europe as they begin to rebuild their future. Second, that the greatest assistance we in the West can give is to share the expertise and opportunity they need. We already provide expert advice. Britain's Know How Fund is helping spread the commercial skills and understanding that can unleash dynamism and enterprise.

But enterprise needs outlets. Free trade requires access to markets. We must provide this. Western Europe already has a good record. Since 1989 EU imports from Central and Eastern Europe have grown by 60 per cent. The Union takes over 50 per cent of the exports of the six central European countries. But problems persist. Significant obstacles remain to agricultural trade. Anti-dumping actions cause particular difficulty. Britain must be a champion of those trying to break down the barriers to trade and prosperity.

By sharing our expertise and opening our markets we can help lay the foundations of lasting prosperity in Central and Eastern Europe. There could be no greater contribution to real security. As I said in Kiev, it is a Marshall Plan for the 1990s, as relevant to the needs of Russia and Ukraine as the Marshall Plan itself was to the ravaged economies of Western Europe. Russia's and Ukraine's needs in the 1990s are different to those of Western Europe in 1945. The ability to expand their trade and have the chance to compete in Western European markets is the key to their future prosperity.

Bosnia

It is of course impossible to speak of the new challenges facing Europe without mentioning the most pressing and tragic crisis before us, in Bosnia. I have just returned from a visit to the region, at a time when the peace process is more promising than for a long time; but with the continuing fighting making the prospects still enormously uncertain.

Britain has done as much as any country to save lives and relieve suffering. We are the largest troop contributor to the UN force, with about 10 000 men and women in theatre. We have given over 270 million pounds of humanitarian aid. The cost has been more than financial: 18 British servicemen and four British aid workers have lost their lives on duty. When I was in Sarajevo the

Bosnian Government were warm in their praise for the professionalism and effectiveness of the British role.

In the wake of the fall of Srebrenica and Zepa, the London Conference in July agreed that further attacks on safe areas would meet with a robust and forceful reply. When a Bosnian Serb shell landed in a Sarajevo market on 28 August, killing 37 innocent civilians, the international community had to respond. UN and NATO military action has not been designed to bomb the Serbs to the negotiating table. It had a clear, limited objective, to deter attacks on safe areas. This has been achieved. Serb heavy weapons are being withdrawn from around Sarajevo. Air and land routes are open and food supplies are flowing again. So military action has been suspended for the time being. But if the attacks were to resume NATO and the UN would respond swiftly and firmly.

The political prospects look better than at any time in four years, thanks not least to the efforts of the US negotiator, Dick Holbrooke. The outline agreement reached in Geneva on 8 September draws on the principles worked up by Britain and our partners in the Contact Group But these principles are only the beginning: the hardest part is still to come. The first priority is to end the fighting. The military tide seems to have turned against the Bosnian Serbs. But it is vital that the Bosnian and Croatian Governments show restraint. Further destruction cannot bring peace to the people of Bosnia.

It is equally clear that only the parties can agree a settlement in former Yugoslavia: we cannot impose one on them. I have the sense that the people of the region yearn for peace. But for this to be achieved their leaders will have to make hard choices. No-one will emerge from the negotiating chamber having achieved 100 per cent of their aims. They must lift their eyes from individual priorities to the common need to end the suffering and bloodshed and avoid another appalling winter of war. We shall do all we can in our own contacts with them to help them to reach this goal.

Britain in a Wider World

Debate on Britain's overseas role often centres on those areas I have discussed, on its policy towards Europe and North America. Getting these twin relationships right is certainly at the heart of a successful and effective British foreign policy. But it is a necessary, not a sufficient condition. I began by describing Britain's global interests. If we are to protect and further all those interests we must lift our eyes beyond the transatlantic community of nations.

An obvious area is that other ocean, the Pacific. We must pay far more attention to a region where one third of the world's population live and where one quarter of the world's gross product is created. Its extraordinary growth seems set to justify the assertion that the 21st century could be the Pacific century. Add to that a revitalised South Asia, and the message of closer engagement becomes more pressing.

It is striking to compare the economic prospects of this new world with the old world of Europe and North America. Over the last two decades annual growth in developed countries has averaged 3 per cent. In the developing countries of Asia it has been 6.5 per cent. In the 1950s South Korea had a per capita income below that of Zambia. Now it is on a level with members of the

EU, and the world's eleventh largest economy overall. Over the last decade the Western Pacific share of world trade has risen from 16 per cent to nearly a quarter. In the same period the growth rate in Guangdong Province in China is said to have been about 20 per cent a year. China is the latest prospective economic giant.

The effects of this transformation are profound. Twenty years ago South East Asia was a major recipient of foreign aid. Now the Asian tigers have graduated out of aid and are becoming donors, helping other countries in turn. A new regional political architecture is taking shape in APEC and the ASEAN Regional Forum. Korea has joined Japan as an increasingly important player in the UN and the World Trade Organisation.

Britain has responded. Two years ago John Major announced a new priority for Asia in our foreign policy. Since then we have reinforced our diplomatic representation and opened new trade and investment offices throughout the region. Last year our exports to the ASEAN countries grew 25 per cent, to over 5 billion pounds, making it our 8th largest market. We are the biggest EU investor in the Asia/Pacific region as a whole, the second biggest exporter of goods, the biggest exporter of invisibles.

But we must do more. Our export performance is less good in countries like Korea and China. The competition for inward investment will grow fiercer: we must maintain our strong record. We must work with APEC to galvanise support for our goals of open international trade and investment rules.

In Asia and more widely we must exploit the priceless asset of the Commonwealth. It contains some of the world's fastest growing economies, some of the leading contributors to UN peacekeeping. With the historical ties it embodies, its common legal framework, the Commonwealth provides a unique entree for Britain in countries across five continents. Our high market shares in Malaysia, Singapore, India and South Africa, demonstrate the benefits we derive from those links.

To make the most of the Commonwealth we must keep it up-to-date and relevant to the needs of its members. With the corrosive stain of apartheid gone, the Commonwealth can move forward. At the Summit in Auckland in November we must apply it to its new agenda, from promoting good government to combatting the threats of money laundering and drug trafficking. A new Commonwealth can benefit Britain and all its members.

Conclusions

This is far from a comprehensive survey of British foreign policy. I have outlined some objectives I consider to be of particular importance to this country. Meeting those objectives does not fall solely to diplomats, or to Government. To be influential overseas is a function of a country's military, political and economic potential. As Douglas Hurd said in his farewell speech, punching above our weight is not enough: we also need to increase our weight.

So there is plenty of work for a Foreign Secretary to do. I approach the task with this encouraging thought.

Many of the political problems we had got used to thinking of as intractable have turned out in recent years not to be so at all. It is nine years since I served as a Minister of State in the Foreign Office. At that time many observers expected South Africa to collapse in a bloodbath. Today South Africa is a multi-racial democracy with a functioning market economy.

In 1986 the Soviet Empire seemed set to last, despite the first stirrings of Gorbachev's new thinking. Today we are building new partnerships with the new democracies of Central and Eastern Europe, and with Russia itself.

Nine years ago the Middle East remained trapped in discord and hostility. In 1995 Israel is urging Europe to help Jordan after the conclusion of their peace treaty. Palestinian police have stormed a Hamas stronghold in Gaza to arrest suspected terrorists bent on the destruction of Israel.

In all these areas progress has taken years. Further advances may be slow. As Henry Kissinger said, foreign policy is a trend, not a hot item. But these examples show that the opportunities for success exist, even with the most seemingly intractable problems.

We are privileged to live at a time when Europe is being reborn, and when the world as a whole is drawing together to deal with global opportunities and global problems. Great Britain has both the power and the influence to make a significant contribution to that common effort. It is a national interest of the highest importance that we should succeed.

Royal Institute of International
Affairs, Chatham House, London,
21 September 1995

Annex 4
The Queen's Speech at the Opening of Parliament

WEDNESDAY 15 NOVEMBER 1995

MY LORDS AND MEMBERS OF THE HOUSE OF COMMONS

The Duke of Edinburgh and I look forward to receiving the State Visit of His Excellency the President of France and of His Excellency the President of South Africa next year. We also look forward to our State Visits to Poland and the Czech Republic in March and to Thailand in October next year.

National security remains of the highest importance to my Government. They will continue to support the North Atlantic Treaty Organisation and to promote Britain's wider security interests by contributing to the maintenance of international peace and stability. The United Kingdom's minimum nuclear deterrent will be maintained.

My Government will encourage a co-operative relationship between NATO and Russia, and will offer further help to countries in Central and Eastern Europe to consolidate democratic reforms and build stability and prosperity in the region.

A Bill will be introduced to bring up to date the legislation governing the Reserve Forces. My Government will also continue to work to preserve and modernise the Conventional Forces in Europe Treaty. During their Presidency of the Western European Union next year, they will work to enhance that Organisation's effectiveness.

Preventing the proliferation of weapons of mass destruction remains a priority. My Government will introduce legislation to ratify the Chemical Weapons Convention. They will pursue negotiations on a verifiable Comprehensive Test Ban Treaty and a Convention to ban the production of fissile material for nuclear weapons and other explosive purposes.

The fight against terrorism, organised crime, and drug misuse and trafficking, in the United Kingdom and elsewhere, will remain a priority.

My Government will continue to pursue the objective of transatlantic free trade in the context of world trade liberalisation.

In the European Union, my Government will participate in the 1996 Inter-Governmental Conference and contribute to preparing the Union for further enlargement. They will work for the continued implementation of the principle of subsidiarity and maintain their efforts to combat fraud. They will promote flexible labour markets and reduced social costs as the best means to improve the competitiveness of the European economy and create a climate for job creation.

A substantial aid programme will be maintained, focused on the poorest countries, to promote sustainable development and good government, including respect for human rights.

Reform of the United Nations, and efforts to enhance the organisation's effectiveness in peace-keeping, will remain an important objective. My Government will work to develop the capacity of the United Nations and regional organisations in the prevention of conflict. They will continue to promote a negotiated settlement in the former Yugoslavia.

My Government will continue working to strengthen ties between members of the Commonwealth.

My Government will work for the prosperity and stability of Hong Kong. In the interests of the Hong Kong people, they will seek to co-operate with China on the basis of the Sino-British Joint Declaration, in order to promote a smooth transition in 1997.

My Government will maintain support for the Middle East Peace Process.

In Northern Ireland my Government will continue to build on the present peace and to create the conditions for political progress through inclusive talks. They will facilitate economic development and promote fair and equitable treatment for all people in Northern Ireland. They will maintain close and friendly relations with the Government of the Republic of Ireland. Legislation will be introduced to continue special provisions required for preserving the peace and maintaining order.

MEMBERS OF THE HOUSE OF COMMONS
Estimates for the public service will be laid before you.

MY LORDS AND MEMBERS OF THE HOUSE OF COMMONS
My Government will continue with firm financial policies designed to support economic growth and rising employment, based on permanently low inflation. Fiscal policy will continue to be set to bring the public sector borrowing requirement back towards balance over the medium term. The share of national income taken by the public sector will be reduced.

My Government will improve the performance of the economy, by encouraging enterprise and competitiveness and offering support for small businesses. They will promote further deregulation. They will introduce a Bill to extend choice and competition in broadcasting by providing for new digital services and easing restrictions on media ownership. Legislation will again be brought before you to authorise the construction and operation of a high speed rail link between London and the Channel Tunnel.

Increased competitiveness will be encouraged by raising educational and skill levels, advancing knowledge, and promoting an efficient and flexible labour market. Legislation will be laid before you to expand nursery education for four-year-olds and to allow grant-maintained schools to borrow on the commercial market. Legislation will be introduced to enable students to choose between private and public suppliers of subsidised loans. In Scotland, legislation will be introduced to reform education and training.

My Government will continue to improve the quality of public services, through the Citizen's Charter programme and by other means.

A Bill will be introduced to streamline further the handling of asylum applications and to strengthen enforcement of immigration controls.

Legislation will be laid before you to enable the Security Service to assist the law enforcement agencies in their work against organised crime; and to reform the procedures in criminal cases, including those for prosecution and defence disclosure.

My Government will bring forward legislation to make better provision for housing and to promote the smooth running of construction contracts.

Legislation will be introduced to extend the Parliamentary Health Service Commissioner's jurisdiction, and to enable local authorities to make payments to particular groups of people who want to purchase their own community care.

My Government will introduce legislation to reform the law governing divorce and other aspects of family law.

Other measures, including other measures of law reform, will be laid before you.

MY LORDS AND MEMBERS OF THE HOUSE OF COMMONS
I pray that the blessing of Almighty God may rest upon your counsels.

Annex 5
Presidency Conclusions: Madrid European Council, 15–16 December 1995

INTRODUCTION TO PART A

The European Council, meeting in Madrid on 15 and 16 December 1995, took decisions on employment, the single currency, the Intergovernmental Conference and enlargement to bring in countries of Central and Eastern Europe and the Mediterranean.

The European Council considers that job creation is the principal social, economic and political objective of the European Union and its Member States, and declares its firm resolve to continue to make every effort to reduce unemployment.

The European Council adopted the scenario for the changeover to the single currency, confirming unequivocally that this stage will commence on 1 January 1999.

The European Council decided to name the currency, to be used from 1 January 1999, the 'Euro'.

The European Council continued its deliberation on the future of Europe, which was launched in Essen and continued in Cannes and Formentor.

In this connection, having welcomed the Reflection Group's report, the European Council decided to launch the Intergovernmental Conference on 29 March 1996 in order to establish the political and institutional conditions for adapting the European Union to present and future needs, particularly with a view to the next enlargement.

It is essential that the Conference achieve results sufficient to enable the Union to bring added value to all its citizens and to shoulder its responsibilities adequately, both internally and externally.

The European Council notes with satisfaction some significant achievements in the area of external relations which have occurred since its last meeting and in which the European Union has played a decisive role:

- the signing in Paris of the Dayton Agreement, which puts an end to the terrible war in former Yugoslavia and builds on considerable European efforts over the preceding months in military, humanitarian and negotiating terms The European Council recognises the decisive contribution made by the United States at a crucial moment;
- the New Transatlantic Agenda and the Joint EU-US Action Plan signed at the Madrid Summit on 3 December 1995, which are major joint

commitments with the United States to revitalise and strengthen our association:
- the signing in Madrid of the Inter-Regional Framework Agreement between the European Union and Mercosur, the first agreement of this type to be concluded by the European Union;
- the Barcelona Declaration, launching a new, comprehensive Euro-Mediterranean association which will promote peace, stability and prosperity throughout the Mediterranean through a permanent process of dialogue and cooperation;
- the signing in Mauritius of the revised Lomé IV Convention by the European Union and the ACP States, which will consolidate the association between the two sides;
- the European Parliament's assent to the customs union between the European Union and Turkey, which opens the way for the consolidation and strengthening of a political, economic and security relationship crucial to the stability of that region.

The European Council began its proceedings by exchanging ideas with Mr Klaus Hänsch, President of the European Parliament, on the main subjects for discussion at this meeting.

Finally, a meeting took place today between the Heads of State and Government and the Ministers for Foreign Affairs of the associated countries of Central and Eastern Europe, including the Baltic States (CCEE), as well as Cyprus and Malta. There was a broad exchange of views on these conclusions, matters concerning the pre-accession strategy and various issues relating to international policies.

Annex 6 An Eagle Star Advertisement (London Underground, 1990)

EAGLE STAR · ALWAYS A GOOD IDEA.

Annex 7
Universal GATT Speech

Combine any phrase from Column I with any phrase in Columns II, III and IV and you will obtain a universal GATT statement.

The number of possible combinations is 10 000. You will be able to speak for about 40 hours.

Column I	Column II	Column III	Column IV
Mr Chairman,	the introduction of effective disciplines and compliance with existing rules	should play a significant role in	the reinforcement of the GATT system
There is evidence to support our view that	the further development of multilateral trade cooperation	ought to be given a prominent place in our current efforts aiming at	a more coordinated attempt to address the global economic problems
In these circumstances it is our position that	a realistic attempt to curb the rising protectionist pressures	requires serious consideration of various proposals directed at	changing the negative trends characterising the present state of affairs
As my distinguished colleagues have rightly noted	a continuous improvement in the north–south trade relations	would provide a valid contribution to the urgent task of	strengthening the non-discrimination principle of the international trading system
In addition,	a balanced and pragmatic solution of the current debt crises	calls for an energetic action with a view to	assuring a further liberalisation of international trade
My government is convinced that	a rapid reduction in the bilateral trade imbalances	is one of the major elements of a successful strategy aiming at	creating an atmosphere of mutual confidence and understanding among the major parties concerned

Many contracting parties share our opinion that	a constant search of mutually satisfactory arrangements on trade in services	necessitates a resolute action on the part of all trading nations targeted at	implementing the standstill and rollback commitments
Recent developments in trade policy clearly show that	a full implementation of the objectives stated in the Ministerial Declaration	requires that substantial progress is also reached in other areas which are essential for	assuring more stability in the field of trade and finance
My delegation is of the opinion that	a long-term solution to the proliferation of grey-area measures	should be given a proper place in negotiations directed at	avoiding the constant deterioration of the trading environment
Neither should we forget that	a balanced attempt at solving the issue of safeguards	constitutes a *sine qua non* for	resolving the current tensions in the trading system

Notes

PREFACE

1 Alfred Marshall, *Principles of Economics*, 8th edition, Macmillan, 1920, Book IV, Chapter XIII.
2 See Lecture 5, especially the definition on p. 87.
3 Lord Strang, *The Foreign Office*, Allen and Unwin, 1955.

INTRODUCTION

1 Quoted in Philarète Chasles, *Voyages d'un Critique – A Travers la Vie et les Livres*, 1868, Vol. 2, p. 407.
2 For a more detailed discussion of the point, see p. 136.
3 See also p. 22.
4 Macaulay, *Essay on Machiavelli*, Edinburgh Review, 1827.

1 DIPLOMACY: A CHILD OF CHANGING TIMES

1 Sir Ernest Satow, *Guide to Diplomatic Practice*, 5th edition, Longman, 1979, p. 3.
2 Lewis Carroll, *Alice's Adventures in Wonderland*, 1865. A shrewd fable.
3 See in particular pp. 13, 52, 91, 122 and note 10 below.
4 Sir Harold Nicolson, *The Evolution of Diplomatic Method*, Constable, 1954, pp. 73–6.
5 John Locke, *The Second Treatise on Civil Government*, 1690, para. 159.
6 *The Federalist Papers*, 1787–8, no. LXIV.
7 Sir Victor Wellesley, *Diplomacy in Fetters*, Hutchinson, 1944.
8 Ibid., p. 26.
9 *Proposals for the Reform of the Foreign Service*, Cmd 6420, January 1943. This White Paper, the full text of which is contained in Lord Strang's *The Foreign Office*, was the basis for the reforms introduced at the end of the Second World War. See Lecture 8 for a discussion of modern Diplomatic Service organisation.
10 This is the first of 'Fourteen Points' in Woodrow Wilson's address to Congress, 8 January 1918. In the event Wilson quickly abandoned open diplomacy at the Peace Conference at the end of the Great War. He realised that attempts to arrive openly at open covenants were doomed to failure.
11 Macaulay, *Essay on Hallam's Constitutional History*, Edinburgh Review, 1828.

12 This aspect of British foreign policy is dealt with most valuably and interestingly in Marett, *Through the Back Door*, Pergamon, 1968. Sir Robert Marett was a businessman and journalist before joining the Foreign Service.

13 See Lecture 3, especially pp. 37–41 and Lecture 5 as regards the developing country dimension of the world economy, pp. 80–4.

14 This major question recurs throughout these lectures. See in particular Lecture 2, pp. 27–8.

15 See Lecture 5.

16 World Commission on Environment and Development, *Our Common Future*, Oxford University Press, 1987.

17 See in particular pp. 84 and 87. The literature on environmental questions is vast. An excellent survey of the international politics of the environment is contained in Brenton, *The Greening of Machiavelli*, Earthscan Publications and the Royal Institute of International Affairs, 1994. Mr Brenton is a member of the British Diplomatic Service.

18 In a speech in Washington on 13 December 1995, US Secretary of the Treasury Robert Rubin listed combating 'global crime' as a priority area for world economic co-operation. 'Organised crime buys and sells drugs, weapons and politicians.'

19 Stuart Eldon, *From Quill Pen to Satellite*, The Royal Institute of International Affairs, 1994. See also Lecture 8, especially pp. 150–1.

20 See p. 23.

21 The difference can easily be exaggerated. The word 'business' has traditionally been used in connection with politics, as for example in Macaulay's verdict on Machiavelli quoted on p. 6. However, management has become of increasing importance. See Lecture 8.

2 THE NATURE OF INTERNATIONAL SOCIETY TODAY

1 Samuel P. Huntington, 'The Clash of Civilisations?', *Foreign Affairs*, Vol. 72, No. 3, Summer 1993.

2 See p. 18.

3 The Historical Branch of the Library and Records Department has produced a series of interesting and entertaining papers on the history of the FCO and its personalities, as well as on issues of policy. History Notes, no. 2, 'The FCO, Policy, People and Places, 1782–1993' is particularly relevant. A more detailed history is contained in Tilley and Gaselee, *The Foreign Office*, Putnam, 1933. Sir John Tilley was Chief Clerk of the Foreign Office, 1913–18, and Stephen Gaselee the Librarian and Keeper of the Papers, 1920–43.

4 See p. 82.

5 See in particular section (d) of Lecture 5.

6 Adam Smith, *The Theory of Moral Sentiments*, 1759. This work preceded *Wealth of Nations* by 17 years. It has regained a measure of prominence, after years of neglect, at the time of the bicentenary of the famous treatise in 1976. The earlier work is essential to a full understanding of the later.

7   This is a key element in the Preamble to the United Nations Charter. See Lecture 4. See also section (e), below.
8   See p. 18.
9   See pp. 100–2.
10 *The Times*, 24 April 1995.
11 See pp. 40–1.
12 The future of Hong Kong will be significant in this regard.
13 The Rt Hon. David Howell, MP, *Easternisation*, Demos, 1995.
14 This general issue affords an excellent illustration of the way in which what may seem to be primarily a matter of internal debate has international ramifications in the interdependent world of today.
15 A phrase made famous by Mr Francis Fukuyama, State Department official and political scientist. His book *The End of History and the Last Man* (Hamish Hamilton) was published in 1992. The 'End of Geography' seems a more apposite phrase to describe a world where distances have shrunk and communications are instantaneous. See Richard O'Brien, *Global Financial Integration: The End of Geography*, Chatham House Papers, Pinter, 1992, p. 7.
16 See Appendix to Lecture 6.
17 Attributed to Edmund Burke, eighteenth-century British political writer and statesman.
18 See also p. 61.
19 See p. 58.
20 See p. 42.
21 See pp. 46–7.

3   NATIONAL SOVEREIGNTY AND ITS LIMITS

1   See p. 44.
2   See p. 32.
3   The originator of the mathematical theories known by this name was John Von Neumann. See Neumann and Oskar Morgenstern, *Theory of Games and Economic Behaviour*, 3rd edition, 1953.
4   Sir Harold Nicolson, *Diplomacy*, 2nd edition, Oxford University Press, 1950, pp. 129–53.
5   The characteristics of British foreign policy are examined further in Lecture 7.
6   Nicolson, *Diplomacy*, p. 131.
7   J.L. Brierly, *The Law of Nations*, 5th edition, Oxford University Press, 1955, p. 1.
8   See p. 7.
9   The International Court of Justice was established by the Charter of the United Nations as the 'principal judicial organ of the United Nations' (Article 92). The Statute in accordance with which the Court functions is annexed to the Charter. See Lecture 4, especially pp. 53 and 55.
10 Sir Ian Sinclair, 'International Law: The Court, Commission and Judges', in *The United Kingdom – The United Nations* (ed. E. Jensen and T. Fisher), Macmillan, 1990, pp. 143–4.

11 Hans Kung, *Global Responsibility in Search of a New World Ethic*, Student
    Christian Movement Press, 1991.
12 See p. 23.
13 David Mitrany, *A Working Peace System: An Argument for the Functional
    Development of International Organisation*, Royal Institute of Interna-
    tional Affairs, 1943.
14 Brierly, *The Law of Nations*, p. 60.
15 Dr Jonathan Sacks, *Faith in the Future*, Darton Longman and Todd, 1995.
16 See pp. 40–1.
17 This familiar slogan has been taken out of its original context. Alcuin, an
    eighth-century English churchman and educator, was a prominent adviser
    to Charlemagne. In one letter he wrote: 'and those people should not be
    listened to who keep saying the voice of the people is the voice of God,
    since the riotousness of the crowd is always very close to madness'.
18 Shakespeare, *Henry IV, Part 2*, III, i, 36.
19 Attributed to Sir James Fitzjames Stephen, nineteenth-century English
    jurist and author.

4   THE UNITED NATIONS

 1 See p. 12.
 2 See pp. 10–11.
 3 The results of the Dumbarton Oaks Conference are summarised in a UK
    White Paper (Cmd 6560, 1944). An official UK Commentary on the
    proposals was published as Cmd 6571, 1944. The UK official commentary
    on the UN Charter itself (Cmd 6666, 1945) contains a valuable
    explanation of the difference between the final text and the relevant
    passages in the Dumbarton Oaks proposals.
 4 It is of interest that there was no Preamble in the text emanating from
    Dumbarton Oaks. It was added at the San Francisco Conference, and is
    thought to be largely the work of the South African Prime Minister, Jan
    Smuts, in the wake of a 'meeting of Commonwealth Statesmen' held in
    London on the eve of the conference, in April 1945.
 5 The word 'democracy' does not occur in the Charter. The democratic
    character of its aims and provisions is, however, apparent. The opening
    words of the Preamble are 'We the Peoples'.
 6 Sir Charles Webster, quoted by Lord Gladwyn in *The United Kingdom –
    The United Nations*, ed. E. Jensen and T. Fisher, Macmillan, 1990, p. 36.
 7 The latest version of 'Human Rights: A Compilation of International
    Instruments' was produced by the UN in 1994 (ST/HR/1 Rev 5, 2 vols).
    The Universal Declaration was adopted as General Assembly Resolution
    217A(III) on 10 December 1948. The Covenants were adopted as
    Resolution 2200A(XXI) on 16 December 1966. The literature on the
    subject is extensive. Particular mention may be made of P. Alston (ed.),
    The United Nations and Human Rights: A Critical Appraisal, Oxford
    University Press, 1992.
 8 See Lecture 6, especially pp. 100–5.

9   There can be few more influential figures in grappling with interdependence than Jean Monnet, French businessman, politician and statesman (1888–1979). His avoidance of the limelight was legendary. He preferred 'to do something than be somebody'.

10 The outbreak of the Great War remains a fascinating subject of study for both the historian and the diplomat. Sir Victor Wellesley (q.v.) maintained that it was several wars 'rolled into one: war between Germany and Russia; between Germany and Great Britain; between Italy and Austria; between Russia and Austria; and between France and Germany'. See his *Diplomacy in Fetters*, Hutchinson, 1944, p. 35.

11 Indeed the United Nations' claim can be regarded as the stronger. European peace after the Congress of Vienna was a precarious affair. See Mr Rifkind's remarks (p. 132) and note 12 to Lecture 7.

12 Cf. the argument that the UN has had the effect of tilting the balance in favour of the state as against the claims of interdependence (p. 57).

13 See pp. 35–6.

14 Security Council document S/23500, 31 January 1992.

15 *An Agenda for Peace*, General Assembly document A/47/277, Security Council document S/24111, 17 June 1992. The ensuing series of relevant documents and decisions has been brought together in an admirable volume *An Agenda for Peace*, published by the UN Department of Public Information (DPI) in February 1995.

16 The relevant documentation was published in a companion volume, *An Agenda for Development*, by DPI in February 1995.

17 The text is contained in *An Agenda for Peace*. See note 15.

18 Cmd 6666 (see note 3).

5 THE WORLD ECONOMY

1   See Vincent Cable, 'What Future for the State?', *Daedelus*, Spring 1995. Vol. 124, No. 2 of the *Proceedings of the American Academy of Arts and Science*. This article contains much valuable analysis of factors affecting globalisation and the responsibilities of governments. See also Lecture 7, note 9.

2   See pp. 10–11.

3   This, while not without risk, would seem a more prudent forecast than that of the 'end of history' (Lecture 2, note 15).

4   The text, finally initialled on 15 December 1993, after seven years of negotiations, runs to some 450 pages.

5   The run-up to the Declaration was almost as frustrating as the Uruguay Round itself. The idea of a further round of negotiations had been mooted soon after the completion of the previous round, the Tokyo Round, in 1979. It was at the centre of a spectacularly disorderly GATT ministerial meeting in November 1982.

6   See pp. 70–2.

7   A milestone was reached with the publication in May 1944 of a UK White Paper on *Employment Policy* (Cmd 6527). This stated at the outset that the government accepted 'as one of their primary aims the maintenance of a

high and stable level of employment after the war'. Keynes is probably the best known of British economists. His seminal work is *The General Theory of Employment, Interest and Money*, Macmillan, 1936. See also p. 311.

8   Figures are published periodically by the Bank for International Settlements of the estimated daily turnover in the foreign exchange markets. In April 1995 the total was put at $1230 billion, the largest share (30 per cent) represented by London.

9   See note 7.

10   Lord Beveridge followed up his *Report on Social Insurance and Allied Services* with his *Report on Full Employment in a Free Society*, Allen and Unwin, 1944.

11   The text of the draft ITO was published in the UK White Paper *Final Act and the Havana Charter for an International Trade Organisation*, Cmd 7375, April 1948.

12   For a political survey of relations between the developed and the developing countries – the North–South Dialogue – see the author's chapter in *The United Kingdom – The United Nations*, ed. E. Jensen and T. Fisher, Macmillan, 1990, pp. 159–208.

13   See also pp. 16–17 and 84.

14   The Earth Summit and the UN ramifications are helpfully explored by Professor Patricia Birnie, 'The UN and the Environment', in *United Nations – Divided World* (ed. A. Roberts and B. Kingsbury), 2nd edition, Oxford University Press, 1993. See also A. Brenton, *The Greening of Machiavelli*, Earthscan, 1994 (Lecture 1, note 17).

15   Baroness Chalker, speech to the All-Party Group on Population and Development, House of Commons, 22 November 1995.

16   Commonwealth Finance Ministers meet regularly on the eve of the Annual Bank/Fund Meetings and have been the occasion for the launching of initiatives. A notable recent example was the granting of terms for debt relief – the 'Trinidad' terms – put forward at the meeting of Commonwealth Finance Ministers in Port of Spain in 1993.

17   See pp. 16–17 and 81.

18   See p. 73.

19   See p. 63.

20   *An Agenda for Development*, para. 3.

21   See pp. 63–5 and Annex 2.

22   Communiqué issued by 'the heads of State and Government of seven major industrialised nations and the President of the European Commission', Halifax, Nova Scotia, 17 June 1995, para. 12. The Halifax Summit was the twenty-first in the series. The role of these Summits is most helpfully analysed in N. Bayne and R. Putnam, *Hanging Together*, 2nd edition, Sage, 1987. Sir Nicholas Bayne was British High Commissioner in Ottawa, 1992–6.

23   John Gordon, *Green Knight to the Rescue?* Centre for the Study of Global Governance, Discussion Paper, No. 12, p. 11. Mr Gordon was formerly a member of the British Diplomatic Service.

24   *Our Global Neighbourhood*, Report of the Commission on Global Governance, Oxford University Press, 1995. See Bibliography for details of the major Commission reports.

25 Ibid., p. 2.
26 Ibid., p. 154.
27 Ibid., p. 342.
28 See p. 80.
29 See p. 86.

6 EUROPEAN ARCHITECTURE

1 The phrase was used by Canning, British Foreign Secretary, in the House of Commons on 12 December 1826 to justify his policy of breaking free from Austria, Prussia and Russia, with which Great Britain was linked in the Holy Alliance. Canning did not take the view that this coalition had a role to play beyond the defeat of Napoleon. In this he differed from his predecessor Castlereagh. He emerged instead as the leader and protector of world liberalism, not least in Latin America. It is not clear that the House of Commons fully understood what Canning was saying.

2 See p. 9 and Lecture 1, note 3.

3 The official documentation relating to all these developments is, of course, immense. References to it will be kept to a minimum in this lecture. It is, however, covered in more detail in the Bibliography.

4 De Gaulle was a towering figure in post-war Europe. A biography 25 years after his death in 1970 is aptly entitled *The Last Great Frenchman*. See Bibliography.

5 See p. 58 and Lecture 4, note 9.

6 Heads of State and Government of the member states meet regularly every six months, that is, once per rotating presidency of six months' duration, as the 'European Council'. The outcome of these meetings is contained in the *Presidency Conclusions*. See p. 134.

7 The British Management Data Foundation produced in 1992 a very helpful publication, *The Maastricht Treaty in Perspective*, containing 'the full text of all the changes and additions proposed by the Maastricht Treaty incorporated into the Treaty of Rome and the Single European Act, together with an analysis of the proposed extra powers of the European Community Institutions'.

8 The Werner Report on Economic and Monetary Union (named after its Chairman, the Luxembourg Prime Minister) appeared in 1970. When they met in Paris in October 1972, that is, before the formal enlargement of the Community from Six to Nine members, the Heads of State and Government reaffirmed 'the determination of Member States of the enlarged European Communities irreversibly to achieve the economic and monetary union . . . The necessary decisions should be taken in the course of 1973 so as to allow the transition to the second stage of the economic and monetary union on 1st January, 1974, and with a view to its completion not later than 31st December, 1980.' (The text of the communiqué was issued as a White Paper – Cmd 5109.)

    At the Summit of the Nine in Copenhagen in December 1974, the unreality of this timetable, as of other projects for closer European integration, was manifest. Generalised currency floating, the Middle East war in October 1973, and the oil crisis had reduced Community co-operation to tatters. However Heads of Government meeting in Paris on 9 and 10 December 'having noted that internal and international difficulties have prevented in 1973 and 1974 the accomplishment of expected progress on the road to EMU affirm that in this field their will has not weakened and that their objective has not changed since the Paris Conference' (Cmnd 5830, December 1974). It was not until 1979 that the more modest concept of the European Monetary System came into being.

9   P. Fontaine, *Europe in Ten Lessons*, European Documentation, 1992.

10   A useful contemporary assessment is made by Evgeny Chossudovsky, *The Helsinki Final Act viewed in the United Nations Perspective*, UNITAR Research Report, No. 24, 1980.

11   H. Kissinger, *Diplomacy*, Simon and Schuster 1994, p. 813. The work as a whole is an invaluable compound of fact, instruction and stimulus.

12   See p. 98.

13   H. Rieben, *Des Guerres Européennes à l'Union de l'Europe*, Fondation Jean Monnet pour l'Europe, 1987, p. 220.

14   The text was communicated to the Secretary-General by the United States Permanent Representative and circulated as General Assembly document A/50/790 and Security Council document S/1995/999.

15   The text was communicated to the Secretary-General by the United Kingdom Permanent Representative and circulated as Security Council document S/1995/1029.

16   See pp. 107–8.

17   See p. 107.

18   NATO Press Communiqué M-NAC-2(95)118, 5 December 1995.

19   United States Information Services SFF 703 and SFF 702, respectively, 3 December 1995.

20   See pp. 134–5 and Annex 5.

21   See p. 70.

22   See pp. 62–3.

23   See p. 87.

24   The question is whether this will be a precedent. Compare the recommendation in the Report of the Commission on Global Government for the Economic Security Council (p. 88).

25   This resolution is based on the Dayton Agreement, the Conclusions of the London Conference and the Secretary-General's own report (S/1995/1031).

26   See p. 55.

27   These issues are covered in detail in S/1995/1031.

28   See p. 65.

29   See p. 33.

7   FOREIGN POLICY-MAKING

1   See Lecture 2, note 6.

2   Foreign and Commonwealth Office, including Overseas Development Administration, 1996 Departmental Report, March 1996, Cm 3203, p. 1.

3   10 September 1994, p. 34.
4   See *Vacher's Parliamentary Companion*, No. 1080, November 1995,
     pp. 144–8. This 'reference book for Parliament, Departments of State,
     Senior Civil Servants and Public offices' is a mine of information. It is
     published quarterly.
5   See p. 52.
6   Quoted by Lord Baldwin (his son) in an address to the Kipling Society,
     October 1971.
7   See p. 13.
8   See p. 80.
9   The question of future international telecommunications policy is the
     subject of a valuable new study by Vincent Cable and Catherine Distler,
     Global Superhighway, Royal Institute of International Affairs, 1995.
10   See p. 13.
11   See p. 49 in particular.
12   The balance of power, which is credited with keeping the peace in Europe,
     was recognised from the start as involving an element of brinkmanship. It
     depended on the accuracy of the assessments by the respective Great
     Powers of one another's intentions and the efficiency of their individual
     diplomatic machines in conveying the right signals. It met its nemesis in
     the outbreak of the Great War. See p. 58 and Lecture 4, notes 9 and 10.
13   See p. 1.
14   See *Hansard*, 18 December 1995, Vol. 268, No. 22, Cols 1219–35.
15   See Bibliography for Lecture 6.

8   DIPLOMATIC SERVICE ORGANISATION

1   Lord Strang, *The Diplomatic Career*, André Deutsch, 1962, p. 14.
2   See p. 121.
3   See p. 2.
4   See pp. 120–1.
5   It is interesting to recall in this connection a prophecy made many years
     ago by Lord Balfour, British Prime Minister, and Foreign Secretary.
     Speculating on the future development of large-scale organisations, he
     suggested that the ever-increasing complication in their working, due to
     new methods of communication and other modern inventions, would in
     the end put them beyond the range of effective human control. The two
     illustrations Lord Balfour gave of this thought were giant business
     'combines' and the Foreign Office (see the Introduction by Sir John Simon
     to Tilley and Gaselee, *The Foreign Office*, Putnam, 1933, p. vii).
6   It was a wise but perhaps apocryphal tycoon who said that he was quite
     willing to be told that one-half of what he spent on advertising was wasted,
     but that he had never found anyone who could tell him which half.
7   1995 Departmental Report, Cmnd 2802, p. 10. In 1914 the Foreign Office
     staff numbered 176, including the doorkeepers and office cleaners.
8   Cmd 6420. See p. 12 and Lecture 1, note 9.

9 *Review of Overseas Representation*, Report by the Central Policy Review Staff, HMSO 1977. See the author's *The Dynamics of Diplomacy*, 1990, pp. 13–20.

10 The conduct of European Union business has a markedly interdepartmental character. The UK Permanent Representative's Office in Brussels is staffed from a number of departments. So far the Permanent Representative has always been a member of the Diplomatic Service.

11 See p. 12.

12 Those of a ready wit might reply that the proposition could just as well be put the other way round.

13 See pp. 17–18.

14 The US Secretary of State John Foster Dulles in the 1950s was an early exponent of this practice. He was said to have 'an infinite capacity for taking planes'. Of the long-serving German Foreign Minister Hans-Dietrich Genscher, it was observed that, if two planes collided in mid-Atlantic, his name would be on both passenger lists.

15 Tilley and Gaselee, *The Foreign Office*, p. 257.

16 Sir Edward Grey, British Foreign Secretary, 3 August 1914, as he gazed out of the windows of his office on the eve of the outbreak of the Great War and saw the lamplighters at work: 'the lamps are going out all over Europe; we shall not see them lit again in our lifetime.'

17 Lord Morrison, *Government and Parliament*, 2nd edition, Oxford University Press, 1959, p. 63.

18 Sir Harold Nicolson, *Diplomacy*, Oxford University Press, 1950, p. 126. See also p. 176.

19 See p. 46.

20 The London Diplomatic List, December 1995, HMSO. It contains an 'Alphabetical list of the representatives of Foreign States and Commonwealth Countries in London with the names and designations of the persons returned as composing their Diplomatic Staff.' It lists the representatives in order of their precedence based on the date of their presentation of credentials. It also lists National Days and contains a Directory of International Organisations based in London, notably the Commonwealth Secretariat and the International Maritime Organisation.

21 See p. 143.

22 See p. 17 and Lecture 1, note 19.

23 A most informative presentation on 'The Impact of Information Technology on Diplomatic Practice' was given by Ian Soutar, the Head of Library and Records Department of the FCO, to the Symposium 'Diplomacy Beyond 2000', held at the Diplomatic Academy of London on 6 April 1995.

24 See, for example, Beryl Smedley, *Partners in Diplomacy*, Harley Press, 1990. A highly entertaining survey.

25 See p. 138.

26 There is a Vienna Convention on Consular Relations (1963), distinct from the 1961 Convention on Diplomatic Relations.

27 See p. 141 and note 9.

9 THE ACQUISITION OF DIPLOMATIC SKILLS: DRAFTING

1 Sir Harold Nicolson, speaking to new entrants to the British Foreign Service, 1945.
2 Blaise Pascal, *Lettres Provinciales* (1657), xvi.
3 Shakespeare, *Troilus and Cressida*, I, iii, 109.
4 See p. 53.
5 The scope for chairmen in all this is an illustration of the dictum current in United Nations circles: 'the chairman who does not abuse his position loses prestige'.
6 Anonymous, quoted by John Chadwick, *The Unofficial Commonwealth*, Allen and Unwin, 1982, p. 73. A comprehensive but readable account of the early years of the Commonwealth Foundation, the body concerned with promoting non-governmental co-operation within the Commonwealth.
7 Sir Henry Taylor, *The Statesman*, 1836, chapter XIII. Taylor's observations, mixing wisdom with wit and what later generations might call gamesmanship, were aimed at producing the higher quality of civil servants (or 'closet statesman', as he called them) the growing complexity of government demanded.

10 A DIPLOMAT'S DECADE

1 Charles Dickens, *David Copperfield*, chapter 11.
2 See p. 38.
3 Sir Henry Taylor, *The Statesman*, 1836, chapter XXIV.
4 See p. 158.
5 See pp. 45–6 and Lecture 3, note 9.
6 See p. 7.
7 Shakespeare, *Hamlet*, I, iii, 58.
8 See p. 146.
9 One of the great diplomatic gaffes was that of Sir Henry Wotton, the English Ambassador to Venice, who on a stop-over at Augsburg in 1604 wrote in the album of a friend, 'an ambassador is an honest man sent to lie abroad for the good of his country.' But he wrote in Latin, which did not convey the *double entendre* in the word 'lie' and left only the concept of telling lies. He was rebuked by King James I.

Select Bibliography

The international relations literature is massive. Any comprehensive bibliography would be book-length in itself. The following is a brief selection, incorporating less well-known material as well as a limited number of familiar texts. For convenience sake the list is divided, of necessity somewhat arbitrarily, on the basis of the subject matter of the individual lectures. The applicability of the works quoted to other lectures will be apparent to the reader.

LECTURE 1

Bull, H. and Watson, A.: *The Expansion of International Society*, Oxford University Press, 1984
Busk, D.: *The Craft of Diplomacy*, Pall Mall Press, 1967
Jackson, G.: *Concorde Diplomacy*, Hamish Hamilton, 1981
Nicolson, H.: *Diplomacy*, 2nd edition, Oxford University Press, 1950
——: *The Evolution of Diplomatic Method*, Constable, 1954
Satow, E.: *Guide to Diplomatic Practice*, 5th edition, Longman, 1979
Wellesley, V.: *Diplomacy in Fetters*, Hutchinson, 1944

LECTURE 2

Fukuyama, F.: *The End of History and the Last Man*, Hamish Hamilton, 1992
Huntington, S. P.: 'The Clash of Civilisations?' *Foreign Affairs*, Vol. 72, No. 3, Summer 1993
Kennedy, P.: *Preparing for the Twenty-First Century*, Harper Collins, 1993

LECTURE 3

Brierly, J. L.: *The Law of Nations*, 5th edition, Oxford University Press, 1950
Frankel, J.: *International Relations in a Changing World*, 3rd edition, Oxford University Press, 1979
Henkin, L.: *How Nations Behave*, Praeger, 1968
Kung, H.: *Global Responsibility in Search of a New World Ethic*, SCM Press, 1991
Mitrany, D.: *A Working Peace System: an Argument for the Functional Development of International Organisation*, Royal Institute of International Affairs, 1943
Sen, B.: *A Diplomat's Handbook of International Law and Practice*, Nijhoff, 1965

Sinclair, I.: 'International Law: The Court, Commission and Judges', in *The United Kingdom – The United Nations*, ed. E. Jensen and T. Fisher, Macmillan, 1990

Taylor, P. and Groom, A.: *International Organisation*, Frances Pinter, 1978

LECTURE 4

The United Nations Charter

The Statute of the International Court of Justice

The Rules of Procedure of the General Assembly

Annual Report of the Secretary-General on the Work of the United Nations (submitted to the General Assembly)

Boutros-Ghali, B.: *An Agenda for Peace* (2nd edition) United Nations 1995

——: *An Agenda for Development*, United Nations, 1995

Commonwealth Secretariat: *The Commonwealth at the Summit* (Communiqués of Heads of Government Meetings 1944–86), 1987

Independent Commission on Disarmament and Security Issues (the Palme Commission): *Common Security: A Programme for Disarmament*, Pan Books, 1982

Independent Commission on International Humanitarian Issues: *Winning the Human Race?* Zed Books, 1988

Jensen, E. and Fisher T. (eds): *The United Kingdom – The United Nations*, Macmillan, 1990

Roberts, A. and Kingsbury, B. (eds): *United Nations – Divided World*, 2nd edition, Oxford University Press, 1993

Smith, A. with Sanger, C.: *Stitches in Time*, General Publishing, 1981 (memoirs of the the First Commonwealth Secretary-General, 1965–75)

Urquhart, B.: *A Life in Peace and War*, Weidenfeld and Nicolson, 1987

LECTURE 5

International Commission Reports:

(i) The Pearson Commission, *Partners in Development*, Praeger, 1969

(ii) The Brandt Commission, *North–South: A Programme for Survival*, Pan, 1980

——, *Common Crisis*, Pan, 1983

(iii) The Bruntland Commission, *Our Common Future*, Oxford University Press, 1987

(iv) The Carlsson-Ramphal Commission, *Our Global Neighbourhood*, Oxford University Press, 1995

Bayne, N. and Putnam, R.: *Hanging Together*, 2nd edition, Sage, 1987 (a history of the G7)

Brenton, A.: *The Greening of Machiavelli*, Earthscan, 1994

Commonwealth Secretariat.: *International Development Policies*, review of the activities of international organisations (quarterly)

The Economist: Pocket World in Figures (annually)

Galbraith, J.K.: *A History of Economics*, Hamish Hamilton, 1987

List, F.: *The National System of Political Economy*, 1840
Marshall, P.: 'The North/South Dialogue: Britain at Odds' in *The United Kingdom – The United Nations*, ed. E. Jensen and T. Fisher, Macmillan, 1990
OECD.: *Twenty-Five Years of Development Cooperation*, OECD, Paris, 1985
——: *World Economic Interdependence and the Evolving North-South Relationship*, OECD, Paris, 1983
United Nations: *The History of UNCTAD 1964–1984*, UN publication, 1985
World Bank.: *The World Bank Atlas* (annually)

LECTURE 6

The Treaty of Maastricht, 1992
HMSO: *Developments in the European Union* (a comprehensive six-monthly survey)
——: *Presidency Conclusions issued at the end of regular meetings of the European Council* (see, for example Annexe 5)
Kitzinger, U.: *Diplomacy and Persuasion*, Thames and Hudson, 1973 (the story of how the UK joined the EEC)
Monnet, J.: *Memoirs* (translated by Richard Mayne), Doubleday, 1978
Williams, C.: *The Last Great Frenchman: A Life of General de Gaulle*, Abacus, 1993

LECTURE 7

Acheson, D.: *Present at the Creation*, Hamish Hamilton, 1969 (an account of his years at the State Department 1941–7 and 1949–53)
'Britain in the World', Proceedings of a one-day conference organised by the Royal Institute of International Affairs in association with HMG, 29 March 1995.
Clarke, M.: *British External Policy-Making in the 1990s*, Macmillan, 1992
Kissinger, H.: *Diplomacy*, Simon and Schuster, 1994
Strang, W.: *Britain in World Affairs*, Faber and Faber and André Deutsch, 1961
Tugendhat, C. and Wallace, W.: *Options for British Foreign Policy in the 1990s*, Royal Institution of International Affairs/Routledge, 1988
Woodward, L.: *British Foreign Policy in the Second World War*, HMSO, 1962

LECTURE 8

FCO: *Departmental Report* (annual)
FCO, Historical Branch.: *The FCO, Policy, People and Places, 1782–1993*, 3rd edition, 1993 (one of a series of 'History Notes'. *Inter alia* it contains very useful bibliographical information)
Official reports:
Proposals for the Reform of the Foreign Service, Cmd 6420, HMSO, January 1943

Report of the Committee on Overseas Information Services (the Drogheda
  Report) Cmd 9138, HMSO, April 1954
Report of the Committee on Representational Services Overseas (the Plowden
  Report) Cmnd 2276, HMSO, February 1964
Report of the Review Committee on Overseas Representation 1968–9 (the
  Duncan Report), Cmnd 4107, HMSO, July 1969
Review of Overseas Representation: Report by the Central Policy Review Staff
  (the 'Think Tank' report), HMSO, 1977
The United Kingdom's Overseas Representation, Cmd 7308, HMSO, August
  1978 (this is principally the government's reply to the 'Think Tank' report)
*Foreign Affairs Committee of the House of Commons: Cultural Diplomacy
  Fourth Report*, Session 1986–87, HMSO, May 1987 (a very useful analysis of
  the cultural aspects of international relations)
Boyce, P.: *Foreign Affairs for New States*, University of Queensland Press, 1977
Commonwealth Secretariat: *Diplomatic Service: Formation and Operation.
  Report on Commonwealth Seminar, Singapore, 1970*, Longman, 1971
Eldon, S.: *From Quill Pen to Satellite*, Royal Institute of International Affairs,
  1994
Garner, S.: *The Commonwealth Office, 1925–68*, Heinemann, 1978
Marett, R.: *Through the Back Door*, Pergamon, 1968
Strang, W.: *The Foreign Office*, Allen and Unwin, 1955
——: *The Diplomatic Career*, André Deutsch, 1962
Tilley, J. and Gaselee, S.: *The Foreign Office*, Putnam, 1933

LECTURE 9

Bacon, F.: *Essays*, 1597–1625
Cornford, F.: *Microcosmographia Academica, Being a Guide for the Young
  Academic Politician*, Bowes and Bowes, 1953
Gower, E.: *The Complete Plain Words*, HMSO, 1954
Kaufmann, J.: *Conference Diplomacy*, 3rd edition, Macmillan, 1996
——: *United Nations Decision Making*, Sijthoff and Nordhoff, 1980
Taylor, H.: *The Statesman*, 1836

LECTURE 10

Connell, J.: *The 'Office'. A Study of British Foreign Policy and its Makers,
  1919–51*, Allan Wingate, 1958
Dickie, J.: *Inside the Foreign Office*, Chapmans, 1992
Dudley Edwards, R.: *True Brits*, BBC Books, 1994 (accompanying an
  entertaining and informative TV series)
Keens-Soper, M. and Schweizer, K. (eds): *The Art of Diplomacy* (translation of
  De la Manière de Négocier avec les Souverains, 1716 by François de Callières,
  an eighteenth-century classic), Leicester University Press, 1983
Machiavelli, N.: *The Prince*, 1532
Oudendyk, W.: *Ways and By-ways in Diplomacy*, Peter Davies, 1939 (memoirs
  of a Netherlands diplomat exemplifying the 'Old Diplomacy')

Smedley, B.: *Partners in Diplomacy*, Harley Press, 1990 (the 'story of many generations of women who have been married to British diplomats serving abroad')

Trevelyan, H.: *Diplomatic Channels*, Macmillan, 1974 (light-hearted reflections of one of the most eminent of twentieth-century British diplomats)

Index